AF557768

ISLAM
Philosophy and Ideology

ISLAM
Philosophy and Ideology

By
Dilshad Hasan

ANMOL PUBLICATIONS PVT. LTD.
NEW DELHI - 110 002 (INDIA)

ANMOL PUBLICATIONS PVT. LTD.
4374/4B, Ansari Road, Daryaganj
New Delhi - 110 002
Ph.: 23261597, 23278000
Visit us at: www.anmolpublications.com

Islam: Philosophy and Ideology

First Published, 2005

ISBN 81-261-2238-2

PRINTED IN INDIA

Published by J.L. Kumar for Anmol Publications Pvt. Ltd., New Delhi - 110 002 and Printed at Mehra Offset Press, Delhi.

Contents

Part - III
Present Scenario

Preface

Islam is a progressive, scientific and logical religion. Nothing in Islam is against reason or contrary to wisdom. Holy Quran is the greatest source of knowledge and Prophetic Tradition is the treasure of intellect. Islam upholds the fundamental rights of the human beings for attaining knowledge and receiving education. Not only that, this religion binds its followers to get educated and commands them to go to far off places for enhancing their academic qualifications. Islam is the only religion, which as a principle, promotes intellect in men and women and encourages the approach of reasoning and logical attitude.

Islam was first among all faiths and 'isms' to teach the lesson of equality, humanity and fraternity to the mankind. Islam believes in freedom of thought and individual's liberty. However, it calls for some limits and restrictions, as it introduces a complete code of conduct for leading a successful and meaningful life in this world and for attaining lasting contentment in the eternal world—our final destination.

In Islam, we have particular interpretations for the usual terms, like intellect, education, society and polity etc. In this book, specially these terms have been discussed in detail, in the light of the historical background and in the context of modern times.

This book has three sections, viz., Islamic Wisdom, Spirit of Governance and Present Scenario. In the first section, Islamic philosophy has been studied, with special reference to Holy Quran, Prophets' Tradition and great Islamic scholars' works. And thus Islam emerges as the fountainhead for wisdom, knowledge and intellect. Further, the faith comes up as a practical discipline of life in the second section, which sheds light on Islamic tenets for administering a state, waging a war and establishing permanent peace. In the third section, Islam's relevance and its role in contemporary world have been examined and evaluated very empirically. This academic and healthy debate, finally depicts the features of a living Islam, in totality.

The undersigned feels pride in presenting such diverse subjects in comprehensive manner, in a single book, as an endeavour to make. Islam's message comprehensible for scholars, students and general readers, who love to read about Islam.

Editor

1

Introduction

The God Almighty (Allah) had created man (and woman) in his own image by giving him three deiform faculties, which he had given to no one else in his creation in the same proportion or combination. These three deiform faculties are transcendent intelligence, free will and gift of speach.

Transcendent Intelligence

There is no blind faith in Islam. In the Quran, Allah invites us to either accept or reject Islam, but with reason. However, while the Quran lays a great emphasis on reason, it does not consider it as a sole means of gaining knowledge and the only criterion for judging truth. Thus, while Islam is a great proponent of reason, it is against rationalism.

The intellect, through which divine knowledge is received, must not be mistaken for reason alone (al-aql-al-juzi). In Islam, the combined faculty of reason and intuition (al-'aql'al-kulli) serves as an instrument for reaching the divine truths, which are super-rational but not irrational. The Quranic term for the seat of knowledge is "fuad" which means both heart and mind. But if this faculty is obscured by the worldly passions, it can become the veil that hides man from the divine and leads him astray. We should therefore be worry of the two-edged nature of the "sword of reason".

Paradoxical as it may seem, while the Quran lays great emphasis on reason, it also requires us to believe in the unseen (Al-ghayb). It will indeed by presumptuous on our part if we tried to comprehend the whole of the Quran strictly in the context of the current framework of the scientific method, which is constrained by a number of severe limitations. At a lower level, these limitations pertain to the direct verification of an occurrence (Null hypothesis) and at a higher level to the fragility of human observation (the Hisenburg principle of uncertainty) and the relativity of observation (Einstein). It is indeed in the recognition of human limitations that the Islamic faith also extends to things which are beyond the reach of human perception.

The faith in Islam (Al-Iman) is connected with transcendent intelligence, which must lead a believer to certainty—certainty of Absolute and attachment of all things to the Absolute. In this context the Quran describes three distinct stages of knowledge. First, "ilm-al-yaqin" (Knowledge of certainty) knowledge through information, second, "ayn-al-yaqin" (eye of certainty) knowledge through experience and third and the highest "haqq-al-yaqin" (truth of certainty) knowledge through being.

Free Will

Man is free to choose his destiny. Without such a freedom, he could not be the pride of God's creation. God knows how a particular individual will behave in a particular situation because He is God. But this in no way contradicts man's inherent freedom. Islam literally means submission (to the Will of God) and it is submission with free will which alone is acceptable to Him. thus, Al-Islam which represents an equilibrium in terms of the Absolute and with the Absolute, is based on the free will and submission with free will to the divine law, which includes ritual prayers, fasting, alms giving, correct conduct, etc.

Gift of Speech

Man has been given the gift of speech for the beneficial communication. The Quran enjoins people to speak well to each other. But, above all, the gift of speach has been given to man so that he may praise his Creator. The remembrance of God (dhikr-Allah) is based on Al-Ihsan (the way: virtue) which reflects excellence and implies that you should worship God as if you see Him and if you do not see Him, He sees you. Al-Ihsan also implies special compensations over and above justice (Adil) for individuals who may be suffering from any deficiencies, whether physical, economic, or spirtual.

The remembrance of God is the quintessential prayer in Islam, which in the Quran is rated higher than other religious obligations. This is because it is the remembrance of God, which by purifying our minds and hearts, will lead us to the "ayn-al-yaqin" (eye of certainty), enabling us to discern the things or creatures of the unseen and thus augment our faith layer upon layer.

Central Framework

To summarize, the central framework of Islam is based on Al-iman, Al-Islam, and Al-ihsan. Al-Iman (faith), which reflects certainly (yaqin) is based on transcendent intelligence; Al-Islam (the law: submission) which reflects equilibrium is based on the free will and Al-Ihsan (the way: virtue) which reflects excellence is based on the gift of speach. Thus, Islam is a religion of certainty, equilibrium and remembrance and is based on three deiform faculties of transcendent intelligence, free will, and gift of speach. Equilibrium implies maintenance of a balance between Allah and His creation and between His transcendence (the law) and immanence (spirituality). Also, it implies an attitude of moderation both in speach and actions.

Another fundamental percept of Islam is that of orientation, which implies that not only our thinking should be correct on purely religious questions, but also on broad social and political issues. The central theme of Islam is welfare and not salvation. Therefore, for Islam the main objective is to attain the state of felicity by following the laws of God and not merely to observe these laws for their own sake. The Islamic law is there to serve man and not the other way around. Also, we should make a distinction between the Islam as such and the cultural practices of various Muslim countries.

Islamic Law

Allah wishes all mankind to lead a happy and a useful life on earth. To attain a state of felicity man needs both an orientation and a set of rules and regulations. The logical conclusion of any laws made by man, based on these are of self-interest, conflict and oppression. Only One God's laws could be attuned to the welfare of all mankind. The central theme of Islam is welfare and not salvation. Therefore, for Islam the main objective is to attain the state of felicity by following God's laws and not merely to observe these laws for their own sake. The Islamic law is there to serve the man and not other way round.

The final source of Islam's laws is the Quran. The life example of the Prophet (PBUH) had illuminated God's laws for us. The Prophet was, so to speak, a living Quran. However, as Quran is the final message of God to man, continuing Ijtihad (independent thinking) on it is necessary in order; to frame Islamic laws for all times to come. The legal interpretations of the Great Imams of the past can serve as a point of reference rather than as an iron-clad framework. It should be remembered that finality belongs to Allah and His Word (the Quran) alone, to ascribe finality to anyone else would tantamount to committing a grave Shirk. No doubt, while the truth of this statement would be self- evident to all true followers of Islam most of them would resist opening the gates of Ijtihad in the fear that once these gates are opened, these will also be opened to the enemies of Islam. However, they should have no such fears. In fact, this may bring the hidden enemies of Islam out into the open. Any way, we should not allow our fears of today to kill our hopes of tomorrow.

Moreover, the Quran is not mere a book of the sources of law. It is the God's all-embracing message to mankind, which give firm guidelines for the spiritual orientation of man. Without a correct spiritual orientation, any code of law would remain but an empty shell. Without the spiritual spring of Islam erupting in the hearts of men and women, no true Islamic order could be established and any attempted outward observance of Islamic laws would amount to no more than an exercise in futility.

Part - I

Islamic Wisdom

2

Knowledge and Scholarship

Islam has insisted that life is to be lived in a positive, gainful and effective manner and that an individual has deep obligations towards the collective welfare of the community. To achieve this objective it is essential to maintain a constant flow of fresh knowledge into the society so that its members can be saved from ignorance and stagnation.

The pre-Islamic Arabia was not entirely denuded of learning, but whatever evidence has been preserved shows that knowledge as something higher, nobler and truer did not exist at that time. The Prophet of Islam for the first time in the history of Arabian peninsula made knowledge an essential tool for understanding realities of life. Under his inspiring guidance, learning acquired respect and reverence which remained the hallmark of Islamic civilization for centuries afterwards.

The Quran itself in lucid and self-explanatory terms has laid great emphasis on the acquisition of knowledge. In the chapter entitled *Al-Adaq* (The Clot) which is considered by commentators to be among the earlier, if not the earliest revelations, the Quran in unmistakable terms points out God's desire to educate men in arts and sciences which are difficult for them to comprehend.

1. Read : In the name of thy Lord who createth,
2. Createth man from a clot,

3. Read: And thy Lord is the Most Bounteous,
4. Who teacheth by the pen.
5. Teacheth man that which he knew not.

There is ample evidence in Quran that knowledge was essential even for the prophets.

And unto Solomon (we subdued) the wind in its raging. It set by his command toward the land which We had blessed. *And of everything We are aware.*

And about the Prophet Lot the Quran says:

> And unto Lot we gave judgement and knowledge, and We delivered him from the community that did abominations. Lo ! they were folk of evil, lewd.

The importance which the Quran attaches to knowledge can further be explained by the frequency with which it has used the word *ilm* (knowledge).

According to one estimate it has been used 750 times in the Holy Book.

The Traditions of the Prophet have also emphasized in unequivocal terms that life without knowledge is hollow and barren. Knowledge is a great fertilizer of the human mind, and to have the maximum harvest out of human existence it is essential to enrich one's life with continuous learning. Al-Bukhari in his monumental work attributes a tradition to the Prophet which says that disappearance of knowledge and absence of scholars from society would spell the demise of human civilization. Abu Dawud (202-275/817-889) also makes several statements to illustrate the basic fact that knowledge alone could make life radiant with spiritual, material and moral richness. The position of the scholar among people, in his opinion, is the same as that of the moon among stars. He copies numerous traditions of the Prophet which accord a very prestigious and reverent position to scholars in a Muslim community. He also emphasizes that knowledge, particularly religious knowledge, should not be sold for worldly gains.

The entire Hadith literature is replete with references from Quran and the sayings of the Prophet which abundantly prove that religion and knowledge are the two main pillars of human life.

Some historians have attributed the following two traditions to the Prophet :

> Acquire knowledge, because he who acquires it in the way of the Lord performs an act of piety; who speaks of it, praises the Lord, who seeks it adores God, who dispenses instruction in it, bestows alms, and who imparts it to its fitting objects, performs an act of devotion to God. Knowledge enables its possessor to distinguish what its forbidden from what is not; it lights the way to Heaven; it is our friend in the desert, our society in solitude, our companion when bereft of friends; it guides us to happiness; it sustains us in misery; it is our ornament in the company of friends it serves as an armour against enemies. With knowledge the servant of God rises to the height of goodness and to a noble position, associates with sovereigns in this world and attains to the perfection of happiness in the next.

There has never been any doubt in Islamic history that knowledge is a benediction of God and it is fully integrated into Iman (Belief). A verse in the Quran reads as follows :

> God will lift up by degrees those among you who have come to believe and those who have been given knowledge.

And those who come to believe know.

And we have set out signs for people who know —for people who understand—for people who have come to believe.

'Seyyed Hussein Nasr has summed up the significance of knowledge in Islam in the following words:

> Many of the verses of the Quran that were to follow affirmed the sacred nature of knowledge and scientia (ilm) one of the God's name being 'He who knows (Al-alim). The Prophet himself though unlettered from the stand-point of human knowledge was at the same time the channel of the revelation of the Book which is considered by all Muslims to be the quintessential sum of all knowledge both human and divine.

> Moreover, he reaffirmed the teachings of the Quran by stressing that the acquisition of knowledge to the limits of one's abilities is incumbent upon every believer, as a part of his religious duties. His sayings such as 'Seek knowledge from cradle to the grave,' 'Seek knowledge even in China' were echoed through the later centuries as the most authoritative arguments for teaching and propagating knowledge (ilm) even though debates also arose as to exactly what the knowledge to which the Prophet alluded, and whose attainment he considered so essential, encompassed.

Islam has insisted that reason and revelations are the two wheels of the vehicle of life, ana in order to reach one's destination, both wheels have to be equal in size, strength and lubrication. In other words, search for knowledge is an act of piety ; it is equivalent to prayer. To make search for fresh knowledge easier, Islam has kept its principles and precepts flexible, and left an ample room for individual interpretation, so that growing complexities of human problems could be resolved in the light of increasing knowledge. Grunebaum says, "There is an element of sober reasonableness in Islam which works toward a human application of its precepts. The Prophet was sent not to make life more difficult but to facilitate it." The emphasis, however, was on the usefulness of knowledge, so that the believer could shape the affairs of his life strictly according to the ethical ideals of Islam.

In short, the role of knowledge in the religio-political life of the Muslim community is decisive and all-pervading. It is considered to be a source of strength for human character. It enlightens the soul, dispels ignorance, enriches the mind, produces excellences in intellect, saves men from omissions and excesses, cures passions and impulses of their waywardness and solidifies faith and belief in the revealed word of God.

Definition of Knowledge

It is very difficult to formulate a concrete and operational definition for an elusive and eternally ambiguous term like knowledge. Difficulties multiply manifold in the case of Islam, because in it secular and religious knowledge are completely intermingled. In the mind of a Muslim, knowledge includes every thing which reason and revelation can unearth for the spiritual and material betterment of mankind. Since the Quran and the Prophet had emphasized the importance of knowledge in unmistakable terms, Muslim scholars in every period of Islamic history took special pains to explain the scope and subject matter of knowledge. The result of all these endeavours, however, has been that Islamic literature is crowded with bewildering variety of definitions.

Franz Rosenthal in his valuable work listed 107 definitions from various source books.

Philip K. Hitti defines ilm (Islamic knowledge) in the following words :

> The Arabic word for science (ilm) like its English correspondent, etymologically means "knowledge" or "learning." It may be used in the broad sense to mean knowledge systematized with reference to general truths and laws, or more specifically, to refer to knowledge as it relates to physical world in which case it is known as physical or natural science.

The term ilm (knowledge) as originally used was a universal blanket for all kinds of intellectual, philosophical and scientific pursuits, which enabled human beings to explore the mysteries of nature, and highlighted the true meanings of the revelation. But at a very early stage of the growth of Muslim scholarship, knowledge was categorized into different areas and instead of ilm (knowledge) singular, ulum (plural) became a common term for scholarship. The general opinion among the historians of Islam is that as territories which had advanced civilization were conquered outside Arabia, realization dawned upon Muslims that knowledge was extremely diverse in nature, and that each branch constituted a distinct area of specialization, requiring specific kind of intellect and a particular kind of education and training.

According to Franz Rosenthal there reached a stage when the number of various branches of knowledge had risen to 150 and according to one account in the sixteenth century, the number possibly could be as high as 316. In spite of this bewildering diversity, however, a belief that knowledge in essence is one, continued to persist in the world of Muslim scholarship. All branches of knowledge were interconnected and in order to understand the realities of life, and resolve baffling complexities which hampered the solutions of problems it was essential to use maximum amount of information from all branches of knowledge.

The Muslim scholars, however, never gave any definitive view on how to relate the original Quranic concept of Ilm to the later developments which produced countless fields of intellectual specialization. The study of the landmark figures in the history of Muslim scholarship clearly demonstrates that compartmentalization of knowledge did not deter them from mastering several branches of knowledge at the same time, pleading that division of human learning into different subjects was only an effort to systematize knowledge and facilitate its assimilation, otherwise knowledge was one compact whole.

In Arabic and Persian the term Hakeem which meant wise was used for physician as well as for philosopher. Very rarely a distinction was made between natural sciences, humanities, and other related subjects. As a general rule the reputation of a scholar depended on the number of subjects on which he could claim mastery, and the amount of light that he could shed on an issue through various interdisciplinary approaches.

Uses of Knowledge

Knowledge is the guardian of soul, architect of morality, and custodian of values and ideals which are the major determinants of human destiny both here and hereafter. Intellect, which is the unique characteristic of human beings, is meant to be utilized for the cultivation of divine attributes. It is the only instrument, which is properly cultivated and effectively used, could narrow the gap between God and man. Ignorant and untutored mind can never hope to develop the ability which uncovers the inscrutable secrets of the universe. Scholars of all shades of opinion in Islam agree that pure reason alone is an insufficient guide. Reason in their opinion needs always to be supplemented with the revealed word of God. Ideal conditions for human thought and action are possible only when a believer uses both the secular and spiritual knowledge in resolving the problems of life. Revelation does not put any serious constraint on the freedom of thought. Except for some fundamental principles relating to the sovereignty of God, the mission of the Prophet, and sanctity of the word of the Quran, all the rest of the fields of human activity are subject to independent judgement, and rational interpretation. Outside the boundaries laid down by Sharia, the entire world of knowledge is a fit subject for research. As a matter of fact such an investigation through reason and logic, it is said, would strengthen the faith of the believer.

In Islam knowledge is not the monopoly of the learned few. Every Muslim according to his needs and means is under religious obligation to accept learning as a continuous process in his life. Reason and debate are considered to be competent instruments for the spread of enlightenment, and independent judgement based on righteous niyya (intention) is a very powerful instrument to overcome difficulties of life. It is due to this insistence on research and inquiry as a religious duty, that the early Muslims produced some of the greatest early heralds of scientific knowledge. Between the ninth and twelfth centuries when the rest of the world was intellectually stagnant, Muslim scholars wrote some immortal works in every branch of scientific knowledge. Schools and academies in the Muslim empire were throbbing with creativity and innovation. A careful examination of some of the fundamental duties of the Islamic faith showed that without scientific knowledge their performance was impossible. Fasting, pilgrimage and numerous other religious ceremonies required careful and scientific understanding of the lunar calendar. Five daily prayers needed precision regarding the movement of the sun. It was essential to devise instruments by which the increasing and decreasing shadows between dawn and dusk could be measured with exactness. Prayers in Islam were congregational, and thus there was all the more reason for finding a universally accepted standard by which everyone could be in time in the mosque. Similarly, the numerous details regarding many other aspects of the sacred law could only be assured by specialized knowledge. For instance, the laws of inheritance, Zakat (Poor Relief) and Wakf (religious endowments) required considerable knowledge of various sciences.

Some Western scholars have tried to minimize the role of

Islam in the sudden upsurge of scientific inquiry in the Muslim lands which followed its advent. Grunebaum says :

> No matter how important the contribution of Muslim scholars were able to make to the natural sciences, and no matter how great the interest with which, at certain periods, the leading classes and the government itself followed and supported their researches, those sciences (and their technological application) had no root in the fundamental needs and aspirations of their civilization.

This statement by a learned orientalist, however, smacks of prejudice. Islam's broad but firm injunctions in favour of knowledge and reason, played a decisive role in unleashing the spirit of inquiry, which led to the sudden upsurge of scientific learning in lands which for centuries had been intellectually barren.

Western View

Western scholars have been critical of Islamic civilization, pointing out that except for one powerful thrust during the 4th and 5th centuries of Hijra it has been intellectually sterile and stagnant. Muslim writers in their opinion were trapped in dogma, and their mind and thought revolved with few exceptions around unalterable stereotypes. Their capacity to widen the horizons was limited by the inflexible and insurmountable theological barriers. These impressions could be the result of prejudice or misunderstanding or may be both. It is not our intention to make another apologetic plea in defence of Muslim scholarship. The approaches of the Muslim scholars were far from being perfect. They had numerous faults of methodology, and many of them were patently careless in the collection of data. It is, however, unfair to think that Islam in any way was hostile to independent intellectual inquiry and that it was a religion which ultimately led to permanent stagnation in Islamic thought.

In order to make an objective estimate, it would be essential to list certain cardinal features of Muslim scholarship which distinguish it from the rest of the world of scholarship.

It was inherent in the thinking of Muslim scholars to believe that the revealed word of God was the main source of knowledge.

All other knowledge derived through scientific experimentation, observation or reflection was meant to support or substantiate the instructions given in the Quran. The only purpose the knowledge has is to strengthen the faith of the believer. Such an approach is diametrically different from the Western views on knowledge, which insist that all scientific learning is meant to refute religious dogma, and find ways of interpreting and understanding the realities of life, which have no spiritual connotations. Judging strictly from Western standards knowledge is an end in itself and not a means to an end. In Islam on the other hand, knowledge is only a means to an end. D. B. MacDonald in his estimate of the contributions of Al-Ghazzali has made the following remarks regarding this fundamental aspect of the Muslim scholarship.

Unfortunately, he was beset by the utilitarianism of Islam, and so could not be content to let his book stand for itself as a human document, nor even as an *apologia pro vita sua.* He must needs make out of it a manual of apologetics suited to his time, and thus, undoubtedly, has dulled the personal touch. In so doing he has furnished perhaps the most striking example of the fatal Muslim didacticism which does not permit an artist, conscious or unconscious, to set a living figure before the reader and leave it to do its work, but must systematize and explain everything. In this, the Muslim writers differ markedly from the poets of heathen Arabia who had a frank delight in the simple expression of themselves without thought of their audience. Al-Ghazzali in his *Ayyuha L-Walad* has in unequivocal terms emphasized the knowledge which cannot be operationalized is only a monumental wastage. Unless research findings are helpful in resolving prob lems of life, in his opinion, they are a futile intellectual exercise. Tehsil-i-Ilm (search for knowledge) he points out, must have some meaning, a purpose and a denned goal. The above treatise was written in response to a young scholar who was encountering certain difficulties in streamlining his thoughts regarding the wisdom of striving and struggling for the accumulation of knowledge and incessant reading of various sciences. Al-Ghazzali says :

> O youth, do not be bankrupt of works, nor empty of states, be assured that knowledge alone does not strengthen the hand—just so though a man reads a

> hundred thousand scientific questions and understood them or learned them, they do not benefit him except by working.

Without implementation, the tree of knowledge will not bear any fruit, and one would never be able to attain the nearness to God which is the ultimate objective of all learning. He says:

> Knowledge is the tree and the working is its fruit, and though you studied a hundred years and collected a thousand books, you would not be prepared for the mercy of Allah the Exalted except by working.

In advocating such a course Al-Ghazzali was only trying to portray the true and essential character of knowledge in Quranic terms. In Islam, religion is not merely a spiritual embellishment of human soul; it provides full guidance to the believers in resolving multifarious problems which they encounter in their search for the Straight Path. According to the Islamic view, religious and secular knowledge are two facets of the same reality. Both complement each other.

In 'Mizan al Amal' Al-Ghazzali says, "whoever thinks faith alone will suffice him is ignorant of the meaning of faith." In other words to make life more gainful faith based on revealed knowledge, and understanding derived from secular learning must go hand in hand. He sums up his thesis with a warning to his correspondent that "O youth, knowledge without work is insanity and work without knowledge is vanity."

The essence of devotion in Islam is to work ceaselessly for the the glory of Almighty God and to abide with His commands in shaping human destiny on this earth. Ibada (prayer) is the only instrument by which this obligation can be fulfilled. But prayer without knowledge remains hollow, and knowledge by itself would be meaningless unless it is translated into action. Both ilm (knowledge) and amal (action) are needed to give enrichment and meaning to life.

Reward in its Own

In Islam knowledge is its own reward. It cannot be sold or bought as a marketable commodity in pursuit of worldly gains or reputation. Search for material rewards and ambition to win widespread fame are the common frailities of human nature, but to acquire knowledge simply for their sake is intellectually sacriligeous.

From the strictly Islamic point of view knowledge is only meant to uncover the truth and strengthen the faith of a believer. Knowledge used for any other purpose is against Quranic principles whose supreme ideal is to make scientific research an additional support for the dissemination of God's message on earth. It is meant to illustrate and substantiate the wisdom of the Holy Prophet as depicted in his words and deeds. In the books of Hadith the following tradition of the Prophet is narrated through Abu Hurairah :

> The second (person to receive sentence on the day of resurrection) a man who shall have obtained knowledge and instructed others, and read the Quran, he will be brought into the presence of God, and will be given to understand the benefits he had received which he will be sensible of and confess and God will say 'What didst thou do in gratitude thereof? He will reply, 'I learned knowledge and taught others and I read the Quran to please thee.' Then God will say 'Thou liest, but thou studiest that people might call thee learned.' Then God will order him to be dragged upon his face and precipitated into hell. The prophet said, 'He who desires knowledge in order to be honoured in the world or dispute with the ignorant and attract the notice of mankind, God will throw him into hell fire.'

Al-Ghazzali has administered the following warning to scholars who use scholarship for material acquisition, official position and popular recognition. O youth, how many nights you have remained awake repeating science and poring over books and have denied yourself sleep. I do not know what the purpose of it was. If it was attaining worldly ends and securing its vanities and acquiring its dignities and surpassing your contemporaries and such like, woe to you and again woe.

Ignorance is the malady of the human heart and soul, which can only be cured with knowledge. Learned doctors in Islam are the physicians who through insight and knowledge diagnose the ailments of mind and then write prescriptions for their ultimate elimination. It would be extremely unbecoming of a physician to have any other objective except to cure the disease.

Divine Knowledge

The idea that knowledge is divine, and that scholars are accountable to God for it, inculcated among Muslim scholars a deep sense of responsibility and objectivity both in the collection of facts and their interpretation. They did not like search for truth to be contaminated with prejudices or selfish interests. In order to arrive at the right conclusions they very often used comparative method of study. Abu Nasr-al-Farabe (258/870-339/950) who ranks among the greatest philosophers of Islam has listed his views on research in natural and social sciences as follows:

> There he should set out next upon the science of man and investigate the *what* and the *how* of the purpose for which man is made what is the perfection that man must achieve. Then he should investigate all things by which man achieves this perfection or that are useful to him in achieving it. These are the good, virtuous, and noble things. He should distinguish them for things that obstruct his achieving this perfection. These are the evils, the vices and the base things. He should make known what and how every one of them is, and from what and for what it is, until all of them become known, intelligible and distinguished from each other.

Abu Raihan-al-Beruni (362/973-442/1051) whose examination of Indian history, geography and society is considered a spectacular piece of scientific inquiry, also laid down certain rigorous rules for genuine scholarship. E. G. Sachau who translated Al-Beruni's monumental work, *Kitab-ul-Hind,* made the following observations on his method and approach to social studies:

> He is a stern judge both of himself and of others. Himself perfectly sincere, it is sincerity which he demands from others. Whenever he does not fully understand a subject or only knows part of it, he will

> at once tell the readers so, either asking the reader's pardon—He is not a friend of those who hate to avow their ignorance by a frank 'I do not know' and he is roused to strong indignation whenever he meets with want of sincerity.

In his preface to *Kitab-ul-Hind,* Al-Beruni himself made the following remarks on scientific reporting and observation in research.

No one will deny that in questions of historic authenticity *hearsay* does not equal *eye-witness,* for in the latter the eye of the observer apprehends the substance of that which is observed, both in the time when and in the place where it exists, whilst hearsay has its peculiar drawbacks. But for these, it would even be preferable to eye-witness; for the object of eyewitness can only be *actual* momentary existence, whilst hearsay comprehends alike the present, the past, and the future, so as to apply in a certain sense both to that which is and to that which is not (i.e., which wither has ceased to exist or has not yet come into existence). Written tradition is one of the species of hearsay we might almost say, the most preferable. How could we know the history of nations but for the everlasting monuments of the pen ? The tradition regarding an event which in itself does not contradict either logical or physical laws will invariably depend for its character as true or false upon the character of the reporters, who are moved by the divergency of interests and all kinds of animosities and antipathies between the various nations. We must distinguish different classes of reporters. One of them tells a lie, as intending to further an interest of his own, either *by lauding* his family or nation, because he is one of them, or *by attacking* the family or nation on the opposite side, thinking that thereby he can gain his ends. In both cases he acts from motives of objectionable cupidity and animosity. Another one tells a lie regarding a class of people whom he likes, as being under obligation to them, or whom he hates, because something disagreeable has happened between them. Such a reporter is near akin to the first-mentioned one, as he too acts from motives of personal predilection and enmity.

Another tells a lie because he is of such a base nature as to aim thereby at some profit, or because he is such a coward as to be afraid of telling the truth.

Another tells a lie because it is his nature to lie, and he cannot do otherwise, which proceeds from the essential meanness of his character and the depravity of his innermost being.

Lastly, a man may tell a lie from ignorance, blindly following others who told him.

If, now, reporters of this kind become so numerous as to represent a certain body of tradition, or if in the course of time they even come to form a consecutive series of communities or nations, both the first reporter and his followers form the connecting links between the hearer and the inventor of the lie; and if the connecting links are eliminated, there remains the originator of the story, one of the various kinds of liars we have enumerated, as the only person with whom we have to deal.

That man only is praiseworthy who shrinks from a lie and always adheres to the truth, enjoying credit even among liars, not to mention others.

Value of Truth

It has been said in the Quran, 'Speak the truth, even if it were against yourselves' and the Messiah expresses himself in the Gospel to this effect: 'Do not mind the fury of kings in speaking the truth before them. They only possess your body, but they have no power over your soul.' (cf. St. Matt. X, 18, 19, 28; St. Luke, xii, 4). In these words the Messiah orders us to exercise *moral courage.* For what the crowd calls courage—bravely dashing into the fight or plunging into an abyss of destruction—is only a *species* of courage, whilst the *genus,* far above all *species,* is to *scorn death,* whether by word or deed. Now as justice (i.e., being just) is a quality liked and coveted for its own self, for its intrinsic beauty, the same applies to *truthfulness,* except perhaps in the case of such people as never tasted how sweet it is, or know the truth, but deliberately shun it, like a notorious liar who once was asked if he had ever spoken the truth, and gave the answer, 'If I were not afraid to speak the truth, I should say, no.' A liar will avoid the path of justice; he will, as matter of preference side with oppression and false witness, breach of confidence, fraudulent appropriation of the wealth of others, theft, and all the vices which serve to ruin the world and mankind. In his other famous work called *Chronology of Ancient Nations,* Al-Beruni also emphasizes that historical research should be free from emotions and prejudices which so often blur human vision and disable men from comprehending the truth with clarity. He points out that rigorous comparative method alone can insure objectivity and impartiality in research. In the preface to the above book he says that his purpose "cannot be obtained by way or ratiocination with philosophical notions, but solely by adopting the information of those who have a written tradition—and by making their opinions a basis on which to build up a system; besides we must compare their traditions and opinions among themselves, when we try to establish our system. But even that we must clear our mind from all those accidental circumstances which deprave most men, from all causes which are liable to make people blind against the truth, e.g., inveterate custom, party spirit, rivalry, being addicted to one's passion, the desire to gain influence."

From the Greeks the Muslim borrowed their tremendous love for logic. Although theologians like Ibn Taimiyya condemned Greek logic vehemently as something against the canons of Islam, the history of Muslim scholarship shows that logic as an instrument of intellectual synthesis and philosophical articulation continued to exercise considerable influence in research and studies in Islam. Josef Van Ess has explained its uses for the Muslims as follows :

> This assertion seems somewhat in question; no Islamic jurist, or any other jurist, could do without logic ; he had to use most subtle hermeneutic methods to interpret the Quran, and he had to apply all kinds of logical processes to adjust the commands found by this interpretation to the individual cases of daily life. The same is true of *kalam,* Islamic theology : theology is by definition nothing more than logical demonstration of believed truth.

Abu Said Al-Sirafi (280-368/893-979), a reputed theologian of his time in Baghdad, made distinction between two types of logic. One which was used by Muslim theologians (Ulema) and Fukaha (Jurists) and the other which was strictly of Greek origin. In his opinion scholars in Islam were keen and anxious seekers after truth. They looked into each issue diligently and spread no effort in uncovering right and wrong through intelligent interpretation.

Their achievements he believed were impressive and intellectually satisfying. The strict logicians on the other hand wasted most of their time in wallowing around in barren argumentation. In other words, logical argumentation should not be an end in itself; it must further the cause of knowledge. Logic which does not help either in resolving problems of life, or in strengthening our beliefs is a wastage. Some scholars knowing that Islam does not allow meaningless hairsplitting, have castigated it as a religion based on intolerance and fanaticism. Such a view, however, is patently contrary to the spirit of Islam. There is nothing in the Quran or the Traditions of the Holy Prophet from which it could be construed that independence of judgment or difference of opinion are disallowed. In fact all the available evidence goes to prove that Islam perhaps among the great religions of the world, is the only religion which maintains that difference of opinion, provided it is not based on malice is the surest way to wisdom and rectitude.

The Tolerance

Intellectual and religious tolerance is a sign of social and emotional maturity. In all areas of Islamic scholarship, i.e., philosophical, theological and mystical, there were always deep and unbridgable divergencies. Ikhtilaf (difference) was considered to be a legitimate right of the individual. The result was that intellectual saber-rattling became a very prominent feature of scholarly circles in Islam. Most of the *Asul-ul-Fiqh* (Principles of Islamic Jurisprudence) were products of continuous debate and discussion, and endless controversies which were generated by serious differences among various schools of thought. The only time when Ikhtilaf would not be tolerated was when it was apprehended that scholars were indulging in dangerously innovative interpretation of the Quranic faith. Jean-Paul Charnay has summed up the role of Ikhtilafat (Divergences) in the intellectual life of Islam as follows :

> Ikhtilafat played a primary role in the development of Muslim thinking : intellectual technique, practical utilization, function in the Muslim community's evolution through diverse historical phases. Ikhtilaf is first an expression and consequence of the creative

> intellectual flowering of demogeographic conquests, of local and social disparities. It multiplies as it is influenced by political and religious passions and regional deviationism.

Concept of Education

An attempt has been made in following few lines to articulate certain philosophical and conceptual aspects of the nature of Prophethood and Prophecy and to use these concepts in outlining an Islamic theory of education.

Nature of Prophethood

The first thing to notice about Prophethood is that the birth of a Prophet had invariably taken place in a noble family with a long tradition of piety and good deeds. If this event is to be explained in the modern political terms, then the relevant concept would be that of 'elitism' and not of 'democracy'. Allah had choosen His Prophets entirely according to His own Wisdom.

The second thing of which we must take note of is that before the mission of Prophecy was bestowed upon an individual, he had already shown, without doubt, that he was a person of exceptional conduct and character and of outstanding merit. In other words, a person on whom the Prophethood was to be bestowed had to meet certain pre-qualifications.

The third thing of which we must make a special note is that a would be Prophet was, without exception, a thinker. He was an individual who was not satisfied with the prevailing environment of morality and human conduct. He was pained to notice the prevailing injustices. All this led him to think about the social order in which there would be no more injustice and usurption of the rights of the poor. We thus find that the individuals on whom Allah had bestowed the mission of Prophecy had usually faced a fairly long period of intellectual struggle and personal anguish. We see them withdrawing into deserts or into the hills. It is interesting to note that there appeared to be, mutatis mutandis, a certain optimum period for this intellectual and spiritual striving; it was neither too short for the tempering of the Prophetic soul nor too long that it might have led to frustration. Thus, it is not that

Allah had thrown away the honour of Prophethood on anyone; the person awarded the Prophetic mission had already been searching for the Truth and was eventually granted a vision of the Truth.

A paper read at the auspicious occasion of Eid Milad-un-Nabi celebrations at the Embassy of Pakistan, Cairo, Arab Republic of Egypt on 12th Rabi-ul-Awal, 1400 H (30th January, 1980).

Allah had used various means for conveying His word to His Prophets, while Allah had rewarded some of the Prophets with His own Vision or with the reflection of His own Vision, a larger part of His message was received as perceptions and inspirations of truth or in other words as Revalations (Wahy). The Ascension of the Prophet Muhammad (Peace and Blessings be upon him) to 'the Heavens (Miradj) was the ultimate grace of Allah bestowed upon him, wherein he was admitted into the presence of Allah. There is a deep philosophical meaning of the Ascension. This event points to be the place of man in Allah's Design. It tells us that man has been bestowed with an inherent capacity to rise the threshold of Allah, but by following the 'Straight Path'. The 'Miradj' points to the highest point, which the human intellect or ego could possibly attain. Thus, it also fixes the outer limits of knowledge.

In the above context, it would seem desirable, to distinguish between the mystic experience and the Prophetic perception. The mystic feels the bliss of his finite personality melting in the infinite ocean of Reality. The mystic, given a choice, would never wish to return from the repose of 'unitary experience' and his experience remains largely private and incommunicable. On the other hand, the Prophet perceives the reality in its totality. His return is creative and he asserts himself to mould the forces of history with a view to creating a fresh world of ideals.

Islamic Theory of Education

The above important facts serve as a background to the articulation below of an Islamic theory of education.

The first duty of a Muslim student is hardwork in the search of knowledge and knowledge should lead him to Certainty (Yaqin), which in turn should strengthen his Faith (Iman). Please note that Islam does not believe in blind faith; in Islam faith is based on intelligence (Aql) and not only on emotions. Quran describes three distinct levels of knowledge: First is ilm-al-yaqin, knowledge through information; second, 'yn-al-yaqin, knowledge through experince and third and highest, haqq-al-yaqin, knowledge through being.

The second duty of a Muslim student is to do the above search with good intentions, because if his intentions are not right, his hardwork would come only to a naught. Good intensions mean good intentions for all. It is important to note here that the Quranic concept of 'Good is based not only on justice (Adl) but also on the principle of 'Ihsan', which means that not only we should do 'Adl' but also on the principle of 'Ihsan' which means that not only we should do 'Adl' but also make special compensations for the individuals who are suffering from various deficiencies, whether physical, economic or spiritual.

The third point in this theory of education is that of "Blessings" (Faydh), which on one hand, is a product of our own good intentions and on the other, of the grace of our teacher. Unless we are able to establish a special bond between ourselves and our teacher and give him all the due respect (Adab), we will not have these 'blessings' and therefore, our knowledge would remain incomplete.

Another factor of great importance to keep in mind is that unless we purify our heart of all ill will and evil, we could not possess good intentions for all. Therefore, in the first place, we have to cleanse our heart, if we want to perceive true knowledge. One Quranic word for heart is 'Fuad', which means both mind and heart.

With the Westernization of our minds, we have forgotten about one very important source of knowledge. One pillar of knowledge, of course, is the objective knowledge, based on the concepts of deduction and induction and the emprirical knowledge about causation, but we have forgotten about the other equally important pillar of knowledge - the intuitive knowledge. A Prophet's perception of truth is the most advanced form of this knowledge. Of course, a common individual cannot be privy to Prophetic perception (Wahy), but he can strive towards its lesser aspect i.e. 'Basirah'. We could build a sort of equation for this qualitative knowledge. We can prepare the ground for it by our hard work; we lay its foundations with our good intentions; we cement the foundations with the blessings of our teacher and we correct the direction of this building by the purity of our hearts. We are then ready to receive this knowledge in a great abundance. Indeed, Allah is the Great Grantor of knowledge to those who seek.

However, when we have read all the books and claim to have acquired all the Knowledge, we may still face a great danger, which may nullify all our previous efforts and life's work and this destruction may be brought about by the doubts created in our heart about the Truth (Haqq). In other words, we may lose our faith (Iman) of course if we lose our faith, we lose everything. Therefore we must always pray to Allah that He should not put us in doubt and make us faithless. A faithless person is like a building built on sand. But, if we have faith, then we would have that great quality of mind which would further brighten the building of our knowledge i.e. the 'unity of thought' (Wahdat-ul-Fikr).

Now if we have passed all the above stages, indeed we have done extremely well and deserve the praise of our brothers. However, our work is not finished yet. In fact, our real work starts from now onwards. Its now that we must assume the role of preaching good and in Islam, only preaching of good is not enough; simultaneously, we must also forbid evil and do that with a force and if necessary lay down our lives in doing that. However, many of us may lack enough courage to do that. But, we can have this courage by developing this great quality, this final force which cannot be readily explained by an English word. This force is that of 'Ishq' - Love of Allah and his Prophet.

True Objectives

Of course, we should direct this 'force' toward the true objective, otherwise there is a danger that we may become ineffective. This direction is given by the vision of a better world, as outlined in the Quaran-a world in which everyone is equal and free, in which there is complete justice and in which there is no poverty. We must, therefore, strive to establish the Quranic Social Order of the 'Rububiyyah', which would enable full realisation of the latent potentialities of every individual through both sustanance and fostering of his body, as well as the fulfilment of his personality and spirit, which indeed is the ultimate purpose of Islam. We must not forget that the central theme of Islam is 'Welfare' and not 'Salvation'.

3

Scientific Attitude

Exploration of the mysteries buried deep in the bosom of nature, is an endless activity of human mind. Science and religion are generally considered to be the two major contendors in this eternal endeavour of man. Religious and scientific views in most cases are irreconcilable. Scientists ridicule the theologians as irrational and mythical and the theologians in turn castigate the scientists as atheists or materialists. Both tend to claim the monopoly of truth. In Islam however, the struggle between science and religion was never so acute or critical. In fact during most of the Islamic history science and religion remained in a very healthy combination in uncovering the secrets of the universe and in fortifying the beliefs and ideals of the Muslims. There is a general consensus among historians of Islamic civilization, that religion in Islam instead of being a barrier to scientific investigation provided a powerful thrust for greater and wider inquiry into the unresolved mysteries of the relationship between man and nature.

Islam and Scientific Knowledge

The Quran in very clear terms has brought home this message to every believer. A passage in the fourth chapter reads as follows :

> He it is Who sendeth down water from the sky, and therewith We bring forth buds of every kind; We

> bring forth the green blade from which We bring forth the thick-clustered grain; and from the date-palm, from the pollen thereof, spring pendant bunches ; and (We bring forth) gardens of grapes, and the olive and the pomegranate, alike and unlike. Look upon the fruit thereof, when they bear fruit, and upon its ripening. Lo ! herein verily are portents for a people who believe.

Floods, rains, clouds, insects, are all God's creations. He is the sole Provider and Protector. He enjoins upon every believer to understand these manifold manifestations of nature, as Ayats (signs) of the Creator. There are numerous verses in the Quran which repeatedly emphasise this theme. Some of them can be reproduced as follows :

> So We sent against them the flood and the locusts and the vermin and the frogs and the blood—a succession of clear signs. But they were arrogant and became a guilty folk.

And He it is Who sendeth the winds as tidings heralding His mercy, till, when they bear a cloud heavy (with rain), We lead it to a dead land, and then cause water to descend thereon and thereby bring forth fruits of every kind. Thus bring We forth the dead. Haply ye may remember.

He sendeth down water from the sky, so that valleys flow accoıding to their measure, and the flood beareth (on its surface) swelling foam—from that which they smelt in the fire in order to make ornaments and tools riseth a foam like unto it— thus Allah coineth (the similitude of) the true and the false. Then, as for the foam, it passeth away as scum upon the banks; banks, while, as for that which is of use to mankind, it remaineth in the earth. Thus Ailah coineth the similitudes. What, have they not beheld heaven above them, how We have built it, and decked it out fair, and it has no cracks ? And the earth—We stretched it forth and cast on it firm mountains, and We caused to grow therein of every joyous kind for an insight and a reminder to every penitent servant. We sent down out of heaven water blessed, and caused to grow thereby gardens and grain of harvest and tall palm-trees with spathes compact, a provision for the servants, and thereby We revived a land that was dead. Even so is the coming forth.

All commentators of these verses agree that uncovering the secrets of nature is a religious duty of every believer. Scientific and philosophic explorations and the results derived out of them should help the believer to fortify his faith in God. In order to facilitate rational enquiry and save human knowledge from stagnation, Quran allows intellectual and ideological disputations among the learned because that is the only way one can sort out truth from falsehood. The Quranic verse in this regard is as follows :

> Call thou to the way of thy Lord With wisdom and good admonition, and dispute with them in the better way.

The Muslim scientists used this verse to demonstrate that knowledge acquired through research is valid and does not in any way contradict the revealed word of God. Arberry has given the following interpretation of the verse :

> When the Quranic term 'hikma' (wisdom) came to be used loosely to signify philosophy, this text fortified the philosophers in their contest with the obscurantists. The verbal noun derived from 'jadalhum' (dispute with them) was to acquire the technical meaning of 'reasoned debate.' As for 'mauiza' (admonition) that was the chosen method of the preachers. This verse would be taken to confirm Aristotle's threefold differentiation of proof into demonstrative, rhetorical and dialectical.'

There is ample evidence in the Traditions of the Prophet that he too believed that life without intellectual activity is fruitless. He once pointed out that intellect was the first thing created by God. Therefore, effective and gainful use of intellect was a kind of prayer which would be pleasing to God.

In spite of the clear indications in the Quran and the Traditions of the Prophet that scientific and rational investigation in human life, and natural phenomena was a religious duty, the relationship between scientific knowledge and religious learning in Islam was often very uncomfortable. Suspicions between the protagonists of the two increased after the Greek thought under the patronage of the early Abbasides became almost an official doctrine in the

Muslim kingdom. The clash between the knowledge based on reason and the one derived through revelation kept on mounting, until it became a permanent feature of the world of scholarship in Islam. Such a clash was natural because the Semetic mind for ages had made revealed knowledge the chief pillar of human life, while the Hellenic thinking had relied solely on rational and logical enquiry. The theological circles were disturbed particularly when the rationalists started questioning some of the fundamental principles of Islam. Attributes of God, the nature and character of prophesy, the authenticity of revelation, and numerous other issues relating to miracles, angels and life hereafter were subjected to very critical examination by the rationalist thinkers. The increasing popularity of such concepts created widespread fears among religious scholars about the future of the religion. Seeds of dissension sown between secular and religious knowledge early in Islamic history persisted for along time. In this controversy the scientists unquestionably were at a disadvantage. The hold of religion on the masses was so strong that they would easily be ralied in defence of any religious cause. Moreover, their contact with the religious leaders was constant. In each mosque, five times during the day, hundreds of them congregated for prayers and listened to the learned theologians with reverence. Scientists and philosophers on the other hand were mostly cloistered in their ivory towers; and their technical and abstruse writings could not be comprehended by the vast majority of the illiterate people. Another point which needs to be kept in mind is that learning in Islam to a large extent depended on royal patronage, and the kind of knowledge that would be encouraged and developed was determined by the outlook of the ruler. Even a cursory glance at the Islamic history would reveal that, although not practicing Muslims in the true sense of the term, most of the Muslim rulers proclaimed themselves to be defenders of the faith. A large number of theologians held powerful positions in government and exercised deep influence on all aspects of public policy. Even under the most rationalist of the rulers, Sharia was the law of the land, and religious scholars held the monopoly of interpreting its principles. Judgments given in the religious courts could not be contested in any other court of law, and opinion pronounced by Qadis and Muftis, in most cases used to become precedents for later decisions. From this however, it should not be construed that theologians had an absolute veto in the affairs of the government. There is no question that as an elitist group they wielded considerable power in a Muslim state, but their decisions could be vetoed by the rulers.

Scientists and philosophers were also consulted very often by the rulers but since their advice had no religious backing it lacked the impact of a Mufti's fetwa (religious pronouncement of a Juro-consult). In extreme cases, the theologians used to declare rationalists as Kafirs (infidels), which could be extremely detrimental to their reputation.

The result of this prepondering influence of religion was that secularism as it is understood in the West, never flourished in the Muslim civilization. Irrespective of their private opinions and intellectual proclivities, all public officials in a Muslim state had to show some deference to the word of God.

Even the renowned scientists of Islam, with all their undiminished commitment to reason, never thought that religion in any way was a barrier to their scientific researches. They remained firmly anchored to the religious faith, and there is no evidence that they ever felt intellectually thwarted by the laws of the Sharia. George DeSantillana has made the following remarks on the approach of the Muslim scientists to religion :

> One wishes only at times that he had not drawn so tight the web of orthodox piety as to leave in an uncomfortable and slightly alien position, along the course of time, men who stand out more clearly as representing the scientific temper. These men do not belong to the phase of withdrawal, but to the phase of world leadership; they are good Muslims and true, and a glory of their civilization. Therefore, since this is a history centered on science, I feel they should have been presented in bolder relief. In Al-Beruni, the greatest scientist of Islam, we meet a mind in no way different from the Western lay scientific mind at its best. His religious faith is secure but carried lightly, without protestations. It does not impede his freedom of judgement, his love of fact, his free-wheeling curiosity, his easy sarcasm, his strict and watchful cult

> of intellectual integrity. We recognize soon, in Al-Beruni, the scientist without qualifications as we mean him, as he has been understood again and again, and the same may be said of the other great men of his ilk-observers, experimenters, analysts, such men as Rhazes, Alhazen, Al-Battani, Averroes. This is what the Islamic intellect was able to bring forth during the golden age, as well as later, and they surely need no apologies for their perhaps-a-shade-too-secular attitude, nor deserve the hint that they were out of step with their own culture.

Wider Perspective

In order to get broader perspectives on the relationship between science and religion in Islam it would be in the fitness of things to make a synoptic survey of the views held by some of the leading Muslim scientists. Scientists selected are those whose achievements and contributions are always highlighted in the history of science. It is difficult to say with certainty what were their private opinions on religion, but in their writings and public pronouncements, they always professed un-deviating adherence to religion. On the whole they seemed to believe that Islam encouraged scientific research and favoured creative endeavours which opened new pathways to human understanding. In their opinion scientific findings provided support and strength to the believers faith in the eternal wisdom and truthfulness of the Quran.

Abu-Yousaf Yaqubi-ibn-Ishaqal Kindi ranks among the greatest scientists of Islam. Attached to the court of Caliph-al-Mamun, he had the opportunity to read and assimilate the latest Greek works which were being translated in large numbers at that time. To attain richness in philosophy and scholarship he had laid down the following six prerequisites :

> For a seeder of learning aspiring to be a philosopher six prerequisites are essential, a superior mind, uninterrupted passion, gracious patience, a free-from-worry heart, a competent introducer and a long time, should one of these prerequisites be lacking, the student is bound to fail.

Al-Kindi was fully equipped with these qualities of head and heart, and his genius under the royal patronage of Al-Mamun who was a great lover of free thought, got every possible chance to develop. He was deeply impressed by the logic and reasoning of the Hellenic thought and spared no efforts to convince his contemporaries that search for divine truth would be strengthened if reason was kept in close companship with religion. Knowledge, in his opinion, should be accepted from all sources. It is not a monopoly of any one region or religion. He said : We should never be ashamed to approve truth and acquire it no matter what its source might be, even if it might have come from foreign people and alien nations far removed from us.

In his opinion reason and revelation are the two main streams of knowledge in human life. True knowledge always stems out only when ideas flowing out of two sources are cross-fertilized. Hitti has summed up Al-Kindi's tireless zeal to harmoniously blend philosophy and theology, and dispel thickening clouds of suspicions from the minds of the theologians regarding secular learning, as follows:

> He argued that theology was a branch of philosophy, one depends on revelation, the other on reason, one employs logic, the other faith, but the truth attained by theology is not in conflict with that attained by philosophy. As a Mutazilite thinker, Al-Kindi had a special fascination for non-Arab sciences. His sympathetic attitude towards knowledge acquired through foreign sources, and the gusto with which he tried to integrate it with basic theological views and opinions, introduced a patently new approach to the religious researches in Islam. His writings created a tremendous impact on the religious circles of the day and mitigated considerably the built-in antipathy of the theologians towards scientific inquiry. He typified the new trend among Muslim scholars to synthesise traditional theological knowledge with the latest findings of scientific studies. In this way he increased the prestige of the secular learning without diminishing the reverence for religious scholarship.

Not Contrary

In other words Al-Kindi was, convinced that the wisdom of the Greek philosophers, as he had been able to construe from the translations of their writings, was not contrary to the spirit of Islam. He found perfect harmony between the revelations of the Quran, and the reasoning of the Greek texts regarding life and society. All that one needed was to establish a working relationship between the two.

Abu Rihan-al-Beruni, who ranks among the greatest scientists of Islam includes his classic work Kitab-ul-Hind (India) with the following words :

> We ask God to pardon us for every statement of ours which is not true. We ask Him to help us that we may adhere to that which yields Him satisfaction. We ask Him to lead us to a proper insight into the nature of that which is false and idle, that we may sift it so as to distinguish the chaff from the wheat. All good comes from Him and it is He who is clement towards his slaves. Praise be to God, the Lord of the worlds and His blessings be upon the Prophet Muhammad and his whole family.

Al-Beruni, like most Muslim scientists, believed that all knowledge was inherently religious. It was difficult for him to disbelieve that the universe was the creation of God, and that all the material glories of life on earth, including the blessings of human reason and intelligence were diverse manifestations of His eternal and universal benediction. All learning and every enquiry was sacred because with every new discovery, man's faith in God was strengthened and it proved the truth of the Holy Prophet's message. He believed that the universe was the handiwork of God and its study constituted the noblest pursuit of human mind. Labels given to various sciences were immaterial, physical sciences, history, or studies relating to man and society, all had religious character. Al-Beruni in all his writings continued to emphasize that examination of visible phenomena, provided a clue to the invisible world, and this reconciliation between the secular and the spiritual knowledge, in his opinion constituted the hall-mark of Islamic civilization !

Ibn Sina (Avecena) another outstanding figure in the history of science in Islam, also insisted that the motions in heavens and movements on earth were due to the will of God. Life with all its trials and tribulations was devoted entirely to the search of Supreme Truth, which directed the multifarious activities in the universe.

Mastery over Science

Ibn Sina worked very hard in the acquisition of knowledge and even before he was twenty, he had mastered practically all the sciences. In his autobiography he proudly refers to the fact that at eighteen he had reached the acme of his intellectual attainments. Most accounts agree that his education was thorough and comprehensive and included both religious and secular sciences. Ibn Khallikan in his Kitab Fafayat Ayan (Biographical Dictionary) says :

> Abu Ali (Ibn Sina) laboured in the acquisition of natural philosophy, divinity and other sciences, he reads the texts with the commentaries, and God opened for him the gates of knowledge. Several contemporary scholars criticized him for his philosophical ideas, thinking that his writings were deeply influenced by Hellenic thought. But there is ample evidence in his encyclopaedic compilations that he continued to adhere to the fundamentals of Islam. His faith in the ultimate power of God remained unshaken and he never questioned the indisputable competence of the prophet to produce knowledge through revelation. Ibn Khallikan has mentioned his overwhelming devotion to ..... in the following words :

> And when he met with an obscure point he used to perform a total ablution and proceed to the great mosque, where he would pray to Almighty God to facilitate its comprehension to him, and unlock the gate of difficulty.

In his Aqsam-al-ulum, Ibn Sina said that "through this part of practical philosophy we know the existence of prophecy (as something necessary) and that the human race needs the Sharia for its existence, preservation and future life."

To his critics he replied that "if there is in the world a man like me and that man should not be a Muslim, then there is no Muslim at all in the entire world." He also believed in the immortality of the human soul and life hereafter which brought rewards and punishment for deeds done on this earth. This view was strictly in consonance with the orthodox interpretation of the Quranic injunctions.

Ikhawan-al-Safa wal Khullam-al-Wafa (Brethren of Purity) is another classic of cosmological knowledge which has earned tremendous popularity among scholarly circles of the Muslim lands for several centuries. These Rassails (Treatises) are known traditionally for many of their excessively rationalistic views on religio-political and spiritual aspects of life in a Muslim community. But in spite of their deep interest in Aristotalian logic the authors have abstained from preaching anything which would throw doubt on basic principles which constitute the corner-stone of Islamic ideology. The authors main purpose was to emancipate the human mind from the captivity of ignorance, and enable it to grasp the realities of life in a scientific and rational manner.

J. H. Kramers has made the following estimate of the "Brethren of Purity." Parallel with the fixation of orthodox theology there appeared in Iraq a philosophical movement that was equally unfavourable to the free development of unprejudiced scientific research. We know this movement through the encyclopaedic writings of the so-called "Brethren of Purity" or "Brethren of Basra." These writings were composed about 950. In the fifty-two treatises of which they consist all the sciences known at that time are placed in a general scheme. Its system, as far as there is any system is mainly influenced by neo-Platonic views, which consider the world as the result of a series of emanations from the divine unity. This philosophy is outwardly Islamic in that it makes use of allegorical interpretations of the Quran. In its application to the sciences this system points to the hidden meaning of connections between various phenomena in nature, as expressed in numbers. On the whole the theories of the "Brethren of Purity" are scientifically less important than the work of Al-Kindi and his contemporaries.

The treatises consist of epistles or long essays which were

written during the Buwayhid period and had the support and patronage of the rulers who being Shiate were comparatively more tolerant of free thinking. The essays deal with all varieties of subjects from magic and mythology to mathematics and metaphysics. There are also detailed discussions about theology and astrology, and on matters relating to reason, revelation and prophecy. DeLacy O'Learey has made the following comments on the contents of the epistles of the Brotherhood of Purity :

> The doctrine contained in these letters is eclectic, the world is described as an emanation from God, the human soul as of celestial origin and striving to return to God and to be absorbed in Him, a consumation to be attained by wisdom, the Gnosis of Gnostic and neo-Platonic writers. The rationalism of the authors, and their excessive reliance on reason in resolving the mysteries of life, however, did not minimize in their estimate of importance of the revealed word of God. In one of the epistles the importance of divine knowledge is depicted as follows :
>
> Know, my brother, that the prime support of faith and its most powerful pillar is subservience to the bearers of the divine Laws (nawamis) in that which they command of obedience and that which they forbid of rebellion; it consists of harkening to them and obedience to them. This is so because the noblest works of mankind, the most delightful deeds of humanity and the highest rank to which the wise may attain next to the rank of angels is the establishment of the divine laws.

Fakhr-ad-Din Razi, who had a very questioning mind and seemed to disagree with many of the precepts of Islam, professed publically that religion was a repository of immeasurable knowledge. His lectures at Herat were attended both by theologians and philosophers and earned him the title of Shaikh-al-Islam (Chief Interpreter of Islam). It is said that he had memorized by heart the whole of Imamal-Haramains treatise on fundamental theology entitled al Shamil. In the same manner, Ibn Rushd who ranks among the greatest physicians and philosophers of Islam, was vehemently criticized among the orthodox circles for many of his views which were deemed to be heretical. But there is ample evidence in his writings that even he never denigrated the importance of religion in the moral, spiritual, and material welfare of the Muslim community. He once said, "he who studies anatomy increases his belief in God." A common belief has been established among commentators of Muslim philosophy that Ibn Rushd was a staunch rationalist, and that his expressions of religiosity were only an expediency to avoid annoyance of his royal patrons who in spite of their enlightened view were strict believers in Orthodox Sunni doctrine. W.J.J. Rosen that however, is of the opinion that in the absence of any definite evidence, it is wrong to contend that Ibn Rushd was guilty of intellectual dishonesty.

Enriching Knowledge

Like the rest of the philosopher-theologians of Islam, Ibn Rushd was convinced that Islam as a religion had to contribute a great deal towards the enrichment of every branch of knowledge. The knowledge of God, soul and spirit can only be acquired through prophecy, and whatever other insights one acquired through philosophy, logic and ethics, were secondary in character. He believed that religion alone can ensure material welfare and moral health of the society. Any knowledge which ensured happiness of mankind in one form or another, could never be contrary to Islam. Ibn Rushd once said that "philosophy is the companion and the foster-sister of the Sharia." He made a powerful case for the unification of revelation and reason. Truth in his opinion was not a monopoly of any particular race or nationality. He was convinced that the Quran and the Hadith did not debar the believers from accumulating knowledge from pre-Islamic sources.

Ordinance itself requires us to look into the books of the ancients, since their intention and goal in what they wrote was the same goal as that towards which Divine Ordinance has urged us. Any man forbidding the study of these books to anyone properly qualified to look into them—anyone that is, who combines sagacity of spirit with religious uprightness and moral virtue—thereby bars mankind from the very door whereby Divine ordinance calls men to get to know God, the door of speculation, leading to the true knowledge of Him.

In other words, he believed cosmological knowledge as found in the books of the ancients provided powerful crutches to the understanding of the word of God. He points out that it is the duty of every ardent believer to understand the universe around him because it testifies to the greatness of the Creator. Blossoms in the oasis of the desert and the stars in distant heavens, earth and water, plants and change of seasons, rain, rivers and oceans, floods, storms and the entire cyclones, and the entire cycle of life and death, are signs meant to speak eloquently for the boundless authority, control, as well as mercy and benediction of God. Exploration of the mysteries buried in the bosom of the universe is a legitimate activity of the human mind. Numerous other instances could be collected from the writings of other Muslim scientists, to prove that the dichotomy between science and religion which highlights the Western Civilization did not exist in Islam. Most scientists were devout Muslims, and in their books and public statements, they professed undeviating confidence in the truth and wisdom of the religious doctrines. They did not have to be atheists or agnostics, in order to perform creative experiments in various sciences. In most cases they believed that by uncovering the mysteries of nature, they were serving the cause of religion. In the religion they found a permanent source of inspiration for their innovative endeavours. There were constant intellectual skirmishes between strictly orthodox circles, and scholars who believed in free will and indulged in liberal interpretation of the Quranic principles, but in the world of Islamic scientific thought atheism was never accepted as prerequisite for enquiry into the realm of sciences. A question is always raised that if religion was such a powerful source of inspiration in Islam for scientific studies, then why after a certain period of time, the scientific activity was abruptly brought to an end. A careful examination of the history of Muslim scholarship will show that the decline in the study of mathematical and natural sciences was not due to religious barriers. It was the result of many causes.

Creative Period

It is true that the creative period of Islamic scholarship was very short lived. It touched the meridian of its achievement with lightening speed, and then suddenly due to certain religio-political reasons it became stagnant and declined. But even during the short time that it led the world, its achievements left an imperishable mark on the later development of scientific knowledge in human history. To everything that Muslim scientists and scholars borrowed from other sources they gave a stamp of their own originality. They clarified many ambiguities of the ancient knowledge, corrected numerous discrepancies in scientific thinking, and through many innovative experiments and verifications they opened countless new vistas in human understanding. For centuries religious prejudices of the Western historians always degenerated the contributions of the Muslim men of science, but in recent years there has been growing realization that the history of learning would have been very poor without the depth and originality of the Muslim scholars. Philip Hitti has made the following comments:

> The question has often been raised, how creative was the thinking of his co-religionist colleagues? Some have claimed that Arab philosophy was a series of footnotes to Plato and Aristotle. But creativity based on nothing takes place only in theology. The creative process pre-supposes the existence of old elements which when combined in new ways or with new elements yield a new and useful product. In this case Arab creativity consisted in combining old philosophic and theologic ideas to produce original and useful ones.

George Sarton's classic work on the history of science has made the following remarks on the contributions of the Muslim scientists.

Some of the giants of medieval times belonged to the Arabic culture, mathematicians and astronomers like Al-Khwarizmi (IX-1), Al-Farghani (IX-1), Al-Battani (IX-2), Abu-l-Wafa (X-2), Umar Khayyam (XI-I), Al-Ghazzali (XI-2), Ibn Rushd (XII-2), Ibn Khaldun (XIV-2) physicians like Al-Razi (IX-2), Ishaq-al-Israili (X-l), Ali Ibn 'Abbas (X-2), Abu-l-Qasim (-2), Ibn Sina (XI-I), Maimonides (XII-2). This enumeration could be greatly extended. Few of these men were Arabs and not all of them were Muslims, but they all belonged essentially to the same cultural group, and their language was Arabic. This illustrates the absurdity of trying to appraise medieval thought on the basis of Latin writings alone. For centuries the Latin scientific books hardly counted; they were out-of-date and out-landish. Arabic was the international language of science to a degree which had never been equalled by another language before (except Greek) and has never been repeated since. It was the language not of one people, one nation, one faith, but of many peoples, many nations, many faiths.

The Arabic culture is of a singular interest to the student of human traditions in general, to those whose greatest task it seems to them is the rebuilding of human integrity in the face of national and international disasters, because it was, and to some extent still is, a bridge, the bridge between East and West.

Range of Scholarship

Richard Sullivan has made these comments on the range of Muslim scholarship.

The range of Muslim scholarship was immense. Theology and religious law commanded primary attention, but other fields of scholarship were also extremely active. In the realm of the natural sciences, Muslim scholars, building on their encyclopaedic collection of ancient knowledge, created scientific manuals that were superior to any found elsewhere in the contemporary world. It is possible to detect in these works the origins of our modern scientific knowledge and spirit.

Scientific Miracle in Holy Quran

There may seem to be an inherent contradiction in the term "sceintific miracle" , because when a miracle can be explained in sceintific terms, it no longer remains a miracle. Yet under another shade of meaning, even a scientifically expalined phenomenon can be a wondrous occurance and thus a miracle.

The Quran, the whole of it, is a miracle in many ways. But as yet it can only be partly expalined in scientific terms. Of course, as our knowledge increases more and more of the Quran will be explained in scientific terms. The Quran has layers upon layers of meanings, which are being gradually revealed to us as our knowledge increases:

> Say: If all the Sea were ink for my Lord's words, The sea would indeed be exhausted before my Lord's Words are exhausted! And [thus it would be] if we Were to add to it sea upon sea.
>
> (Quran 18:109)

In other words indeed all miracles are scientific phenomena. Simply because on the basis of our current state of knowledge, we are unable to comprehend their true scientific foundation, we call them miracles. Allah had created the Universe according to a Plan and all knowledge flows from Him. Therefore, there is an underlying unity in all knowledge, whether ethical, scientific or spiritual. For example, just ponder over the concepts of straight line and equality; how they pervade through all branches of knowledge.

No Blind Faith

There is no blind faith in Islam. The Quran continously invites you to observe, think and reflect.

Allow me to digress here a little to present to you the central framework of Islam, which is based on three fundamental concepts of Al-iman, Al-islam and Al-ihsan. Al-iman (faith), which is based on transcendent intelligence; Al-islam (the law: submission) which reflects certainty (Yaqin) reflects equilibrium is based on free will and Al-ihsan (the way : virtue) which reflects remembrance (dhikr) is based on the gift of speech. Thus, Islam is the religion of Certainty, Equilibrium and remembrance is based on the three deiform faculties of transcendent intelligence, free will and gift of speech. Thus, in Islam the prayer and of course the remembrance of God must be done with free will and intelligence; only then will these be acceptable to Him.

Turning now, to the other side of the coin, we should clearly appreciate that the current 'state of art' of the sceintific method is constrained by severe limitations. At a lower level these limitations pertain to the direct varification of an occurance (null hypothesis) and at a higher level to the fragility of human observation (the Hisenburg principle of uncertainty) and to the relativity of observation (Einstein). The Quran has emphasised the importance of firm observation in the following verses:

The (Prophet's) (mind and) heart
In no way falsified
That which he saw
Will ye then dispute
With him concerning
What he saw?
Behold, the Lote-tree
Was shrouded
(In mystery unspeakable)
(His) sight never swerved,
Nor did it go wrong!
(Quran, 53 : 11, 12 & 16, 17).

In view of the above-mentioned limitations of the scientific method, it will indeed be presumptous on our part if we tried to comprehend Quran strictly in the context of the current framework of the scientific method. It is indeed in the recognition of this human limitation that the Islamic faith ('Iman) also extends to things which are beyond the reach of human perception (Al-Ghayb) :

This is the Book;
In it is guidance, sure, without doubt,
To those who fear Allah:
Who believe in the Unseen,
Are steadfast in prayer,
And spend out of what We
Have provided for them; (Quran 2 : 2, 3)

You have to accept Islam in totality or reject it is in totality, there is no partial acceptance or rejection.

"Accept Islam is its entirety" (Quran 2:208)

You cannot say that we will accept only that part of Quran which falls within the reach of our sceintific percepts:

> Then is it only a part of
> The Book That Ye believe in
> And do Ye reject the rest?
> (Quran 2:85)

Accepted Principle

This Quranic injunction is also an accepted principle in the sceintific method, whereby "either all or none" of the results of an experiment are accepted.

I hope, that this is not in conflict with the Quranic emphasis on reason, is self-evident to you. The Quran beseeches you to strive with reason to understand it but at the same time the Quran asks you to believe in the Unseen (Al-Ghayb).

The Quran asks you not only to use reason, but also to reflect, because it is reflection which will guide us towards layers upon layers of its meanings and its remarkable internal logic. The reason should lead you to ask the question ; Why the "Unseen" or "beyond perception"? The Quran's international logic will lead you to the answer that as the Quran is the book for all times, with human progress over time curtain after curtain will be lifted to reveal the Unseen. Anyway, if the Unseen was never to be revealed, Allah logically would not have talked about it.

Proof of Unseen

The proof of the Unseen for the mankind was provided by Allah through Al-Isra, the night journey of the Prophet (Blessings of Allah and Peace be upon him), which in scientific terms may be at least partly explained by the concept of 'pure time', as discussed by Iqbal in his The Reconstruction of Religious Thought in Islam. But, one miracle of the Quran is that it caries its own proof. While the Quran gives a great importance to reason or logic, it does not consider it as the sole means of gaining knowledge and the only criterion for judging the truth. The Intellect (al-aql-al-kulli), the instrument through which Divine Knowledge is obtained, must not be mistaken for reason alone (al-aql-al-juzi). In the Quran the aql is at once both intellect and reason. But if the 'aql is obscured by the wordly passions, then it can become the veil that hides man from the Divine and leads him astray. Thus, the reason can be both an instrument for reaching the divine truths, truths which are super-rational but not irrational, and a veil which hides these very truths from man. We should, therefore, be wary of this two - edged nature of the "sword of reason".

The Quran describes three distinct levels of knowledge: first ilm-al-Yaqin, knowledge through information; second ayn-al-yaqin, knowledge through experience and thrid and highest haqq-al-yaqin, true knowledge through being:

> Nay, were ye to know
> With certainty of mind,
> Ye would beware!
> Ye shall certainly see
> Hell-Fire!
>
> Again, ye shall see it
> With certainly of sight!
> (Quran 102:5, 6,7)
>
> But verily it is Truth
> Of assured certainly.
> (Quran 69:51)

A Muslim sage had explained these three stages of knowledge more picturesquely with the analogy of fire. If you had not seen fire; only heard about it, that is 'ilm-al-yaqin. When you saw it before you, that is ayn-al-yaqin. But only when you jump into it, you really know what fire is and that is the high stage of haqq-al-yaqin.

It was through beseeching Allah for ayn-al-yaqin that Prophet Ibrahim (on him be peace) strenthened his faith:

> Behold! Abraham said:
> "My Lord! Show me how
> Thou givest life to the dead,"

He said: "Dost thou not
Then believe?" He said:
"Ye but to satisfy
My own understanding."
He said: "Take four birds;
Tame them to turn to thee;
Put a portion of them
on every hill, and call to them;
They will come to thee
(Flying) with speed.
Then know that Allah
Is Exalted in Power, Wise".
(Quran 2:260)

Once you have attained ayn-al-yaqin there remains no need for you to specualte about many things or creatures of the Unseen such as the Jinn. Then you know with certainty what they are. The source of ayn-al-yaqin or being a sahib-al-nazar is available to all of us by purification of our hearts and minds through a constant recitation of the specific verses of the Quran and the dhikr-Allah, the remembrance of God.

Miracle of the Prophet

The miracle of Prophet Muhammad (Blessings of Allah and Peace be upon him) is the Quran. After God, the most powerful instrument in the Universe are neither the Angels nor the forces of the nature but the Word-the Word of God.

The Quran being the spoken Word of God is thus a repository of His Power. Each Word of the Quran has a secret power, which when you learn that Word become yours and can lead you to wondrous things and space-time dimensions. The power of the Word is varified by the Quran among others in the following verses:

He said (to his own men):
"Ye Chiefs! which of you

Can bring me here throne
Before they come to me
In submission?"

Said a bold one of the Jinns:
"I will bring it to thee
Before thou rise from thy
Council : indeed I have
Full strength for the purpose,
And may be trusted."

Said one who had knowledge
Of the Book: "I will
Bring it to thee within
The twinkling of an eye!"
Then when (Solomon) saw it
Placed firmly before him,
He said: "This is
By the grace of my Lord!
To test me whether I am
Grateful or ungrateful
And if any is grateful,
Truly his gratitude is (a gain)
For his own soul; but if
Any is ungrateful, truly
My Lord is Free of all Needs,
Most generous in giving!" (Quran 27: 38, 39, 40)

The status of such persons who rise to this power is described clearly by the following Hadith-al-Qudsi:

....And My slave keeps coming
closer to Me by performing
extra prayers until I love him.

And when I love him, I become his ears
with which he listens; his eys with
which he sees; his hands with which
he hits; his legs with which he
walks and if he asks Me anything
I will give it to him and if he comes
to Me for My protection I will
Protect him (Al-Bukhari)

The most wonderful among these, however, seek not the powers but only him. Please remember that the miracle is the strength of your faith.

4

Scientific Thinking

The study of the rise and decline of intellectual movements is a fascinating and very instructive aspect of the history of scholarship. The matter which surprises most about Islamic civilization is, that in spite of the fact that learning and inquiry were the integral part of the faith, the period of truly creative scientific activity was very shortlived. With one major thrust the scholars and scientists in Islam reached the meridian of their scientific and philosophical achievements; but then there was a sudden-decline. The short period of widespread creative activity was followed by almost permanent intellectual stagnation. Therefore, it would be interesting and intellectually rewarding to search for factors and forces which led to this unfortunate transformation.

Rise and Decline

The closing of the doors of ijtihad (independent thinking) was the single most important factor which killed the spirit of inquiry. History of Islamic civilization is strewn with countless political and intellectual calamities, but the one which had extremely disastrous effects, was the suspension of independent reasoning. Since Islam was 'not merely a manifesto for the spiritual salvation of man, but was also a compact code of conduct for all areas of worldly existence, the Quran, and the Prophet, had made special provision for the use of independent reasoning for resolving complex problems of the Muslim community. Moreover, Islam claimed that it was the final and eternal message of rectitude. In order to fulfil this mission it had to have built-in flexibility so that it could amicably adjust itself to the changing conditions of life. Reason was applauded as the priceless gift of God, which had to be used for the betterment and uplift of the moral and spiritual standards. Innovation was to be respected as long as it did not conflict with the fundamentals of the faith.

The Quran says :

> And if any tidings, whether of safety or fear, come unto them, they noise it abroad whereas if they had referred it to the messenger and such of them as are in authority, those among them who are able to think out the matter would have known it.

According to Ahmad Galwash the word in the Quranic verse is yastanbitana which is derived from *Istanbat* meaning search of hidden meaning through the effective use of human reason. There is also an authentic saying of the Prophet, which has been frequently quoted in support of Ijtihad. The tradition is as follows; He (the Prophet) was sending a judge to take charge of legal affairs in Al-Yeman, and asked him on what he would base his legal decisions "On the Quran" he replied. "But if that contains nothing to the purpose?" "Then upon your usage." "But if that also fails you?" "Then I will follow my own opinion." And the Prophet approved his purpose. Ahmad Galwash defined ijtihad as "The exercise of judgement to meet the new circumstances". A renowned Muslim scholar of Pakistan, Abul Ala Maududi, has given the following definition of the term:

> The whole of this legislative process which makes the legal system of Islam dynamic and makes its development and evolution in the changing circumstances possible results from a particular type of academic research and intellectual effort, which in the terminology of Islam is called ijtihad. Literally the word ijtihad means to put in the maximum effort to ascertain in a given problem or issuing the injunction of Islam and its real intent.

Vesey-Fitzgerald has explained the concept of ijtihad in Islam as follows :

> The mujtahids are the earliest expounders and architects of the law; and ijtihad (the word literally means hard-striving or strenuousness) is the mental discipline of their profession. The word connotes a power of making law, of deducing new principles and applying them to the new facts. In theory, as we have already said this mental discipline resulted in the discovery of the law of God on the basis of revelation according to the accepted categories of the usul Al-fiqh.

No Evidence

There is no precise historical evidence to show how, where and by whom the doors of ijtihad were finally closed. The opinion commonly held among scholars is that in the evolution of Islamic theology there reached a stage when learned theologians under threat from the rulers or for other selfish reasons were trying to put superimposed or distorted interpretations over Islamic principles. In this way ijtihad became a tool to justify the nefarious designs of the rulers. So the scholars thought that if the process of interpretation was allowed to continue, the time would come when in the bewildering maze of interpretations the true spirit of Islam would be lost. The only way to stop such a tragedy was to declare that the era of independent reasoning in Islam had ended and Islamic Shariah was perfected for all times to come.

The infilteration of the Hellenic thought and unabated passion of Muslim philosophers to Hellenize Islam was also considered a powerful threat to the faith which might have compelled the religious scholars to decry independent reasoning. Many Muslim scholars of the Greek thought had adopted duplicity of attitude to stave off popular criticism. Among their own circle they would profess faith in the sophisticated doctrines of the Hellenic philosophy, but while interacting with the masses they used to advocate the superiority of revelation, or would interpret regulations of Shariah in a manner that they would not seem contrary to the Greek thought.

After closing the doors of ijtihad, the Muslims became a community of muqalladin (blind followers). Search for precedents, and memorizing quotations from the predecessors became the hall-mark of scholarships. Later in Islamic history occasionally a stray voice could be heard in defense of ijtihad, but on the whole the kingdom of thought and letters remained denuded of creativity. The most challenging and outstanding defense of ijtihad was done by Shah Wali Ullah, who ranks among the greatest religious scholars of Islam on the Indo-Pakistan sub-continent. His treatise entitled Iqd al Jadid fi Ahkamal-Ijtihad wal Taqlid was a powerful effort to reintroduce independent thinking in Islam. It is only in the twentieth century however that scholars in the Muslim countries, have seriously advocated ijtihad as means for the rejuvenation of Islamic civilization. Muhammad Abduh, the late Grand Mufti of Egypt and Sir Muhammad Iqbal the poet philosopher of Pakistan, were the landmark figures of this century, who repeatedly warned the Muslims that unless independent reasoning was once again introduced as a basic ingredient of research and enquiry, Islam could not be salvaged out of its present day socio-political difficulties.

Recent Explanation

A more recent explanation of Ijtihad has been done by Muhammad Asad in the following words:

> And this is where ijtihadi legislation rightfully comes in. To be more precise the legitimate field of the community's law-making activity presses (a) details in cases and situations where the Shariah provides a general principle but no detailed ruling and (b) principles and details with regard to matters which are Mubah that is, not covered by Sharia laws at all. It is this method that the Quran has referred to in the words (for every one of you we have ordained a Divine Law and an open road). This Divine Law (Shariah) outlines the area within which Muslim life may develop, within this area an 'open road' (Minhaj) for temporal legislature which would cover contingencies deliberately left untouched by the *nasus* of the Quran and Sunnah.

Sometimes ijtihad is divided into two categories. Absolute

Ijtihad (Ijtihad Mutlaq) which means independent reasoning on critical issues. It can lead to innovative solution to the problems which are new, and for which there are no precedents in fiqh (jurisprudence). In this process one can bypass the established schools of thought, and the sanctified consensus called (Ijmah) of the Ulema. The second category is labelled as Relative Ijtihad, which is merely rejuvenation or revivification of the old principles of Shariah to handle new situations.

Even a cursory review of the history of Muslim scholarship leaves no doubt that the closing of the doors of Ijtihad was a major educational tragedy in Islam. The conditions of learning became so stagnant, and the climate of thought so reactionary, that not to speak of creating something absolutely new for the advancement of knowledge, scholars allowed the existing fund of religious and scientific knowledge to stagnate to an extent that much of it became obsolete. Instead of being of any help in resolving the problems it became an insurmountable roadblock to any kind of dynamic thinking.

Rise of Scholars

The rise of Ulema (religious scholars) as a very closed and powerful elitist group is also listed as a major factor which created numerous barriers to independence of research and expansion of knowledge in Islam.

The social and intellectual history of Islam shows that during the first hundred years of its existence the Ulema (scholars) did not acquire any significant role in the Muslim society. One reason could be that during this period there were large numbers of people who had either direct association with the Prophet, the sole fountain head of knowledge, or they were instructed by those who had the privilege of imbibing wisdom directly from him. Historians of Islam would say that as long as Sahaba (Companion of the Prophet, and the younger generation closely associated with them, lived, the need for scholars as a special class did not arise. Moreover, during this period most of the knowledge was communicated by word of mouth, and there was not enough written material to impart it through organized instruction. Political chaos, resulting from internecine tribal feuds could be another factor which might have hindered the growth of formal religious instruction.

Cultivation of Knowledge

With the passage of time, however, as the earlier generations of Muslims died, need was felt of putting in writing that which was formerly being communicated by word of mouth. Territorial expansion, and contacts with Byzantum, and Persian Civilizations showed that for intellectual and spiritual health of society, cultivation of knowledge, through formal educational structures was a basic necessity. Moreover, to accommodate new socio political realities Laws of Islam were being interpreted and reinterpreted so fast, that without expert guidance it was difficult to know the true spirit of religion. It is also to be kept in mind that knowledge and learning thrive only under conditions of peace and prosperity. The earlier period of Islamic history was racked with internal feuds and external wars, and in that state of chronic instability nothing could be accomplished in terms of intellectual refinement.

Intellectual Upsurge

The rise of Abbasides (749-1258 A.D.) marked the sudden upsurge of intellectual activity. Centralization of Caliphat authority, consolidation and streamlining of administration under Persian administrators, who rose to high positions under the new dynasty, opened an era of peace and order in the kingdom. The result was that under the liberal royal patronage, for the first time, art, science, letters and philosophy got a chance to flourish widely among the populace. The introduction of Greek learning made knowledge more complex and need was felt to organize formal institutes to impart education. It was in these circumstances that learning and teaching became a profession, and Ulemas (scholars) emerged as a separate professional class in the Muslim society. Its members went through rigorous training and prolonged induction into numerous branches of secular and religious knowledge, and after the completion of studies became the religious mentors of the community. The masses in general remained ignorant, and the same was true of the rulers who had the ability to govern and administer, but lacked understanding of the religious law which, in theory at least, was the basis of state legislation. Most of them lacked the competence to know the exact meanings of these laws, and very often even if they understood the legal and moral implications of Shariah, dynastic squabbles, court intrigues, wars and pursuit of pleasures would not leave enough time with them to watch the implementation of religious law. All these factors resulted in the emergence of Ulema as a class of specialists whose guidance was constantly sought by the rulers and the ruled.

Islam had abolished priestcraft as a profession, but in due course Ulema became a powerful aristocracy of knowledge, and they remained so for a long time in the history of Islamic civilization. Their influence and authority further increased, when numerous institutions, borrowed from conquered lands, needed their approval in the form of consensus (Ijma) as specialists of religious law.

The Ijma (consensus of the learned) has been a subject of acute controversy in the history of Muslim jurisprudence. In view of its being one of the major sources of legitimacy, it was a very powerful weapon in the hands of the religious class to maintain its supremacy. Claude Cahen calls it 'the dictatorship of the Ulema' in the Muslim society. Their influence in the Muslim society, however, was not steady or uniform. It used to vary from dynasty to dynasty and sometimes from one king to another in the same dynasty. For instance, during the Mutizala supremacy under Al-Mamun, the Ulemas were eclipsed by philosophers, but immediately after the decline of the Mutazalite doctrine, the Ulema re-emerged as a potent social and political force in the Abbaside kingdom.

Many of them became top administrators of the state, and occupied important positions at the seats of higher learning and in Judiciary. As Muftis (Jurists) they gave Fatwas (Authoritative Interpretations) to determine the right and wrong of public policy and as Qadis (Judges) they presided over courts of law to resolve religious disputes and other litigations relating to civil and criminal justice in Islam. Very often they also administered charitable endowments for the general benefit of the community.

Afaf Lutfi Al Sayyid Marsot has given the following reasons for the expansion of the role of Ulema in a Muslim society.

Basic Function

The basic functions of the Ulema were to teach Islam and interpret, that is to be the teachers, lawyers, qadis, and religious mentors. But since almost every aspect of daily life was regulated by the Shariah (holy law) or required a ruling in the light of Shariah the services of the Ulema became necessary in every walk of life, political, social and economic, and they were called upon to play a vast variety of parts.

In due course the Ulema because of their all-pervading influence almost became a ruling class. One thing fortunate, however, was that this class did not become hereditary. Anybody irrespective of caste or colour, who had attained a certain level of scholarship in religious laws could be recruited into their ranks.

Constructive Role

The history of Ulemas shows that as a class at one stage they played a very constructive role. Some of them were bold enough to uncover the fallacies of the Muslim rulers. They acted as a loyal opposition to the government in power. They were the custodians of the religious laws and were expected to keep its fundamentals free from spiritual and moral contamination. They were consulted by Sultans practically in all matters relating to religion and politics.

While each Muslim was obliged to tread the path of rectitude, Ulemas installed themselves as the custodians of religious morality for the society as a whole. They were expected to tame those propensities among individuals which produced heresies, and endangered the purity of canonical law.

Their role, as the enlightened critics of the rulers, however, did not last for a long time. Wisdom and knowledge did not save them from the corrupting influences of wealth and power. They exploited the widespread and deepseated religious sentiments of the Muslim masses—a tendency which unfortunately became the permanent feature of the Ulemas as a class during the later periods of Islamic history. This deterioration in the standard of integrity among religious scholars was a common topic of discussion in the literature on Islamic ethics. They became hirelings or parasites of the rulers. Al-Ghazzali who was an eye witness to the unholy alliance between the princes and the Ulemas made the following remarks:

> And the third thing to avoid is not to mix with princes and Sultans, and not to see them, for seeing them and sitting with them is great mischief, and if you are impelled to do this, avoid praising them and

> commending them, for Allah The Exalted is angered when an oppressor and an impious man is praised, and whoever has called for the lengthening of their lives has delighted that Ailah be disobeyed in his land.

Keddie has made the following comments on the role of Ulemas in Egypt after 1500 A.D. :

> An important role of the Ulema has been to justify the *status quo* and to guard both themselves and secular rulers from attacks by the dissatisfied or dispossessed. They formed an important part of the ideological underpinning of the rulers, needed to justify submission to existing landlords and government agents. They thus helped perpetuate the hierarchical and traditional order of things by teaching submission even to unjust rulers and maintaining that the hierarchical social order was both natural and good.

It was not only in Egypt, but in the rest of the Muslim kingdoms also, that the religious scholars showed marked signs of degeneration in their caliber and moral integrity. Inducements of wealth, and lust for power made the vast majority of them merely lackeys of the rulers. In theory they still continued to enjoy the privileges which had hallowed their role in the past, but in practice the latter image was only a pale reflection of their former grandeur.

They loved *status quo,* and would not hesitate to sacrifice all their convictions at the alter of expediency. Many of them suffered permanently from the crisis of the conscience, because there was a conspicuous gap between the theory and practice of their profession. In theory they were still a beacon light of prudence and religious wisdom for the masses, but in practice their knowledge had become shallow. Constant dependence on rulers killed their creativity and independent thinking.

They had acquired the reputation as time-servers, opportunists, and bearers of double moral standards. By repeated compromises with the glaring breaches of the law they had forefieted the confidence of the masses. Uriel Heyd has given the following picture of the eighteenth century Ulema in the Ottoman Empire, which was more or less typical of their class in most Muslim kingdoms in the Middle Ages.

Lack of Unity

Lack of unity among them was one of the fundamental causes for this. Not only, as mentioned above, were the leading 'Ulema' families and high Mollas separated by a deep gulf from the rank and file, but within the leadership itself the struggle for promotion to the highest positions led to constant intrigues. These became particularly violent when in the eighteenth century an excessively large number of Muderrises and Mollas were appointed because of favouritism and nepotism, thus increasing the number of candidates for the few top positions in the corps. Hence it should not be surprising that a Molla was often willing to yield to the Sultan's wishes and even agree to innovations of Western origin, as the price for gaining ascendancy over a rival. Moreover, the prestige of the 'Ulema' had declined greatly during preceding generations because of the growing corruption in their ranks. Posts were given or even sold to unsuitable men, such as followers and servants of high 'Ulema'.

In some cases people who were not even able to read their names were appointed Cadis. The venality of the judges had become proverbial. While in olden times, a leading 'Alim' lamented, people came to the Cadi to complain of oppression by the governor and his subordinates, it was now the other way round. Instead of the 'Ulema' restraining the Government from infringing upon the holy law, the Sultan had to issue innumerable Firmans warning the judges not to violate the Shariah.

Since to be an Alim (religious scholar) brought a lot of power and prestige, it was the desire of every young man to enter the ranks of this profession. The result was that scholarship became a playground for fortune-hunters. In short, when Muslim scholars became functionaries of the state, they lost their independence, and in order to maintain their position, very often they had to sell their conscience. When scholarship became a marketable commodity it lost much of its pristine dignity, and its custodians then naturally became a subject of adverse comments and popular ridicule. In theory, from platform and pulpit, religious scholars continued to preach in a convincing manner that 'pen is mightier than the sword,' but in practice the pen was subservient to the one who wielded the sword.

Another possible cause for the decline of scientific enquiry in

Islam could be the ultimate triumph of the science of theology over other sciences. It was noticed earlier, great scientists like Abu Nasr al Farabi (258/870-339/950), Abu Raihan-al-Biruni (362/973-462/1051) and Abul Walid Muhammad ibn Rushd (520/1126-595/1198) in spite of their great passion for science, and deep interest in rationalism, never questioned at least publically, the importance of religion as the ultimate source of knowledge and enlightenment. But the typical orthodox circles never trusted them, and a simmering controversy between religion and science remained an integral part of the scholarly debate and discussion in every part of the Muslim world. It was however religion which in the end won the battle, and science was condemned as something which produced agnostics and sowed seeds of distrust and doubt among the simple-minded people. The theologian who led this triumphant crusade was Al-Ghazzali. In his writings he launched a scathing criticism against scientists and philosophers.

Doyen of Scholars

Even a cursory glance at the history of Islamic scholarship can show that Al-Ghazzali had the largest following in the Muslim lands. He earned the reputation of being the doyen of religious scholars and his encyclopaedic production *Ihya al Ulum al Din*—(The Revivification of Religious Science) has been a popular textbook of theology throughout the sweep of centuries and his fame as a leading exponent of truly Islamic point of view has remained undiminished. In the religious literature of Islam he is generally referred as *Hujjat-al-lslam* (Proof of Islam). It is an agnomen which is not given to any other theologian in Islam. In his writings he vehemently criticized the rationalist philosophers who preceded him and called them unbelievers. Aristotle and Plato in his opinion were unbelievers and all Muslim scholars who were influenced by them were also thrown out of the fold of Islam.

> We must therefore reckon as unbelievers both these philosophers themselves and their followers among the Islamic philosophers such as Ibn Sina, al Farabi and others.

This criticism is greatly elaborated by him in his famous work entitled *Tahafut al Falasifa.* (The Incoherence of the Philosophers of the Philosophers). In it he unleashed biting criticism against practically every aspect of scientific thought which in his opinion, cast any doubt on the fundamentals of religion. Abu Rushd wrote a strong reply in support of science in his treatise entitled "The Incoherence of the Incoherence", but it failed to dislodge Al-Ghazzali's influence from vast majority of Muslims. Al-Ghazzali had integrated various streams of Islamic thought so skilfully and with such knowledge and insight that it was difficult to refute his argument easily. He blended philosophy with religion in such a manner that supremacy of the religion could not be questioned. His *Ihyal-Ulum al Din* became the most popular book after the Quran. One thirteenth century writer pointed out if all the books on the religion of Islam were destroyed, Ihya alone was sufficient to make up the loss. For a devout Muslim it remained a treasure house of eternal spiritual wisdom and made Shariah the most desirable way of harvesting goodness in life. The victory of the science of theology was not an unmixed blessing. Instead of doing some creative thinking to maintain the dynamic character of the doctrine, theologians wasted their talent and energies in endless debate and discussion on trivial issues regarding grammar, choice of words, use of terms, syntax and other etymological rules.

The dependence of the scholar on the patronage of their royal masters, in due course became another factor which proved extremely detrimental to the advancement of knowledge. In fact, it became the major source of corruption among them and ultimately eroded their integrity. The tradition of the scholars depending entirely on the funds and facilities provided by the rulers developed very early in Islamic history. Academies and schools, where secular and religious knowledge was imparted, were built and maintained at state expense. In times of peace and prosperity, or of decay and anarchy, the Muslim rulers were always anxious to extend their patronage to scholars and men of science.

Al-Mamun (815-833) the Abbaside Caliph established his famous academy called "Bait-al-Hikma" (House of Wisdom) at Baghdad which became one of the major sources of the dissemination of philosophical knowledge in the Muslim empire. The history of this "House of Wisdom" shows that the scholars associated with it were mostly non-Arab and its library consisted mostly of Greek and Persian books. Later the Persian rulers of Buwaid dynasty and Fatimid rulers of Egypt established . similar academies, where instruction was imparted in every conceivable branch of human knowledge.

Islamic University

Just a quarter of a century before the sack of Baghdad by Hulaqu Khan a university called Mustansiriyah was founded in this city in 1234 A.D. G. Le Strange has given the following comprehensive account of the intellectual climate and physical environments of this institution :

> We are told that in outward appearance, in stateliness of ornament and sumptuousness of furniture, in spaciousness and in the wealth of its pious foundations, the Mustansiriyah surpassed everything that had previously been seen in Islam. It contained four separate law-schools, one for each of the orthodox sects of the Sunnis, with a professor at the head of each, who had seventy-five students (faqih) in his charge, to whom he gave instruction gratis. The four professors each received a monthly salary, and to each of the three hundred students one gold dinar a month was assigned. The great kitchen of the college further provided daily rations of bread and meat to all the inmates. According to Ibn-al-Furat there was a library in the Mustansiriyah with rare books treating of the various sciences, so arranged that the students could easily consult them, and those who wished could copy these manuscripts, pens and paper being supplied by the establishment. Lamps for the students and a due provision of olive oil for lighting up the college are also mentioned, likewise storage places for cooling and drinking water; and in the great entrance hall stood a clock doubtless some form of clepsydra, announcing the appointed times of prayer, and marking the lapse of the hours by day and by night. Inside the college a bath house . . . was erected for the special use of the students, and a hospital ... to which a physician was appointed, whose duty it was to visit the place every morning, prescribing for those who were sick; and there were great store-chambers in the Madrassah provided with all requisites of food, drink, and medicines.

Network of Libraries

Widespread network of large and well-equipped private and public libraries, and flourishing book trade also provided eloquent testimony to the strength and calibre of intellectual activity that characterized practically every Muslim kingdom. Book collection was a great hobby with the aristocracy and an important symbol of its social prestige. Palaces of the princes and chambers of aristocrats boasted of vast collections of books on all subjects. In due course mosques and madrassahs also started having libraries of their own.

"There was, however, no uniform pattern of royal patronage to religious and secular knowledge. It used to differ from ruler to ruler. It mostly depended on the personal proclivities of the patron. If he was inclined to rational and abstract philosophical thought, his leanings towards secular knowledge would be obvious, but if he was a devout orthodox Muslim, religious learning definitely would interest him more. For instance, under Mamun, secular and rational knowledge had precedence because the ruler himself was a staunch supporter of rationalism. Similarly under Seljuk rulers when defenders of religious orthodoxy like Nizam-ul-Mulk came at the helm of the affairs, government's primary concern was to support and strengthen the instruction of religious science, Nizam-ul-Mulk during his term as Prime Minister of the most powerful Muslim kingdom of the day, established a network of madrassahs. (religious schools), the most important of which were in Baghdad and Nishapur. They were generally attached to the mosques and their objective was to propagate true Islamic learning so that defenses against heresies could be fortified.

Scholars and students in these schools received government stipends and the state also provided financial and administrative support to these institutes. Abu Jubair, a famous Arab traveller, visited Baghdad in 1184 A.D. and found that in the eastern part of the city alone there were thirty madrassahs. He has given the following description of these colleges:

> The ordinary mosques in both the eastern and the western parts cannot be estimated, much less counted. The colleges are, about thirty, and all in the eastern part, and there is not one of them that does not outdo the finest palace. The greatest and the most famous

of them is the Nizamiyah which was built by Nizam-ul-Mulk and restored in 1506 A.D. These colleges have large endowments and tied properties that give sustenance to the faqihs who teach in them and dispensed on the scholars.

Over and above the facilities provided for the cultivation of knowledge, each Muslim ruler had an overwhelming desire to adorn his court with renowned scholars. He provided them with pensions, and gave free access to state libraries and observatories. The scholars in turn gave him medical and astrological advice, and were very often instrumental in building weapons of war. They also helped him to resolve problems of public policy which needed knowledge and prudence.

Accumulation of Talent

Kings vied with each other in their efforts to accumulate talent and scholarship in their courts. Luster and radiance of scholarship around the throne was considered essential to increase the international reputation and prestige of the dynasty. For physicians, scientists, poets and artists attachment to the court was a coveted prize, because this was a shortcut to professional fame and social prestige. This close relationship between rulers and Muslim scholars remained a permanent feature of the history of Muslim scholarship.

Practically all the leading scientists and philosophers of Islam were attached to the royal courts. Al-Kindi was attached to the court of Caliph Mamun, whom he served in various capacities, the most important of them being that of a consultant and tutor to the princes. This opportunity had tremendous bearing on Al-Kindi's achievements, because it enabled him to meet the best minds in the realm, and he was able to use the biggest and the most useful libraries of the Muslim world.

Fakhr-ad-Din Razi was attached to the court of Sultan Muhammad Ibn Tukush surnamed Khowarzm Shah in Khorasan.

Ibn Sina spent most of his professional life as a courtier. His career in this respect was very adventuresome. Reputation and ambition took him to various courts. It would be interesting to reproduce the detailed account of his intellectual and professional adventures in various princely courts recorded by Ibn-Khallikan.

Unmatched Talent

The emir Nuh Ibn Mansur as-Samani, prince of Khorasan, having heard, during a fit of sickness, of Abu Ali Ibn Sina talent, sent for him and was restored to health under his treatment. Abu Ali was then received into the favour of that prince, and he frequented his library, which was of incomparable richness, as it contained not only all the celebrated works which are found in the hands of the public, but others not to be met with anywhere else, and of which not only the titles but the contents were unknown. Here Abu Ali discovered treatises on the sciences of the ancients and other subjects the essence of which he extracted, and with the greater part of which sciences he became acquainted. It happened, some time afterwards, that this library was consumed by fire, and Abu Ali remained the sole depository of the knowledge which it contained. Some persons even said that it was he who set fire to the library, being induced to do so for the reason that he alone was acquainted with its contents, and that he wished to pass off as his own the information which he had there acquired. He had not reached his eighteenth year when he had completely mastered all the sciences to the attainment of which he had directed his studies. At the age of twenty-two, he lost his father, in the vicissitudes of whose fortune he had partaken, and with whom he acted as admil for the Sultan. When the affairs of the Samanide dynasty fell into disorder, Abu Ali left Bokhara and proceeded to Korkanj, the capital of Khowarezm, where he frequented the court of Khowarezm Shah Ali Ibn Mamuri Ibn Muhammad. He wore the dress of a jurisconsult with the talisman, and obtained a monthly stipend for his support. He afterwards departed from Korkanj and visited Nasa, Abiward Tus, and other cities, during which period he paid his court to the emir Shams-al-Maali Kabus Ibn Washmakir. When Kabus was arrested and confined in the castle where he died, (a circumstance of which we shall give the particulars in his life,) Abu Ali went to Kihistan, where he had a severe illness, and then returned to Jurjan. From Jurjan Abu Ali proceeded to Rai and was attached to the court of Majd-ad Dawlat son of Fakhral Dawlat. He went afterwards to Kazwin and then to Hamadan where he became wazir to Shamsal-Dawlat.

Similarly Ibn Rushd after the completion of his studies as a physician and jurist was attached to courts at Corodova and

Marrakush, and under Al-Mansur (1186-1199) he was given the highest rank among the courtiers. The same can be said practically about the rest of the scholars and scientists who have earned a permanent place in the history of Islamic civilization.

The relationship between scholars and their royal patrons, however, was never smooth or peaceful.

Fortunes of the scholar were linked with the destiny of the ruling dynasty. A change of ruler would very often mean humiliation, imprisonment and even death for all courtiers including the scholars. The result was that treachery and intrigue were the common features of the court life. Scholars were chased in and out of courts frequently. Many of them seemed to be fortune hunters as they moved from court to court either in search of better worldly gains or looking for safety against a whimsical master. Naturally such instability must have hampered the creative energies of many a Muslim scholar. Moreover in spite of the greatest of efforts, their objectivity must have been marred by views of the patron. Such constraints must have dissuaded many scholars from uncovering truth with confidence and integrity. Under these circumstances the scope of independent thinking was considerably curtailed.

Heirs of the Prophet

The Prophet had said that 'the learned are the heirs of the Prophets,' but as ill-luck would have it most of them in Islam became hirelings of the heirs to the thrones. They were expected to be men of integrity, piety and independent thinking. Their main job was to be the moral and religious mentors of the community. Dispensation of truth and wisdom, without fear and favour, was the cardinal characteristic of their profession. These ideals, however, were shattered to a vast extent, once the scholars and scientists had placed themselves under intellectual captivity of the royal patronage. They fell low in popular prestige.

Although dependence on royal patronage was a universal trend among Muslim scholars, occasionally a disenchanted soul used to raise a voice of protest against the baneful effects of such a practice. In his Revivification of the Sciences of Religion, Al-Ghazzali unrolled a discussion on the relationship of scholars and rulers and his conclusion was that dependence of scholars on princes was a pernicious practice. It was a source of moral and religious corruption, and against self-respect and independence which distinguished a scholar from other human beings. Knowledge in his opinion was a sacred trust which should not be easily betrayed and traded with ordinary worldly gains.

The courts of princes, in his opinion were great temptations which enticed scholars to tell lies and practice duplicity. They supported policies and decisions which they knew to be untrue, and against reason and religion.

It was for this reason that Al-Ghazzali advised the Ulema to stay away from the princes as much as they could. In his *Nasihat ul Maluk* (Counsel for Kings) he says :

> Know that you can have three sorts of relations with princes, governors, and oppressors. The first and worst is that you visit them, the second and better is that they visit you, and the third and surest that you stay far from them, so that neither you see them nor they see you—There is also the Hadith 'The Ulema are God's trustees for the servants of God, so long as they do not mix with the rulers, and if they do that, they have betrayed the prophets; beware of them and stay far from them'. Sufyan-al-Thawri said "In Hell there is a valley entirely inhabited by Quran readers who used to visit kings." Muhammad Ibn Salama said, "A fly on a pile of excrement is finer than a Quran reader at the door of those people."

Rumi, the famous mystic and poet of Iran also pointed out that receiving robes and favours from princes was derogatory to the dignity of scholarship.

Another possible corrupting influence in the history of Muslim scholarship could be the tendency among Muslim scholars to be slavishly subservient to the precedent. Students spent considerable part of their educational career in searching passages from the writings of the leading authors of the past. This wasteful intellectual exercise must have frustrated the abilities, and crippled the creative urges of many a brilliant mind. Scholars spent countless hours of patient and anxious research to find out some evidence in support of their thesis from the writings of their forerunners. The result was that most of their works were crowded with quotations and references from the past, which made their reading very often an insufferable intellectual drudgery. Probably they were inhibited against creative thinking, and whenever anything new struck them they would like to shift its responsibility on someone else.

As the distance between the earlier writers and later scholars increased this passion for authoritative references to former works kept on consuming more and more time of the researchers.

Heaps of Books

With the passage of time the volume of literature in each field of human knowledge had increased so much, that it became difficult for a student to sort out the real from the spurious. Year after year he burnt his midnight candle to examine and assimilate truth out of the bewildering maze of interpretations and distortions, which very often left him confused and frustrated. Historical perspectives provide richness and depth to research, but it should be only means to an end and not an end in itself. Unfortunately for most Muslim scholars search for historical evidence became an end in itself. The tragedy was further compounded when some of the authorities of the past were permanently declared to be sacrosanct, and whose ideas were accepted uncritically. This kind of captivity of the past adversely affected the creative ability. In a dynamic and creative civilization, authorities which have outlived their usefulness, are always replaced by new ones. This creates an atmosphere of intellectual freedom, and creates willingness to question the retention of such propositions which no longer help men to resolve their problems of life. In the history of Muslim scholarship, such an attitude, however, did not last for a long time. After the initial outburst of creativity, the majority of later scholars stagnated because they failed to replace the old authorities when their thesis had become defunct and inoperative. This intellectual tyranny of the past was a major calamity which wrecked originality in Muslim scholarship.

The discrepancies which stemmed out from fruitless search for authorities, ' and the blockade of mind which resulted from undue reverence to their expositions, were further aggravated by faulty documentation. In the absence of printing, the great works of scholarship were circulated in manuscript form in various parts of the Muslim world. Copies were made by a professional copist called (the Katib). Although these copists were professionals, and fairly knowledgeable in various sciences, still in making copies of manuscripts there were always unavoidable omissions and additions. Moreover scholars had the habit of writing comments on the margins of the books, and as the works passed from generation to generation, at some stage, the reader could confuse the marginal comments of the other readers with the text of the original author. Very often at one place, there would be only one manuscript and the researcher had no opportunity of comparing its contents with another's copy. These limitations created considerable confusion and hindered dispassionate and objective research. The world of scholarship in Islam was also plagued with considerable plagerism, and it is mentioned that authors used to indulge in numerous unethical practices in humiliating and denigrating their rivals. Some of them used to write bad books and attribute them to great authors so that their reputation could be ruined. Very often, renowned writers in order to avoid carping criticism of vindictive and unfair critics, used to write anonymous books.

Intellectual Dishonesty

Obviously this kind of intellectual dishonesty multiplied difficulties of research in natural and social sciences manifold. Research workers always remained suspicious regarding their sources, and spent a lot of time in sorting out genuine information from the doubtful one. The absence of printing not only greatly increased the chances of this intellectual dishonesty, but also created scarcity of books. Muslim scholars always complained about the non-availability of the books, the serious-minded and honest among them had to spend a considerable part of their life in travelling from place to place in search of manuscripts which were distributed over wide areas of the Muslim world. This inability persisted for a long time, and must have been a tremendous strain on the time and resources of the authors.

Part - II

Spirit of Governance

5

People's Welfare

It is extremely misleading to apply non-Islamic terms to Islamic concepts and institutions. The ideology of Islam has a social orientation peculiar to itself, different in many respects from that of the Modern West, and can be successfully interpreted only within its own context and in its own terminology. Any departure from this principle invariably tends to obscure the attitude of Islamic Law toward many of the burning issues of our time.

Concept of Welfare State

The concpet of "Welfare State" is a quantitative concept and not a qualitative concept. This has important Connotations for Afro-Asian countries, having their own sense of destiny. Also, it is in this context, that we must view the disenchantment or disillusionment which is felt in Britain about the 'Welfare State'. This disillusionment arises primarily from the awareness of the fact that the British system now no longer produces 'Empire Builders.' the ears stands on hearing such words as 'Empire' and 'Empire Building'. But these are used here only as a concept and also perhaps to catch the attention of the reader. The 'Empire' in the modern world is akin to the 'Area of Influence' or a 'Block'. Was it not Allen Dulles who had said:

> "Our conflict is world wide and we must intervene in order to protect our global interests."

We should not, however, blame Mr. Dulles for what he says. Every great power in any time would have had to same interests. In fact in the history of the world, one cannot find a great country which has also not been an empire building country. There are numerous references to this phenomenon in the poetry of Dr. Muhammad Iqbal. It must, however, be understood that the word 'Empire' has a different connotation in Islam, that what this word is commonly understood to imply. The Quran says:

> "You are the best community that has been sent forth unto mankind: you enjoin the Right and forbid the Wrong: and you have faith in the Laws of God"
>
> (Al-Quran 3:110)

Promotion of the Right

Allama Muhammad Asad commenting on this issue says:

> "This is the moral justification of the aggressive activism of Islam, a justification of the early Islamic conquests and of its so-called 'imperialism'. For Islam was 'imperialist', if you insist on this term; but this kind of Imperialims was not prompted by love of domination, it had nothing to do with economic or national selfishness, nothing with the greed to increase Muslim comforts at other peoples' cost; nor has it ever meant the coercion of non-believers into the fold of Islam. It has only meant as it means today, the construction of a wordly frame for the best possible spiritual development of man. For, according to the teachings of Islam moral knowledge automatically forces moral responsibility upon man. A mere Platonic discernment between Right and Wrong, without the urge to promote Right and to destroy Wrong, is a gross immorality in itself. In Islam, morality lives and dies with the human endeavour to establish its victory upon earth."

Right to Conquer

If one goes back in history, one finds Aristotle preaching to his disciples, one of whom came to be known to the world as Alexander of Macedon that Greeks as a civilized nation had a right to conquer and civilize the barbarians and, if need be, to destroy them.

The 'State' is nothing but a sum total of the ideology, aspirations and hopes of a people. These act and react to produce (that is, if these actions and reactions occur in the right direction and are of sufficient force) a prototype personality to whom the name of 'Empire Builder' is given. This 'Empire Builder', acts on one hand on the idelogy, aspirations and hopes and on the other on the education, culture and religion of his people. This action and reaction produces the needed personality-type i.e. the person which ideally reflects the image of a nation. When a nation has succeeded in producing the needed personality-type in adequate numbers, their actions and reactions on the previous blocks of the model would tend to lead to the fulfilment of a nation. The name 'Empire has been given to this state of fulfilment.

Let us put some flash on our 'Empire Builder'. What type of man is he? To do this, we must first select a 'State'. Let us select Great Britain for this purpose which has been after all most recent of the 'Empires'. In a somewhat lighter vein, we may find a caricature of the Britain 'Empire Builder' in Major Thompson the dynamic impact of the others can be gauged in the following quotations:

> "He (John Jacob) was remarkable man, possessing both physical and moral courage to an extra-ordinary degree. Whatever he thought was right and just he would do it....I seldom get above three hours sleep in the twenty-four, and the work will kill me which I do not regret, for I have proved and established principles and built foundations on which other will be able to work"

> "In August, as the situation steadily deteriorated, John Nicholson rose from his bed, though in a raging fever, and headed south for Attack with sixty Pathan horsemen, leaving orders for 150 levies to follow him on foot. Riding hard through the night, he reached the Indus with about half his horsemen, in the early hours of the morning, and dashed up to the gate of the fortress. Rousing the garrison from their sleep, he demanded that the gates be opened for him, and

> when this was done ordered that the men arrest their mutinous leaders. For some moments the situation looked ugly, and if the Sikhs had set on him Nicholson could not possibly have escaped with his life. But he was of the stuff that great heroes are made (twenty years later mothers in the Punjab would threaten their naughty children that 'Nikal Seyh' would get them) and his language and presence made a shattering impression. The Sikhs were cowed, and did as they were told; Nicholson took over the fort and prepared it for a siege, then, leaving it under a loyal commander, began scouring the countryside with his cavalry, putting down disorder whenever he found it".

John Nicholson had once written to Henry Lawrence:

> "I feel I am little fit for regulation work, and I can never sacrific common-sense or justice, or the interest of a people or the country to red-tape"

Empire Builders

Some of these 'Empire Builder' were vain and proud while others were modest and considerate, but all possessed one quality which was their complete devotion to duty, and above all a cultivated sense of self-righteousness. Now we come to the Islamic Empire, the memory of whose glorious past has haunted the Muslims throughout the ages. It is the memory of dynamic Islam which rose like a storm from the wilds of Arabia and enveloped the world in a short span of 125 years, pulling down from their high pedestal gods who had ruled over man since the beginning of history, up- rooting centuries old institutions and superstitions and replacing all civilization that had been built on enslavement of humanity. Who were these people then, who created this greatest of the empires, the Muslim 'Empire Builder' in addition to the above mentioned qualities of the British 'Empire Builder', had one more advantage, that was his devotion was not to man-made ideals but to the concept of 'Tauheed', which enabled him, while remaining fuly involved in the affirs of this world, to cultivate a sense of detachment and spirit of sacrifice for other fellow beings. Belief in Tauheed meant that their devotion to Allah was absolutely complete; that is they had no fear but that of Allah and fear of Allah means consciousness of the disadvantages of acting against laws of God given to man through the Quran. These people in the Muslim terminology are called 'Mumin' and 'Muttaqi' and only these are fit to be the rulers and administrators in an Islamic State.

In the affairs of the nations, it is mot important to maintain a balance between socio-economic idelogy and the spiritual ideology. It was in fact this balance which for the first time in the history of world was presented by Islam. It is felt that the present Chinese Cultural Revolution initiated by Mao Tsetung is nothing but an arrangement to fill the gap which has arisen between the great economic ideology of China and the lack of a supporting spiritual ideology. It will not be out of place to mention once again Allama Asad who says:

> "It was the religious teaching of the Quran that gave a solid foundation and the life-example of the Prophet Muhammad (Peace and Blessings be upon him) that became a band of steel around that grand social structure. The Roman Empire had no such spiritual element to keep it together; and therefore it broke down so rapidly."

It is most important to appreciate that imitation — physical or ideological — is a most dangerous course for any nation to follow "and only very superficial people can believe that is possible to imitate a civilization in its external appearance without being at the same time effected by its spirit. A civilization is not an empty form, but a living energy. The moment we begin to accept the form, its inherent currents and dynamic influences set to work in ourselves and mould slowly, imperceptibly, our whole mental attitude."

It is in perfect appreciation of this experience that the Prophet said:

> "Who imitates other people becomes one of them"

Also there is feeling among the intellectuals of the Afro-Asian countries that the ideals of 'Welfare State' are purposely being imposed upon the developing countries by the West. The Western Powers, it is felt, are interested in extending 'Welfare State' to the developing countries, with a view to counteract the popular political reactions in these countries in the overall interests of their 'Global

Strategy' and diverting these countries from their drive towards real economic viability based on a sound and self-expanding infrastructure of capital and technology.

It is also feared that Western concept of 'organized welfare' leads to a crisis of identity and that its organized propagation by West aims at creating an 'awareness' leading to general dissatisfaction, frustration and drift. This state of affairs, then naturally diverts the attention of developing countries from nation building tasks of real importance.

Scholars have laid much emphasis on Islamic Charity'. His idea of a 'Modern welfare state' being a heaven of charity, though having some superficial similarity with some limited functions of an Islamic State, is practically an antithesis of Islamic concept, simply for the reason that this idea of charity results in building a makeshift barricade against the emergence of a true Islamic order. The countries of Asia and Africa need a revolutionary concept if they aspire for self-sufficiency and real independence. Only such a concept can extol them to an honourable position in the community of nations. The changes in social structure may be drastic, violent or evolutionary. But makeshift concepts or patchwork ideas simply would serve no real purpose.

The scholars while advancing their ideas of charity so vehemently overlooks the revolutionary concept of Islam in human, economic and social structure. Islam in its pristine ideology, does not envisage society composed of 'haves' and 'have nots', where a vast majority of people are perpeturally degraded to the position of beggars, asking for alms from a minority of charitable and benevolent ruling class. This is diametrically opposed to Islamic principles of Akhuwwat and 'Musawat' and hinders any real progress of the society. It is a concept born out of western capitalism and neo-colonialism. Islamic concept, as can be understood from the Quran and authentic hadith, aims at building a classless society obeying the laws of the Quran:

> "And what do you understand what the Era of faith is; again, what do you understand what the Era of faith is? It is the Era in which no man shall have any control over any other man; and the reign in that Era shall be entirely of Allah's Laws."
>
> (Al-Quran 82:17,18,19)

Thus a country, aspiring to become an Islamic State, must declare its faith and pledge at the very outset to create such classless society governed by the Laws of Quran, as illustrated by the life of the Last Messenger of Allah (peace and blessings be upon him) and his four closest companions, Khulafa-i-Rashideen. It will be a waste of time and energies for Muslims to grope in the dark labyrinth of Western political and social theories. All charitable activities in an Islamic state are meant to cover the interim period till the conditions of a true Islamic society are reached and to meet exigencies of curing maldistribution of wealth. Allama Muhammad Asad commenting on the following hadith says:

> "The faithful are like one man, if his eye suffers, his whole body suffers; and if his head suffers, his whole body suffers. You will recognise the faithful by their mutual compassion, love and sympathy. They are like one body; if one of its part is ill, the whole body suffers from sleeplessness and fever".

Sociological Lesson

"This, then, is the deepest sociological lesson of Islam: there can be no happiness and strength in a society that permits some of its members to suffer undeserved want, while others have more than they need. If the whole society suffers privations owing to extra-ordinary circumstances (as, for instance, happened to the Muslim community in the early days of Islam), such privations may become the source of spiritual strength and, through it, of future greatness. But if the available resources of a community are so unevenly distributed that certain groups within it live in affluence while the majority of the people are forced to use up all their energies in search of their daily bread. Poverty becomes the most dangerous enemy of spiritual progress, and occasionally drives whole community away from. God-consciousness and into the arms of soul-destroying materialism. It is undoubtedly this that the Prophet had in mind when he uttered the warning words:

Poverty may sometimes turn into unbelief (Kufr).

Poverty in the midst of plenty is a negation of the very principle of brotherhood by which Islam stands and falls."

The scholar have suggested the collection of 'Zakat' by Union

Councils. In Islam 'Zakat' is a central responsibility and obligation and must be collected centrally by an Islamic State. Furthermore, if a state is not Islamic in its positive basic concept by virtue of its declarations and actions, it cannot collect 'Zakat' whether centrally or through such agencies as Union Councils, as it no longer remains obligatory on Muslims to pay 'Zakat' to an un-Islamic State, no matter whether it is entirely composed of people paying lip-service to Islam.

In this connection, it is also important to note that:

> "Behold, God has bought of the Faithful their persons and their possessions, offering them Paradise in return".
>
> (Al-Quran 9:111)

Government's Rights

It follows, therefore, that a government ruling in the name of Allah and His Prophet and in obedience to the Law of Islam has the right to call upon all the resources of the citizens —including their personal possessions and even their lives — whenever the interests of the community and the security of the state demand such an effort. In other words, the government is entitled (a) to impose, over and above the Zakat- tax immutably laid down in Quran and Sunnah, any additional taxes and levies that may be deemed necessary for the welfare of the community, (b) to impose, whenever necessary, restrictions on private ownership of certain kinds of properties, means of production, or natural resources with a view to their being administered by the state as public utilities, and (c) to subject all able-bodied citizens to compulsory military service in defence of the state.

It will not be out of place to point out here that most of the present day problems of concept in Muslim world are the outcome of attempts to amalgamate. Western pseudo-social and political theories with wrong notions of Islam. This will lead us nowwhere. The absolute truth of Islam does not accept any compromise with man-made fallacies.

> "Accept Islam in its entirety"
>
> (Al-Quran 2:208)

Acceptance in Totality

Either we shall have to accept Islam in its full application to our social and political life or reject it totally and be damned. There is no midway. There is a very big difference between a state run by Muslims of today and a true Islamic State. We have to discard many legacies of Muslim Monarchism and Western Imperialism in order to become an Islamic State. The Quran provides us the required sound basic concept of such a state without hankering after alien and doubtful ideologies.

Islamic Format

The great scholar of Islam, Allama Muhammad Asad said that: "We should not underestimate the difficulties that will confront us should we decide to give to our polity the contents and forms demanded by Islam. For one thing, it is not an easy task to achieve a truly Islamic polity after the centuries of debasement and slavery which have sapped the strength of the Muslim community and undermined its social morale. During the period of their political decay, the Muslims have lost a good deal of their cultural self-confidence as well, and many of them find it difficult today to avoid thinking in Western terms of 'state and nation' and to think in Islamic terms instead. They blindly follow Western patterns of thought in the naive belief that every thing which comes from the West must be more 'up-to-date' than anything which they, the Muslims, could produce out of themselves; and this conviction leads them to an irresponsible application of Western political concepts to all that happens in their own society. On the other hand, many conservative Muslims who, in word and deed, insist on the maintenance of all traditional forms and, consequently, oppose the Westernization of their community, base their opposition not so much on the real values of Islam as on the social conventions evolved in the centuries of our decadence. Their minds seem to work on the assumption that Islam and the conventions of Muslim society are one and the same thing (which every thinking person knows is an utterly false assumption) and that, therefore, everything that implies a departure from the conventions evolved in the course of our history — both with regard to our social habits and our approach to the problems of state and government — goes against Islam; and that, therefore, it would be the duty of an Islamic state to give permanance and legal sanction to all the social forms in which we have hitherto been living. In other words, these conservative elements within our society seem to take it for granted that the survival of Islam depends on the maintenance of the very conditions which, because of their sterile rigidity, now make it impossible for Muslims to live in accordance with the true tenets of Islam....Apart from the difficulties arising from our own cultural decadence and the centuries-old stagnation of Muslim thought, any attempt to reorganize our countries on truly Islamic lines invariably arouses apprehensions in the non-Muslim world and causes ;it to place all manner of obstructions, direct and indirect, in our way towards this ideal. Ever since the Crusades, Islam has been misrepresented in the West, and a deep distrust — almost hatred — of all Islamic propositions has become part and parcel of the Wertern cultural heritage. The Westerners see in the tenets of Islam not only a denial of many of the fundamental beliefs of their own religion but also a political threat. Under the influence of their historical memories, of the centuries of passionate warfare between the Muslim world and Europe, they attribute to Islam — quite unjustifiably — an inherent hostility towards all non-Muslims; and so they fear that revival of the Islamic spirit, as manifested in the idea of the Islamic state, might revive the slumbering strength of the Muslims and drive them to new aggressive adventures in the direction of the West. To counteract such a possible tendency, the Westerners are doing their utmost to prevent a resurgence of political power in Muslim countries and a restoration of Islam to its erstwhile dominant position in Muslim social and intellectual life. Their means of combat are not merely political; they are cultural as well. Through the instrumentality of Western Schools and of Western-oriented methods of education in the Muslim world, the distrust of Islam as a social doctrine is being systematically planted in the minds of the younger generation of Muslim men and women; and the principal weapon in this campaign to discredit Islam is being supplied, unconsciously, by the reactionary elements within our own society".

6

Theory of Administration

Spirit of Administration

In Islam religious and secular spheres of human life are harmoniously and inextricably blended. Religion provides a comprehensive view of life for both here and hereafter. Spiritual, political, cultural and social aspects in a Muslim society are closely intertwined. It is very difficult to distinguish one from the other. The Prophet, who is an eternal guide to the faithful in his march on the Straight Path (Sirat-i-Mustaqim), signifies the highest ideals of perfect life. He was a prophet, a ruler, a commander of the armies, and a judge, and in all these areas his leadership was a beacon light for the believers.

Be emphasized in unmistakable terms that submission to Allah means that one should practice the spirit of the revealed word of God in every sphere of human activity. Revelation is an absolute reality, and is a general umbrella for the temporal and spiritual affairs of man. Islam, like other social philosophies, believes that sociability is a basic need of man. It is in the framework of the community that our capabilities fructify in their fullness.

In society, an individual is a part of a, dynamic group life, outside it he just withers away. In order to effectively participate in community, a comprehensive code of conduct has been laid down so that peace, order and prosperity could be maintained. Individual rights and duties have been defined in concrete terms and they are deeply rooted in the infallible principles of Sharia.

Another fundamental characteristic of Islamic thought is the indissoluble bond of unity among the members of the Muslim community. The Prophet called his followers Khair-ul-Umamum (the best community), and in his opinion it is unified 'like a single hand, like a compact wall whose bricks support each other.' In another tradition, the Prophet said, 'the believers are as a single body. If one of its members is afflicted it is felt by the rest of the body." The obligations entailed by social cohesion, demand a comprehensive administrative machinery because human propensities for cooperation and non-cooperation are equally strong. Man is loving and affectionate, but at the same time he is selfish and aggressive. His untamed emotions and irrational fixations could be very disruptive for the social order. His behavior in society is often influenced by avarice, malice and suspicion, and if these traits are allowed to persist in him, he can be a threat to peace and harmony. To ward off such dangers a society needs a government, or a central authority, which could extract legitimacy and allegiance from the bulk of the population. It can watch the wicked, punish the wrong-doer and reward the honest and just. Commenting on human nature, the Quran says, "men are the enemies of each other," and again that, "were it not for God (causing) the restraint of one man (by means) of another, the earth would have been corrupted". This makes it abundantly clear that for the preservation and integration of Umma, and to put curbs on the evil instincts of man, some kind of governmental machinery is an indisputable necessity.

In other words, the community, in order to fulfill its mission of peace, order and prosperity, needs an authority which has formal organization and unquestioned legitimacy. The legally constituted authority has at its disposal the coercive power to punish the wrong-doer, and establish a social, climate wherein law-abiding citizens can live in peace and harmony. Need for such an authority has been depicted by Ibn Khaldun in the following words:

> "Human society having been achieved there arises the need for restraining each man from another owing to his animal propensities for aggression and

> oppression there must exist accordingly a restraining force which must be sought from one man, who will be entrusted with power and authority, so that no longer will an individual be attacked by another. This is what is implied in the term *mulk* (sovereignty or statehood) which exists by nature in man is necessary for his existence."

The Quran has emphasized in very clear terms that organized machinery of government is indispensable for the ultimate good of the community. Administration envisioned has to be supremely effective and efficient because its responsibilities are more than mere maintenance of law and order. The Quranic ideal is a service state wherein functionaries are expected to dedicate themselves to the cause of general welfare, and more than that, they have to maintain a moral and religious climate in which people can practice goodness without any hindrance. The following verses of the Quran indicate the need of government:

> "Relation is prescribed for you in the matter of the murdered."

> "Lo Allah commandeth you that ye restore deposits to their owners, and if ye judge between mankind, that ye judge justly."

Ethical and Spiritual Basis

Obviously such an obligation and hundreds of other matters relating to inheritance, distribution of wealth, maintenance of Zakat and organization of Baital Mal could not be administered without systematic and fully streamlined administrative machinery. In other words, Islamic Sharia is a comprehensive code delineating broad, and general principles of social organization for the Umma, and without administration this code could not be operationalized into the daily life of the people.

There are no specific and concrete provisions regarding the structural framework of administration, but it has been emphasized that the basis of administration in a Muslim state should be spiritual and ethical. To provide additional guidance, the Prophet himself organized the city state of Medina, in which broad principles of political organization were laid down to help the later Muslim rulers. Hitti, commenting on the Prophet's role in politics and administration, says, "He performed the functions of prophet, lawgiver, religion, chief judge, commander of the armies and civil head of state." Another important feature of the Muslim polity is that ultimate sovereignty belongs to God. The Quran says :

> "Unto Allah belongs the East and the West, and withersoever ye turn there is Allah's countenance. Lo Allah is All-embracing, All knowing."

Moreover, the titles which have been used by God to depict His control over the universe leave no doubt in the mind of the faithful about His indisputable sovereign authority. Some of these titles are listed below :

> (i) The Lord of the Worlds. (ii) The Sacred King. (iii) The Owner of Sovereignty. (iv) The King of Mankind. (v) The Best of Judges. (vi) Say: O Allah, owner of the sovereign power, Thou givest power to whom Thou willest, and withdrawest power from whom Thou willest, Thou exaltest whom thou willest, and Thou abasest whom Thou willest. In Thy hand is all good and over all things Thou has power.

The principle of the sovereignty of God is pivotal to the ideology of Islam. It is not merely a spiritual concept meant only to provide solace to the soul and spirit of man, but is a principle which, according to the, Quranic edicts, must guide and determine the course of action for every Muslim. Fear of God is considered to be a moral equipment which keeps men on the path of rectitude. Rulers and ruled both are accountable to His authority. All scholars of law and politics agree that sovereignty of God is the sole determinent of public policy in a Muslim state. Grunebaum says,

> "Islam is the community of Allah. He is the living truth to which it owes its life. He is the center and, goal of its spiritual experience. But he is also the mundane head of his community which he not only rules but governs. This makes the Muslim Army the Army of Allah, the Treasury of Allah, what is more, it places the life of the community in its entirety as well as the private lives of the individual members under His direct legislature and supervisory power."

David DeSantillana has; summed up the Muslim view of the sovereignty of God as follows:

> The rule of Allah over his people is immediate and direct. The gods of the ancient Arab tribes had been the patrons and protectors of their worshippers. Allah, patron and defender of his chosen people, now takes the place of the ancient gods, and rules the Muslim community. When the chief of a tribe that had adopted Islam said to the Prophet, 'Thou are our prince', the Prophet answered quickly: 'The prince is God, not I.'

Governance by Allah

Islam is the direct government of Allah, the rule of God, whose eyes are upon his people. The principle of unity and order which in other societies is called civitas, polis, State, in Islam is personified by Allah; Allah is the name of the supreme power, acting in the common interest. Thus the public treasury is 'the treasury of Allah,' the army is the 'army of Allah,' even the public functionaries are 'the employees of Allah.'

Explaining the same point of view, Gibb says;

> "The Head of the Umma is Allah, an Allah alone. His rule is immediate and His commands revealed to Muhammad, embody the law and constitution of the Umma."

A belief in the sovereignty of God helps people to rid vices like greed, jealousy, and hypocrisy, By subjecting all human beings, irrespective of caste, colour, race and rank, to the will of God, Islam introduces a moral element in its social thought which could check galloping ambitions which are a source of injustice and tyranny. It is an ethical tonic which rescues people from the evil effects of pride, conceit and ostentation.

And above all, faith in the supremacy of God strengthens righteous convictions and endows the believer with spiritual courage to fight for every right cause. He would not be cowed down with fear or favour. The Quran says:

> "Verily those who say, 'Our Lord is God' remain firm (on that Path) on them shall be no fear."

Allah's Supremacy

Later in Islamic history, the idea of God's unimpeachable supremacy led to emergence of mystical cults which, contrary to the spirit of Islam, preached self-abnegation, ascetism and passivity. The actual purpose of such a doctrine, however, was not to breed inactivity and deprive human beings of the use of reason and rationality in handling their worldly affairs. The primary objective was to defend human existence against excesses, to which men are so easily seduced. The Quran has only imposed limits called "Hadud Allah" within which people have been given maximum freedom to fashion their destinies. Biographers of the Prophet and Arab historians have recorded an authentic incident which is an eloquent testimony that, in spite of the revealed injunctions of the Quran, the role of human judgment is still very decisive.

The Prophet at the time of sending a judge to Yemen asked him the question as to how he was going to administer justice among people entrusted to his jurisdiction. The judge replied that he would base his decision "on the Quran." The Prophet again asked:

> "But if that does not provide sufficient guidance for the purpose?"

The judge answered:

> "Then I will seek light from your usage or practice."

The Prophet once again questioned:

> "But supposing even there you do not find any solution?"

The judge spoke:

> "Then I will follow my own opinion."

The Prophet blessed the judge and wholeheartedly approved of his views. The Pious Caliphs also adopted similar attitudes in administering the affairs of the kingdom. In their instructions to the state functionaries, they frequently insisted on the use of reason and common sense. Umar I, in his letter to a judge in Kufa in 18 A.H., instructed him that in writing his judgments he should first of all focus all his attention on the Quran and Sunnah (Usages of the Prophet), but in case he failed to find guidance there, he is authorized to use his own wisdom or individual interpretation.

Vast Reservoir

Islamic jurisprudence, a vast reservoir of legal principles, is mostly based on scholarly interpretations of Quranic verses, organized common sense, and rational insight of the jurists. Ray (opinion), Qiyas (analogical deduction), and Ijma (consensus) were frequently used by them to disentangle confusion and complexity from human decision-making. Ijtihad (independent reasoning) is an Integral part of the Islamic way of life. Its primary function is to widen the scope of Sharia and create circumstances, which would enable the Muslims to develop a flexible attitude in handling the changing realities in society.

The Quran says:

> "And if any tidings, whether of safety or fear come unto them, they noise it abroad, whereas if they had referred it to the Messenger and such of them as are in authority, those among them are able to think out the latter would have known it."

The above verse read in conjunction with the Prophet's advice to the judge of Yemen gives a clear proof that in the conduct of political and administrative affairs of a Muslim state, human reason has its proper and legitimate place. An Egyptian writer, Ahmad A, Golwash, has defined Ijtihad as "the exercise of judgment to meet the new circumstances." Abulala Maududi has made the following remarks on this issue:

> "The whole of this legislative process, which makes the legal system of Islam dynamic and makes its development and evolution in the changing circumstances possible, results from a particular type of academic research and intellectual effort, which in the terminology of Islam is called Ijtihad."

In the early centuries of Islam, scholars and statesmen made frequent use of this vital instrument of law-making, but there came a time when Ijtihad was totally abandoned and Muslims, instead of being Mujtahids (innovators in intellectual endeavors), became Muqalids (Traditionalist or slavish followers of precedent). "The closing of the doors of Ijtihad" as the maxim is popularly used in Islamic literature has been considered a great intellectual disaster. Islamic ideology, which was dynamic and progressive, became stagnant, and creative thinking ceased to be an important aspect of Muslim civilization. Historians have not been able to determine the time and the precise reason for the closure of the doors of Ijtihad. It is suggested that at some stage of Islamic history, scholar-jurists, in order to avoid growing pressure from the despotic Muslim rulers to interpret the Quran to suit political expediency, intentionally closed the doors of Ijtihad. The jurists thought that indiscriminate use of independent reasoning with ulterior motives would ultimately subvert the true meanings of the faith.

Law, politics, and administration, which constitute the pivot of socio-economic organization suffered the biggest setback, when the doors of ijtihad were closed. The result was that stagnant law, corrupt politics and incompetent administration became the disappointing aspects of large periods of Islamic history.

Early Administration

The administration over which the Prophet himself presided in Medina was simple. His preoccupation with wars against infidels did not leave enough time for him to lay down some exhaustive plan of administration. Moreover, territory, which the Muslims controlled in his lifetime, was small, which did not require a large number of agencies or departments. Most of his attention and that of his leading companions was focused on creating a religious identity and strengthening the bonds of unity. Under his immediate successor, Hazrat Abu Bakr, administration was also personal and paternalistic in character. The primary purpose of his administration was to frame such public policies which could eradicate pre-Islamic tribal practices which were inimical to the Islamic way of life. Unity, sense of direction and perfect religious identity were the chief objectives, and all governmental resources were geared to their realization. Under Hazrat Umar I, however, there was lightening territorial expansion, which necessitated a completely fresh look on administration. Religious integration still had priority, but there was also a growing realization that, without an efficient and elaborate administrative system, the future of the community would be in jeopardy.

First Step in Formation

Umar I is credited with the first formal establishment of governmental machinery in Islamic history. He found the existing administrative institutions to be inadequate to meet the growing needs of an ever expanding empire. Communication with conquered provinces, collection of revenues, levying of taxes, appointment of officials, and maintenance of records became crucial issues for the peace and stability of the kingdom.

Umar I, thus was compelled to establish new departments and offices, which could effectively administer wide range of public policies. He is credited with the establishment of the office of the Diwan (Registrar) in Muslim history. It was a record office, in which names of the person, who received assistance from Baital Mal were registered. He also created several other governmental bureaus relating to the collection of revenues, supervision of markets and administration of justice. It would, however, be wrong to say that Umar I established an elaborate machinery of government which was entirely new. He infused a truly Islamic spirit in the management of public affairs, but retained the structures and procedures of administration as he found them in the conquered lands. In Syria and Persia, he allowed the administrative offices to continue to function as before. Even the official language of the new provinces was not suddenly changed to Arabic. In Syria Greek, and in Persia, Persian remained the official languages of the administration. Similarly. Amrbin, as the commander who, under Umar I, conquered Egypt decided to retain the coptic machinery of government in that country. Philip K. Hitti has made the following comments on the administration of Umar I :

> "The problem then of administering a hastily assembled, far-flung empire with a multiplicity of languages, religions, and ethnic elements first arose during the reign of the second Caliph. Umar followed the line of least resistance. He left Virtually intact the Byzantine framework of provincial government in Syria and Egypt as well as the Sasanid administrative machinery in Persia, and tried to incorporate in it whatever Islamic-Arabian theories he had. Old

> functionaries and bureaucrats were left in their positions; they could not be replaced. The military register he-instituted was of Persian origin as indicated by its designation (diwan)."

De Lacy O'Leary also testifies that the early Islamic conquerors left the intellectual, cultural and legal framework of the conquered territories undisturbed. He says :

> "The Arab conquest of 632 did not check the religious or intellectual life of either the Nestorian or Monophysite community. The Arabs exacted tribute, but so had the Persian and Roman governments. The tribute paying communities were left free to follow their own laws, religion and customs and to lead their own cultural life."

Richard Sullivan has summed up the policy of non-intervention in the conquered territories followed by early Arab conquerors as follows:

> "Living in exclusive military cities, they tended to permit local religious practices, customs and even governmental institutions to continue in their conquered lands. Contrary to what is often believed, they did not try to force Islam on their subjects, preferring instead to keep the true faith as their chief mark of distinction. The policy of non-interference with existing ways of life made Muslim conquest relatively painless to the victims."

These arrangements were continued by Umar I's successors. The institutions were simple and rudimentary in character, because the period of the Pious Caliphate was stormy and chaotic. In spite of their impeccable honesty and genius for governing men, most of their energies were consumed in the restoration of law and order and consolidation of conquered territories. There were internal convulsions, external wars, tribal rivalries and personal bickerings among several contenders to power, which made peaceful organization of the community rather difficult.

After the end of the Pious Caliphate, the sceptre of authority in the Muslim kingdom passed into the hands of the Umayyads.

Muawiyya, the founder of the dynasty, was endowed with immense administrative capabilities. After transfering the capital from Medina to Damascus, he focused all his attention on the creation of a powerful machinery of government which could effectively and efficiently handle the work of administration which had been growing in volume and complexity very fast. He thought that centralization of bureaucratic decision-making was the only antidote against centrifugal tendencies, which were almost endemic. The functions of the government from the point of view of modern standards were rather limited Mobilization of armed forces, consolidation of conquered territories, and the collection of revenues were the main responsibilities of the government.

New Experiences

In Damascus, the Arabs were thrown in the midst of alien socio-political environment and came into contact with highly advanced legal and administrative institutions.

At the time of Arab conquest, Syria was part of the Byzantine empire, and its central and municipal administration had a great reputation for efficiency. The central government was maintaining a very effective control over the provincial units of administration. The Umayyads decided to retain the administrative structures as they found them and gave the state functionaries the choice to leave and settle in areas, which were still under Roman rule or accept jobs in the new Muslim state. Many of them decided to stay under the Arab rule and obtained positions of respect and distinction in the Umayyad bureaucracy.

New Official Language

In the beginning, the official language of administration remained Greek and government offices were staffed mostly with Christians. During the period of Caliph Abd-al-Malik (685 A.D.-705 A.D.), however, racial and religious frictions started simmering in the administration, but the Muslims were not yet sufficiently trained to replace the Christians in offices. The only thing which Abd-al-Malik could do was to replace Greek with Arabic as the official language.

The Umayyad dynasty established powerful central agencies. At Damascus, a number of diwans (ministries) were constituted to look after government work in various spheres of the state. Some of the important central agencies were :

Diwan al Khatum : In this office, records of official correspondence were kept and outgoing letters were sealed.

Diwan al Rasail : Officers working in this department used to write and polish the language of official letters.

Diwan al Mustaghallat : It was in charge of receiving rents from state lands.

Diwan al Kharaj : It acted as a state treasury.

Diwan al Barid : It maintained the postal system throughout the country. Officers in this department only carried official messages from the center to the provinces and worked as agents of central intelligence.

The officers working in these agencies were servants of the ruler and not the employees of the state. They had very little discretionary authority and for each act of omission or commission every officer was personally accountable to the ruler; whose authority in all matters was indisputable. The functionaries of the state had virtually no job security. Everything depended on the fleeting whim of the ruling autocrat, who alone could make or unmake the fortunes of his kingdom. The character and caliber of the administration also depended on the wisdom and insight of the ruler. His image was always projected in the behavior of the administrators. If he was honest, conscientious, God-fearing and anxious to protect the interests and welfare of his subjects, there was every possibility that the functionaries of the state would also be imbued with the same spirit; but if the ruler was corrupt, dishonest and tyrannical, the officials of the state also used to act in the same way. The administration was excessively centralized and paternalistic, but it was efficient. It inducted the Arabs into the complexities of centralized administration, and trained them for shouldering political and administrative responsibilities in various parts of the world.

Richard Sullivan has made the following remarks on the success of the Umayyed administration :

> "The success of the Umayyad system of government marked one of the highlights of early Muslim history, for never had the Arabs been as well organized and disciplined. By initiating the governmental techniques of more civilized peoples, the Arabs succeeded in establishing and ruling a great empire."

Variety of Changes

The Umayyads were succeeded by the Abbasides, who moved the capital of the Muslim empire to Baghdad. The new dynasty, though Arab in origin, was deeply Persianized in cultural and administrative institutions. This was natural, because the rulers of the new dynasty had risen to power with substantial help of their Persian supporters. The proximity of the new capital to Persia further helped the non-Arab elements to occupy positions of eminence, in the administration of the new Caliphate. Under Abbasides the Muslim empire expanded still further, which necessitated a wide variety of changes in the organization of the governmental machinery. With the help of their Persian Viziers (Prime Ministers) like the Bermecides, they were able to streamline the existing administrative structures and added several new offices to increase the efficiency and output of work in the government.

The institution of Vizierat had its antecedent in the Sassanid tradition, but it was considerably changed to suit the conditions of new religo-political order of the Muslim Caliphate. Vizier, as the highest functionary of the state, was all-powerful, but still he had no job security. Harun-al-Rashid's sudden dismissal of the mighty Bermecides is a classic example of the fragility of this office.

Abu Muhammad Ibn-al-Muqaffa was perhaps among the earliest leading Persians who introduced swift Persianization of the socio-political institutions in Islam. He was an employee of Isa Ibn Ali the uncle of as-Saffah the founder of the Abbasid dynasty. He translated several old Persian works from Pahlawi (Ancient Persian language) into Arabic. He translated the biographical history of the ancient Persian kings called *Khudainama* into Arabic under the title *Siyar muluk al Ajm.* In Arabic he wrote *ad-durra-al-*

yatima fi taat a muluk (a treatise on obedience to the kings). He is also credited with works relating to manners and duties of civil servants and court etiquette. Some of the new ministeries created by the Abbasides were as follows :

Diwan al Nafagat : Head of this department was a comptroller of the royal household.

Diwan al Jaysh : It was a military department dealing with army recruitment and acted as a paymaster of the armed forces.

Diwan al Dar : This was established as an agency to coordinate the work of various revenue collecting agencies.

Bayt Mal Mazalim : It handled the confiscated property of the corrupt officers.

Diwan al Mawrith al Hashriay : It was an office which took care of eschated estates. The practice was that, if an officer dies, his property, after legitimate deductions for dependents, was deposited in the state treasury.

Sahib ul Shurta : He headed a police force to maintain law and order. The organization was a part of the justice department.

Qadi al Kuzzat : His department looked after the administration of justice in the kingdom.

The emphasis in a Muslim kingdom was generally on central administration. Long distances and absence of easy means of transportation hindered effective control by the center over the provincial administration. In theory, the administration was highly centralized, but in practice it lacked the effective control mechanism to supervise and coordinate the administration in provinces of the sprawling empire. The primary concern of the center was the collection of revenues. As long as the center was receiving the fixed revenues, its intervention in the provincial administration was minimal. Philip K. Hitti has made the following comments on the provincial administration :

> "The earlier provincial organization of the empire was not radically altered. In theory, the governor held his position at the pleasure of the Vizir, and behind the Vizir, the Caliph. But in all lcoal affairs, the governor tended to become supreme and his office hereditary. The increase in his authority over the

> judiciary and taxation varied in direct proportion to his personal ability, Caliphal weakness and distance from the imperial capital."

Within each province the administration was also extremely centralized. The provincial governors, although they held mandates from the ruler, were in reality, considerably autonomous in their jurisdiction. Notions of merit or careerism did not exist at all. Recruitment was mostly based on the spoils system or patronage. Since there was no job security, even the most meritorious civil' servant lived in a state of tension and uncertainty. Fall of a ruler could mean the dismissal of all leading administrators of the state. A climate like that was not conducive to any kind of permanent bureaucratic institutions, which could be anesthized against the impact of political changes. Administration, particulary at the higher echelons, was integrated into the political process. Like every other autocratic system, the Abbasid administration had built-in centrifugal tendencies, which continued to aggravate as the dynasty, after its earlier successes and glories, moved swiftly towards its downfall. After 850 A.D., the growing corruption in the central government at Baghdad and chronic revolts and rebellions in the provinces had become the permanent features of the Abbasid rule.

As noticed earlier, the scope of legislation in a Muslim state was very limited. The primary responsibility of the government was to implement the revealed word of God. The Caliph and other rulers were only expected to devise means, by which the law enunciated by the religious doctrine could be effectively implemented. As juristic interpretations of the revealed word, precedents and religious proclamations in the form of *fetwas* kept on multiplying, the privilege of the secular ruler to do something independent of this vast pile of religious law kept on shrinking. Philip K. Hitti has given the following picture of the state of law in Islam :

> "The sharia, according to the traditional view, is eternal, universal, perfect, fit for all men at all times in all places. It preceded the state and the society. It recognizes no difference between the sacred and secular. It sets forth and regulates man's relations with and obligations to God as well as his relations

> with his fellowman. All Allah's commandments—about ritual, civil and other matters—with their punishments are recorded in Quran. Of the roughly six thousand verses therein, some two thousand are strictly legislative."

Thus, even a cursory glance at Islamic administrative law can easily reveal that its foundations were laid mostly on Juristic interpretations as they flowed from the courts of the *Qadis, fetwas* of the *Muftis* and studies of the learned theologians. Statutary law, with rigid legal sanctions as we understand it today, did not exist in the early Islamic history. State could not openly compete with Sharia in legislative matters. Its sole purpose, in theory at least, was to implement the revealed law. With the passage of time, however, a deep wedge appeared between theory and practice. In theory, Sharia embraced everything from cradle to grave in a citizen's life, but under growing strains of territorial expansion and doctrinal complexity, the Caliphs or Sultans were constrained to create numerous offices which were purely of secular character. More often than not, they interfered in strictly religious affairs, and disobeyed injunctions of religion to achieve secular objectives. In many cases customary law took precedence over religious law. There is, however, one chief feature of Islamic administrative law, that irrespective of the differences of time and clime, its ideal was never decried in any Muslim society. Deviations and malpractices, there were many, but reverence to the ideal remained undiminished.

Judicial Administration

As noticed earlier, that bulk of the legislation in a Muslim state was divine, its implementation could not be entrusted to a person unless he was well-versed in religious law. Judiciary, therefore, was always in the hands of functionaries who specialized in the various interpretations of Quranic injunctions and the rules of Sharia. Since one of the primary responsibilities of the Muslim head of the state was to defend the faith and help the people in moulding their lives according to the true spirit of Islam. Judges always occupied a very respectable social position, and their opinions and decisions' were always sought by the ruler and other public officials in formulating the policies of the state. In theory at least, their role was quite different from the rest of bureaucracy, because although they were servants of the state, they were expected to be independent in their judgments. Although they were appointed by the ruler of the day, their accountability and loyalty to him was limited. In fact, it was a major part of their responsibilities to uncover irreligious acts of the government and nullify them by *fetwas* (Judgments). If the various branches of Islamic Judiciary had followed strictly their original religious terms of reference, Muslim politics and administration would have been able to retain some of their pristine virtues like justice, integrity and incorruptability. The history of Islamic Judiciary, however, shows that Judges, working in the different branches of the religious law, more often than not, abdicated from the role assigned to them by the faith, and like the rest of the bureaucracy became an integral part of a monolithic administrative machine, whose sole purpose was to support the ruling dynasty.

The Judge

The office was first created by the Holy Prophet, but most of its professional and procedural trappings were developed later in Islamic history.

In pre-Islamic Arab *hakam,* whose primary responsibility was to arrange arbitration among tribesmen could not handle, complex judicial problems of a new urban society. The office of Qadi was created to resolve the wide variety of legal issues for which precedents did not exist. The Qadis, who were appointed in the Umayyad administration, through their interpretations of the canonical law and use of 'sound judgment' (ray) in cases where relegion was silent, laid the foundations of Islamic Fiqh (Jurisprudence) on which the later Jurists built a fine super-structure of the Muslim Judicial system. As the gulf between ideal and reality widened and countless problems emerged which had no clue in the Quranic legislation, Qadi's court became the only administrative instrument which could guide the state in law-making. Qadi's were always specialists, and commanded a lot of prestige and respect in society, but it would be wrong to construe that in Islamic administration, Judiciary was independent. They were appointed by the political authorities, generally the Caliph or the Governor, and like every other functionary, they could be dismissed at any time.

The ideals with which the office of Qadi was established in Islam were very high. A letter written by Caliph Umar I to Abu Musa-al-Ashari embodies some of the highest ideals commonly associated with this office.

Some of the highlights of this letter are as follows:

> Make all Muslims equal in your sessions and in your sight, so that the highborn will not expect your favour, and the weak will not despair of your justice.

The plaintiff must adduce evidence, and if the defendant denies, he must take an oath. Compromise between the parties is permissible, unless it makes the forbidden lawful, or the lawful forbidden.

Use your understanding for the matters which perplex your heart for which there is neither a Quranic text nor any precedent (Sunna). Know the similarities and like cases, and then make an analogy after that and base yourself on what is most pleasing to God and appears to you to be what is right.

All Muslims may be legal witnesses except those, who have been flogged for an offense which carries a Quranic punishment, or have had false witnesses proved against them or are suspect on grounds of their friendship or kinship to the parties. God must judge the secrets of the heart; He leaves you to judge the evidence. Beware of displaying fatigue and weariness and annoyance in the place of justice, wherein God allows you to win a reward and earn good pay at the same time.

Muhammad ibn Abdun, who was himself a Qadi in Seville during the twelfth century, laid down, that knowledge in the laws of God was the fundamental prerequisite for Qadi's position. This was the only way he could distinguish between right and wrong or the oppressor and the oppressed. He should set aside his personal ambitions and desires as he gives judgment. He should not act in haste, and should not give the people a chance to construe that he is ease-loving and comfort seeking. He will be a great success if his character radiates clemency, gentleness and compassion, and has urbane personality. Mere possession of these qualities, however, is not enough. He must also have the reputation for these excellences, so that people can repose confidence in him. Abdun further adds that Qadi is advised not to delegate his authority because it would be a sign of incompetence or criminal evasion of responsibility. Before pronouncing his judgment, the Qadi must take into consideration the opinions of at least two Jurists, although the ultimate decision always lies with him. Bailiffs employed in his court should also be men of calm disposition, who are sedate and free from vices like drinking and gambling. Abdun has some harsh words for advocates, who appear to plead others' cases. In his opinion, they deceive people who are in trouble with the law. If their appearance at some point becomes indispensable, it is the duty of the Qadi to do rigorous screening of their credentials in terms of piety and learning. Arbitrators are disallowed from pronouncing their awards at their houses. They can do so only in the presence of the Qadi.

The Ideals

The ideals about the Qadi's role, however, were seldom realized in fullness during the Islamic history. Like every other functionary of the state, he was reduced to the position of utter dependence to the ruler. Since the post had great temptations and wide opportunities for bribery and nepotism, many eminent theologians with a strictly puritanical outlook disdained the office and would not accept it. The result was that more often than not, men of less calibre and poor moral integrity were assigned to this office, which weakened the Judicial process a great deal. The greatest setback, however, was the loss of the independence of judgment by the Qadi. He became a minion of those, who wielded authority in the state and who had the power to implement his decisions.

Particularly Muslim governments tended to restrict his jurisdiction in criminal matters, and reserved the right to accept or reject his judgment.

The administration of justice in a Muslim state was extremely complex and elaborate, because according to Sharia human actions were divided into five specific categories :

Fard : Undeviating Divine Command.

Manduh : Which is not ordained but has a divine approval.

Mubah : Something which is neither approved nor forbidden. The divine law is neutral for such an object.

Makruh : Object which needs to be disliked and condemned.

Haram : Things and actions which are totally forbidden.

Except for *Fard* and *Haram,* the other three categories were foggy and confused and left considerable room for difference of opinion and a variety of interpretations. Things were further complicated when the four schools of *Fiqh* demarcated their boundries by listing, what was right or wrong from the point of view of Quran. Local customs, which were not contrary to the fundamentals of religion were also included into the legal framework of Islam to verify the authenticity of the traditions, which were being used as precedent, also consumed considerable time of the courts. All these facts increased the chances of the miscarriage of justice. Another cause for the error of judgment could be the absence of any specialization in Islamic law. Civil and criminal cases were heard in the same court.

The Accountability

It is amply proved through available historical evidence that administration was fully integrated in the political process, and political vagaries of the time would greatly influence its efficiency and integrity. Political neutrality or public accountability of administrative decision-makers were entirely alien to the theory of Islamic administration. There were, however, repeated injunctions in religion for rulers and administrators to keep the interest of the people closer to their hearts, and exercise strict vigilence over standards of public morality. This does not mean that the level of public ethics was always high in Islam. Corruption, nepotism and the rest of the vices commonly associated with autocratic bureaucracies were not uncommon in the Muslim administration. The extent to which these vices were rampant cannot be determined with exactness, but the popularity of the books on public ethics called 'Mirrors of Prices' or 'Counsels for kings' is sufficient indication that more often than not the moral fiber of administration in the Muslim kingdom was weak.

It was to ensure moral rectitude in administration and save the people from tyranny and injustice that the institutions of *Muhtasib* and *Mazalim* were created in the Muslim kingdom. The primary responsibility of the *Muhtasib* was to see that the life of the people was not contaminated with unislamic beliefs and practices; but in normal circumstances, he would have several other administrative duties, which were not directly connected with religion. He was appointed by the king or the Vizier and in rank and status he was always below the Qadi. The office in its original form was borrowed by the Umayyad from the Byzantine administration, where it was known as agoranomos (Inspector of the Market). During the Abbaside period the office was Islamacized and its jurisdiction was widened to include numerous religious and ethical functions. He was authorized to investigate all cases where people had transgressed *haduds* (boundries) laid down by the Quran. With the passage of time, *Muhtasib* was given the authority to give summary judgments also in cases where the laws of Sharia had been violated.

The term *Muhtasib* is derived from the word *hisba* which means to make the will of God an all-pervading phenomenon in the Muslim community. According to Quran, the Muslim community is *Khair al Umamum* (the best of the communities). The verse in Quran says:

> "You are best community brought forth to men, bidding unto good, rejecting what is disapproved, believing in God."

To inculcate goodness, and dissuade fellow members from doing wrong is a moral responsibility of every Muslim. Each muslim in his own little world is a reformer, he is *mujahid* (a crusader) because purification of society from sin and vice is equivalent to Holy War. It is also the collective responsibility of the community to see that the climate of thought and action among its members is not contaminated with impurities which are forbidden by the Quran, and that there are ample opportunities for every individual to cultivate and practice goodness. Morality in Islam is not a private affair of a citizen. Every Muslim is publically accountable for his moral life. The creation of the office of the *Muhtasib* was meant to fulfil this need of public accountability for ethical and religious standards in public life.

Muhammad Ibn Abdun (439 A.H. A.D. 1100) has pointed out that Muhtasib in the performance of his duties worked very closely with the Qadi. In his opinion, the office was necessitated by the corrupting and exploitative propensities of human nature. Men, he says, are crooked and wicked and the only way to keep them on the straight path is to establish official vigilence over their behaviour. He says:

> "It is better to mend a thing than to endure it; like a garment, if it is mended it will yet give service, but if worn it will quickly go to rags."

Ibn Abdun has given an exhaustive list of the main duties of the *Muhtasib*. He was expected to keep strict watch over beggers, who besides being a social nuisance, used to disturb citizens in the performance of their religious duties by clustering around mosques. He was also responsible for keeping the city clean from filth and dirt which resulted from the traffic of the beasts of burden. Educational institutions were also under his jurisdiction, and he was expected to exercise constant vigilence over the conduct of schoolmasters, who were forbidden to attend dinners at peoples' houses and they were disallowed to increase the number of students in their classes. It was also part of the Muhtasib's responsibility to take care of the cemeteries. He regulated the markets and supervised the basic food products, like vegetables, oil, rabbits, poultry, eggs and the slaughter of animals. Public baths and weights and measures were also controlled by his office. Due to unsettled political conditions, spiritual dishonesty had also become a common feature of the Muslim civilization. Masses were very often victimized and deceived by quacks and fake mystics who used to fleece them of their money. It was also the duty of Muhtasib to save them from such deceit and deception. Ibn Abdun has summed up Muhtasib responsibility towards other professions as:

> Professions: No one may be allowed to pretend to mastery in something he cannot do well, especially the profession of medicine, which involves the loss of life, for the mistake of the physician is covered by the earth. The same is true of the house builder. Each should be fitted for his profession, and not lay claim to it unless he knows it, especially when it has anything

to do with women, for ignorance and error are most frequent with them.

Muhtasib was also authorized to adopt strict measures against prostitutes and money-changers, because they had an extremely baneful effect on the moral climate of society. Malpractices in the sale and purchase of goods and non-payment of debts also formed a part of his jurisdiction. His duties were semi-judicial in nature because he could hold summary trials in certain specific cases. His other functions related to enquiries into the conduct of those, who intentionally abstained from the performance of religious duties, particularly he was expected to keep watch on habitual absentees from Friday prayers.

In short, everything which was against canonical law or derogatory to the ethical standards of the Quran was a part of his jurisdiction. He had to keep an eye on slanderous attacks on religion, or any morally unhealthy innovation which was likely to change Islamic view on life and society. He was to watch anxiously that no Muslim drank in public. There was, however, one major restriction on his prerogatives. He was responsible only for sins and immoralities which people committed in public and was forbidden by law to raid the private houses of citizens. Ibn Khaldun has summed up the duties of *Muhtasib* in the following words:

Market Supervision

The office of market supervisor (hishab) is a religious position. It falls under the religious obligation to command to do good and forbid to do evil, which rests with the person in charge in the affairs of the Muslim. He investigates abuses, applies the appropriate punishments and corrective measures. He sees to it that people act in accord with the public interest in the town. For instance, he prohibits the obstruction of roads. He forbids porters and boatsmen to carry too heavy loads. He orders the owners of buildings threatening to collapse to tear them down and thus remove the possibility of danger to passers by. He prevents teachers in schools and other places from beating the young pupils too much. His authority is not restricted to cases of quarrels or complaints, but he has to look after, and rule on everything of the sort that comes to his knowledge or is reported to him. He has no authority over legal claims in general, but he has authority over everything relating to fraud and deception in connection with food and other things and the connection with weights and measures.

In other words, *Muhtasib's* primary responsibility was to supervise morals and markets, and to see that people did not indulge in acts forbidden by law. According to Al-Mawardi, his supervision of public morality was very comprehensive; for instance, he had the right to reprimand a person who dyed his grey hair to attract women. In short, *Muhtasib* was a "proctor, inspector-general, guardian of law and morality, and chief constable." He was guided by a detailed code of instructions relating to general Quranic terms of *maruf* (legal) and *munkar* (illegal).

Ibn Abdun has made the following remarks about the character and qualifications of a Muhtasib:

> The muhtasib must be continent, honest, pious, learned, well-to-do, accomplished, experienced, seasoned and sagacious. He should not be partial or accept bribes, so that he loses his dignity and is taken lightly, and so that those, who are brought before him do not blame him and upbraid him to his face. The office must not be entrusted to people of low condition, or those who would eat up the wealth of others by false practices and reprehensible methods, for it is suited only for those, who have property and prestige.

Thus this office, if one sees to it properly, brings contentment and happiness to the world, the prince, and the people altogether, because in its observance lies the performance of many affairs of religion, the law, and traditions, as well as physical labours and trades and the livelihood of the people and all the matters which concern them, for the competence and administration of this office is not concerned so much with matters of litigation and protecting property, as with what is incumbent upon the individual in the law of Islam. Look into this : thou shalt find that it is so, O man!

The Ombudsman

Even more important than the office of *Muhtasib*, was the department, of *nazr-al-mazalim* (review of wrongs) which came into existence during the caliphate of Hazrat Ali. The officer was in a way the Ombudsman of a Muslim kingdom.

Hazrat Ali introduced the practice of personally presiding at a special court, where cases against administrators were examined, and people, irrespective of rank, status, wealth or position could just walk in and lodge a complaint against any public authority.

During the period of the first four Caliphs, however, the need to institutionalize the practice of hearing public complaints, was not considered such an important matter. Al-Mawardi (A.H. 450/ A.D. 1058) has given the following explanation for the absence of regular mazalim courts during the early history of Islam :

> "None of the first four caliphs were called upon to hold courts for mazalim, because they lived at the first period when the religion was in the ascendency among people, who turned to the right with alacrity or whom a mere admonition would deter from wrongdoing. The disputes which arose among them were only among perplexing matters which the Qadi's decisions could set straight, and if one of the wild bedouins did behave tyrannically or try to, a warning would set him right or a little roughness would leave him to improve."

The mazalim court was institutionalized by the Umayyads, many of whom sat personally in their court and listened to grievances against civil servants. The Abbasides continued this practice in Baghdad, and from Mahdi (775-785 A.D.) to Muhtadi (892-902 A.D.). The Caliph presided over this administrative court in person. But later as political uncertainty increased and central authority became weak, this responsibility was handed over to the vizier. Sometimes the Caliph appoints a special deputy to fill this post in the important cities, and in different quarters of the capital. Caliph Muqtadir (910-932 A.D.), at the request of his mother, appointed a woman named Thumal to preside over the review court in the Rusafa quarter every Friday. The procedures in this court were very simple. Petitioners had just to walk into the court and could lodge a complaint orally.

Joseph Schacht, a renowned authority on Islamic law points out that the institution of mazalim was a continuation of the practice of the Sassanid kings of Persia. The administrative tribunals of *mazalim* in his opinion signified the breakdown of the administration of justice in the Qadi's court.

The historians of the Muslim administration have listed the following duties of the "Reviewer of Wrongs :"

(1) To find remedies against acts of oppression committed by men in authority over the subject of the Caliph.

(2) To inquire into cases where injustice had been done by tax-collectors in levying various taxes.

(3) To find out errors in the judgments of scribes (secretaries) holding public offices.

(4) Government used to pay various kinds of stipends to certain people and any arbitrary reduction in these stipends by a public official was a fit subject for this administrative court.

(5) Any irregularity noticed by a member of the public in the administration of awqaf (religious endowments; could be submitted before the reviewer.

(6) If the decisions of the regular courts presided over by Qadis were not being enforced, because the convicted person was a person of high rank and authority, a complaint could be lodged with the Reviewer to enforce the court decision.

(7) The Reviewer of wrongs had over-all jurisdiction to curb evil propensities of the people, and was supposed to help the muhtasib in implementing the latter's decisions.

Al-Mawardi has given a detailed list of the duties of the mazalims in a Muslim kingdom :

(1) Act of injustice committed by governors.

(2) Tyranny by tax collectors in levying or collecting taxes.

(3) Arbitrary acts of secretaries of state offices.

(4) Complaints of the army against shortages in rations.

(5) Restitution of things seized wrongfully, of two sorts :

(a) Things seized by those in authority; here restitution must be made as soon as it is known (as, from records) even without any complaint having been made.

(b) Things seized by powerful individuals; here a complaint must be made and witnesses appear.

(c) Surveillance of pious bequests and foundations (waqf) of two sorts, general and particular. General foundations must be investigated even if no-one has alleged any wrong-doing, to see if they fulfill their purpose according to the condition established by the donors, after these have been established by one of three sources:

   (a) Registers of the officials in charge of caring for waqfs.

   (b) State archives, to the extent that they mention the operations (of foundations; or name them and thus establish their existence).

   (c) Old writings which are obviously genuine, if there are no litigants (who might have reason to falsify them).

   Jurisdiction in these matters is broader than in the case of particular foundations. In their case, investigation takes place at an allegation of injustice, by those concerned, and evidence is taken from the registers of the waqf officials. It is not permitted to refer to the state archives or to what is stated in old writings, unless there is right evidence that they are genuine.

(7) Enforcing decisions of Qadis not carried out due to the weakness of the law enforcement machinery.

(8) Investigation of matters which those in charge of the injunction to do good and reject the reprehensible (Al-hisba) were powerless to enforce in the general interest, and making people respect the rights of God, exalted be He, and ordering that these be carried out as they should.

(9) Surveillance of the public acts of service to God, such as Friday prayers, feasts, pilgrimage, and holy war, if they are curtailed or wrongly performed, for the rights of God are those most worthy to be upheld, and His orders those most deserving of performance.

(10) Looking into disputes and judging between those making allegations, without however departing from the rules and procedures of Qadis.

Wide Jurisdiction

The officer in charge of mazalims (civil wrongs) had vast power and wide jurisdiction which made him some-what superior to Qadi (judge). He had power to intimidate a defendant if circumstances warranted. He could eliminate unnecessary evidences and short circuit the procedures for speedy justice. He could appoint arbitrators and administer oaths to witnesses if their veracity was doubtful and, more than that, he could summon any person to provide him with relevant information, a power which was denied to officers presiding over the regular-courts. If the Caliphs and Viziers presided over the reviewer's court, they used to fix certain days of the week for hearing public complaints, but if a regular officer was appointed he used to hold court every day. Code of conduct for the Reviewer's office was very strict, and negligence on his part was always considered a gross dereliction. The existence of the courts of mazalim is a clear indication that in spite of the widespread degeneration of ethical standards laid down by the Quran, welfare of the people remained among the top priorities of the state.

Source of Authority

Accordingly Al-Tabri the Abbaside Caliph-al-Mamun at his deathbed gave the following advice to his brother :

> "Do not neglect the welfare of the common people, because they are the source of authority."

The difference between the Qadi's court and mazalim was more or less the same as is usually observed in a modern state between the ordinary courts of law and the office of the Ombudsman. According to Al-Mawardi, the jurisdiction of the mazalim was wider and his decisions were not fettered with rigidities and encumbrances which accompanied the normal administration of justice. In dignity and power he was higher than the Qadi. He could pick up any administrative wrong and give prompt judgment. He could appoint an arbitrator without waiting for the consent of the contestants. He had the authority to demand security from both parties, if he noticed that the contentions were dubious. He could demand oaths from witnesses, and he did not have to wait far the parties to produce witnesses. These responsibilities and the powers conferred on mazalims provide ample testimony that, in Islamic administration there was a positive realization that the public at large had a right to be protected against bureaucratic sins of omission and commission.

There was a lot of confusion in early Islamic administration. Strictly from the point of view of organizational theory, the early Islamic administration had many glaring discrepancies, but this was the normal price which a small religious community had to pay when it became a sprawling empire over many lands. The Arab leaders, who presided over the destiny of the community during the early decades after the death of the Prophet had piety, courage and sincerity in abundance, but the organizational problems they encountered were unprecedented. There was nothing in the history of their tribal life, which could help them to grapple successfully with the complex issues of the centralized political structure of a multiracial empire. To tide over this difficulty, the early Arab rulers adopted the tax system of the Byzantine and the Sassanid rulers. In most cases, even the personnel of the previous regimes were also retained. There was no general plan of administration. Each conquered territory retained its indigenous regulations relating to the major areas of revenue collection, taxation, and fiscal policy. For centuries after the inception of Islam, particularly during the Umayyad and Abbaside period, in every government office Muslim and non-Muslim staff always worked together. It was only after the rise of Seljuks when, under the leadership of Nizam-al-Mulk, a network, of madarassas (religious school) was established, that the practice of employing heretics in the service of the Muslim state was discontinued. These schools were training academies for government administrators and not merely educational institutions.

In theory, the power resided in the Caliph, who combined in his person the sword and the altar, but as the community drifted towards chaos and disintegration sword alone was left as the sole arbitrator of the political destiny of the Muslims. Realizing how difficult it was to maintain order, the Muslim scholars and philosophers evolved the new theory of legitimacy, which enjoined upon the subjects to comply with the dictates of the rulers, irrespective of the fact whether the power exercised by them was good or bad. Power in any shape or form was preferable to anarchy. Source of power was immaterial as long as commands emanating from it were being implemented effectively. Islam was to be 'moral order,' but the dissension and factionalism and ceaseless struggle for power among the early leaders did not allow the community to evolve an institutional framework, which could translate ideal into a political actuality. The result was that Islam, which was essentially democratic, failed to maintain the spirit for a very long time. The emergence of dynastic and authoritarian regimes after the Pious Caliphate produced among the Muslims an oppressive sense of resignation. They ceased to be an effective or integral part of the decision-making processes in administration and politics. Even as great a savant and scholar as Al-Ghazzali, knowing fully well that all material and territorial acquitions of the Sultans, strictly from the Quranic point of view were haram (illegal), wrote the following passage in his famous Ihyaulum-al-din, harkening the Muslims to obey a tyrant, if disobedience was going to produce civil disorder:

> "A tyrannical and barbarous sultan, so long as he is supported by force and cannot be deposed without difficulty, so that an attempt to depose him would cause a bitter civil war, must of necessity be left (undisturbed), and obedience is due to him such as that rendered to the emirs— the government of our days is the result solely of force (shanka), and whoever may be a person to whom the possessor of force owes his allegiance, that person is the Caliph."

To avoid the rigidity of divine law, more often than not, the Muslim rulers used to promulgate many legislative measures in the form of administrative regulations. Knowing that they could not enact any law, they would confuse the masses by saying that they were issuing only certain procedures to operationalize the spirit of the sacred law. The Muslim community had to live with this fiction for practically the whole of its history.

7

First Constitutional Charter

Introduction to the Charter

The word, 'constitution' in its legal sense is of recent origin.

A modern writer defines constitutions as "codes which aspire to regulate the allocations of functions, powers and duties among the various agencies and offices of the government...." When we apply it, to a document which was signed within a few months of the Hijrah of the Prophet (PBUH), fourteen hundred years ago, we do not get the exact sense and meaning given to it by either the Prophet (PBUH) himself or those to whom the document was being given. He had called, the document under study, as:

"A Writing from Muhammad, the Prophet of Allah."

Basis of Future Statutes

It could also mean a letter and a document, the last being the most appropriate. This settles one thing. It was neither a 'treaty' nor an agreement, because it was "From Muhammad, the Prophet of Allah," and not an agreement between him and others. They had not—no objection in receiving it as a Charter laying down the Code of Life for Yathrib. They also accepted his position as "The

Prophet of Allah," even though some of them desired to retain their attachment to the religion they already professed. They had, as a matter of fact, no option, but to accept it or else live in Yathrib as aliens.

A few points need to be borne in mind while studying this document. First, that the document must be placed chronologically before any of the other objects is studied. This is necessary, because of two reasons. The first reason is that unless its period is determined it will not be possible to determine the object for which it was promulgated.

We have referred elsewhere to the immediate object of this document. The document is of a permanent nature. There must, therefore, have been other reasons which are of a lasting nature. The Constitution, if we consider it as such, of the first Islamic State, brought into existence by the Prophet (PBUH) himself has to remain, in most respects, if not all, a model Constitution for all states established by Muslims. We, therefore, feel that it needs studying from a number of angles.

Dictated by Prophet

It is important to bear in mind that the document was dictated by the Prophet of Allah (PBUH). He had been receiving Sublime Guidance, for thirteen years, from Allah. A person of his calibre would not issue a document of this nature without an adequate and a set purpose. Furthermore a person of his knowledge, experience and capabilities would not issue a self contained document piece meal. If a document is issued by instalments it loses consistency and results in being misunderstood. His actions subsequent to the issue of this document have also great relevancy. They show, if he was in the habit of tackling problems in a consistent or a disjointed manner. It must be kept in mind that he is The Law Giver and laws given by him have stood the test of time. Persons who create and promulgate laws have to consider problems from all angles, otherwise their laws fail to receive such reception as desired. There has to be logic and consistency in the words and actions of men placed in the position he occupied. Written documents become out of date if they are void of consistency. Lastly it has to be borne in mind that this document was issued under certain conditions. Therefore, to gauge its proper importance we must bear in mind all the time, the circumstances which necessitated its issue. These have been discussed briefly.

We have referred to the document as a Constitutional Charter.

"The form and nature of a constitution are dictated by the relationship prevailing among the various sections or classes of people." There was no organized group with whom the Prophet (PBUH) could have executed a treaty or an agreement. Hence we find that it was neither a treaty nor an agreement. It is important to bear in mind its heading, which also forms the very first Clause.

The heading needs to be given in full.

"This document (writing) is from Muhammad The Prophet of Allah (PBUH) to Quraysh and Yathribite believers and Those who will follow them and fight alongside with them. They will form *One Ummah* to the exclusion of others."

Primarily the document has been issued to administer the affairs of *Muhajir* and *Ansar* believers. Its jurisdiction is then extended to those who live and fight *Jehad* under the leadership of these *Muhajir* and *Ansar* believers. Leadership has been given to the entire Muslim community. The Prophet (PBUH) has not spoken of his leadership. This point has great significance for future generations of believers.

The manner of promulgation of the Charter may also have a bearing on the circumstances at the time of its issue and the keenness of the recipients to be favoured by inclusion in the *Ummah*. From the wording and placing of concessions to various tribes, it creates the impression, that the dictation of the Charter took place in an open *Darbar*, and as the Arab custom was and still is, those to whom a clause did not apply they spoke up to be included and at once another clause was dictated for inclusion.

The document was issued within a few months of the Hijrah of the Prophet (PBUH) which took place in July or August 622 A.C. This is the period when, "a few years earlier, the reign of the grandson of Nushirwan was extended to the Hellespont and the Nile, the ancient limits of the Persian monarchy; the Christians of East were scandalized by the worship of fire and the impious doctrine of the two principles; the Magi were no less intolerant than the bishops, and the martyrdom of some native Persians, who had deserted the religion of Zoroaster, was conceived to be the prelude of a fierce and general persecution. The oppressive laws of Justinian, the adversaries of the Church were made the enemies of the state; the alliance of the Jews, Nestorians and Jacobites, had contributed to the success of Chosroes, and his partial favour to the sectaries, provoked the hatred and fears of Catholic clergy."

The Persian monarch was so full of arrogance that, as his predecessors used to carry away the gods of the defeated, back to Persia, he carried away to his capital the Holy Cross from Jerusalem. The situation, however, altered, within a few years as predicted in the *Quran.* Byzantium, "rallied under Heraclius, who had led his troops in 624 A.C., into the heart of Iran. Chosroes was deposed and executed by his own subjects, and Heraclius recovered the Cross".

A Great Deal

It meant a great deal for the prestige of the Emperor. To have brought back Holy Cross, the symbol of true Christianity, to Jerusalem, where the Jews were supposed to have been instrumental in having Jesus Christ crucified, was a great achievement. Syria, at that time, was a truly Christian land. "In fact this is the only period in which Syria has been a fully Christian country. Not only was the country Christian, but the age was an ecclesiastical age".

It was in this age of persecution, religious prejudices, taboos, ethnical differences, and acute hatred resulting in mass killings, when this document was dictated to an assembly of believers, *Mushrikeen* and Jews, not far from a totally Christian land, where at about the same time controversies raged, which ended in a, "sentence of excommunication on the tomb of St. Peter ; the ink was mingled with the sacramental wine, the blood of Christ and no ceremony was omitted that could fill the superstitious mind with horror ".

It was the same period, when in India, Harsha ruled and according to a Chinese pilgrim, "The penalty of imprisonment, inflicted after the cruel Tibetan fashion, which left the prisoner, to live or die, was freely awarded, and mutilation was often adjudged".

In spite of it all, we are told that in every one of these lands their particular civilization was at its peak and yet man was in bondage and writhed at the feet of other men. Man had forgotten that he and other men were all descended from Adam and Adam had been created from clay:

"He it is Who hath created you from clay". 6:2

How unnatural that men should be regarded as unequals and yet inhabit the same planet. Many prophets had come and tried to teach men and women, that they were equal as human beings, but it was left to the Last Prophet of Allah to establish complete equality in those who believed in Allah and him as His Messenger and Servant.

While he was dictating this document of great consequence he was observing the principle of equality. It would take centuries for mankind to realise the effect and importance of this principle.

The ultimate destination of mankind, while on this planet, is the mastery of elements of nature. He has to achieve vast knowledge of nature of things and elements to an extent that very few can imagine. Acquisition of knowledge at the level of entire humanity demands peace, justice and equality among mankind. This will come about when mankind rises above the level of present ignorance and becomes One Ummah. This is the most important lesson taught by the Last Prophet of Allah, while dictating this unique document. Universal peace will be achieved when the principle of equality of man is universally accepted. The Prophet (PBUH) when dictating this document brought the level of all men on an equal pedestal. Jews who, at the time, were looked down upon, except may be in Iran, were given equality with Arabs of Quraysh and *Ansar* origin. Equality of man appears to be one of the main features of his Mission, and, "It is difficult to portray the events of the life of the Prophet (PBUH) unless we first understand the nature of the Mission entrusted to him".

This Mission, according to the *Quran* is complete guidance of mankind in all walks of life. Man has to enter Islam completely.

"O ye who believe! Come, all of you, into submission". 2:208

And the Prophet has to bring mankind into Islam-submission to the Will of Allah.

"(This is) a Scripture which We have revealed unto thee (Muhammad) that thereby, thou mayst bring forth mankind from darkness unto light, by the permission of their Lord, unto the Path of the Mighty, the Owner of Praise". 14:1.

Eternal Message

The Eternal Message of Allah happens to be placed in a world which, in certain respects, alters with changes in time and geography. And yet this Eternal Message guides men to the straight path. "The glory of Islam is that it distinguishes the universal from the changing particulars".

If we study the *Quran* and try to locate Eternal Commandments we will find that these happen to be all in respect of those aspects of human life and nature, which remain constant and are not subject to any great changes as a result of time and place. Those aspects of life whether at the level of an individual or at the collective level of society, which are subject to changes due to change in surroundings, have been left to the individual or the society, as the case may be, to find the best solution as long as no other Commandment is violated in the process. This means that no restrictions have been placed on "the changing particulars."

It is the same with the *Sunnah* of the Prophet (PBUH). He has set precedents in all walks of life, but restrictions were placed only in the field of universals and particulars left to be decided by the individual and the society, as the case may be. He was the Messenger of the Code of Life Revealed by Allah. He was not sent as a military commander and yet he demonstrated the "why, when and how" of war, because the Ummah needed guidance in it. He was not a statesman and yet he demonstrated how justice tempered with mercy was to be administered in a society of equals. He led his army to many a battlefield, keeping in view the principles of war and compulsions of strategy and tactics dictated by geography and other factors and demonstrated all the qualities of a great commander.

His critics fail to keep his mission in view when commenting on his activities as a soldier or as a statesman because their view of a Way of Life is limited to acts of prayers only. To say that, "Muhammad (PBUH) himself was not a warrior and had few military gifts. In battle, he invariably followed behind the front line, never, if avoidable, himself engaged in hand to hand fighting", amounts to disregarding his role as a guide of commanders. The writer forgets that commanders do not engage, normally, in hand to hand fighting. They have to direct, control and deploy troops as the situation may demand. This vague statement of a British general does not mention those qualities of martial nature, which in his opinion were absent in the Prophet (PBUH). He would have probably liked to see in him qualities displayed by British generals like Kitchener, who, "sword in hand and Bible in pocket he enjoyed a career of spectacular warfare in Russia, China, India, and Africa...." Kitchener's enjoyment of war amounted to perversity, when he had defeated Mehdi's Army he arranged a victory parade, on 10th of April 1898, in which, he treated the captured enemy commander Amir Mahmud in the most cruel manner. "Dragging chains which were riveted round his ankles, and wearing a halter round his neck the defeated army commander was made to walk, and sometimes run, behind the cavalry. His hands were bound behind his back, and he was driven forward by Sudanese guards, who lashed him with whips when he stumbled. Kitchener rode on a white horse in triumph". What a spectacle of British chivalry and martial excellence during the closing years of nineteenth century when European civilization was at its height.

This British general of whom many generations spoke with admiration, gave orders, that the tomb of Mahdi be razed to the ground and his bones to be cast into the Nile. Mahdi's skull which was unusually large was kept aside to be used as inkstand. One suggestion was to use it as a drinking cup. He had ordered Wingate, another famous British soldier, to "loot like blazes. I want any quantity of marble stairs, marble pavings, iron railings, looking glasses and fittings, doors, windows, furniture of all sorts". A victorious general who pardoned his life-long enemies must have appeared to General Glubb, to lack martial qualities common among European generals and conquerers. The objective of the Prophet (PBUH) was to establish peace as a precedent for believers until the end of time. He had to demonstrate what was an ideal life. This included both war and peace. It included the life of a labourer and also that of a ruler. He demonstrated the life of a man of all walks of life, when he was being persecuted and we find no change in the way he lived, when he was the ruler of entire Arabia and his army had a successful round of exchange of arms with the Byzantine Imperial Army, at the battlefield of Mowta. As a general his strategy was not only to win the war, but to succeed in the days after the war as well, and his war stands alone in the annals of military history, which brought happier days both for the winner and the vanquished although a winner in earlier battles he had accepted armistice on the enemy's terms.

It has been recorded by his biographer "When there was peace and war was abolished and men met in safety and consulted together none talked intelligently about Islam without entering it. In these two years double as many or more than double as many entered Islam as before".

Throughout his life he was keen to use all his resources to bring about peaceful atmosphere in which his Message could be understood and accepted. Today, fourteen centuries after him, the world has accepted the point of view that peace alone can solve mankind's problems. A modern writer has said, "In an age of Total War we will need Total Peace". War, however, has to be catered for." Wars do not break out of themselves, but they may change the course of history and the fate of mankind.... War has, therefore, become the greatest of social problems". For him and for Islam war had become the greatest of not only social, but also political problem. He gave to the world, Islam—The Message of Peace—when war had been brought to his doorstep. This document is of great consequence as it gives an answer to a multi-national *Ummah,* as to how they should face an aggressor and survive. One of the outstanding features of this document, which cemented the citizens of Yathrib was Justice with Equality for all. Peace within communities and, at international level, cannot be established without equality and equal status to men and groups of men—the nations. This equality was not acceptable either within Arabia or at the international level at that time. The Arabs of Mecca, steeped in the idea of racial superiority, their minds clouded with racial prejudices, and having a class ridden society, were in no mood to accept equality between Abu Jehl, the high born Quraysh chief and Bilal the Negro slave.

Equality of Men

It was the principle of equality of man which evoked the animosity of the two neighbouring mighty empires of Iran and Byzantium, towards Islam and Muslims. The ruling classes of both these empires were securely entrenched as the high born elites, who held the birth right of princely and regal positions. The birth of an Ideology of "Equality before the Eyes of Allah," both in this and the next world, was a revolutionary reality which had to be nipped in the bud. The rest of the world was to array itself on the side of these two Empires, one after the other. The prophesy of Abbas bin Ubada was fulfilled soon enough, but it was to continue being fulfilled for ever.

It was during the Second *Bayah* at Al-Aqaba that Abbas bin Ubada-al-Ansari, said to the *Ansars* who were swearing allegiance to the Prophet (PBUH), "O men of Khazraj, do you realise to what you are committing yourselves in pledging your support to this man? It is to war against all and sundry. If you think that if you lose your property and your nobles are killed you will give him up, then do so now, for it would bring you shame in this world and the next. But if you think that you will be loyal to your undertaking even if you lose your property and your nobles are killed, then take him for by God. It will profit you in this world and the next".

The men from Khazraj and many others who followed their footsteps are still being challenged by the enemies of Justice and Equality for all. It is, outwardly, that people oppose Islam, while their real opposition is against the principle of equality of man, by those whose vested interest are in danger of being jeopardised. It was a question of life and death in that age. Religion during that age made men of religion oblivious of cruelties perpetuated in the name of religion. Minor differences or even suspicion of minor differences led men to throw others into flames. As has been remarked, "It remained for the Medieval Church, however, to put cruelty and burning and gruesome public executions on the firm popular basis of exalting religious spectacles".

There can be no peace in the world unless the world led by Muslims observes laws relating to *Jehad* in the Path of Allah and in conducting their foreign affairs as ordained in the *Quran*. This document was the first writing, directing towards the principles and the policy according to which human societies should conduct their affairs. It has been universally accepted that in the world of today there is no International Law, relating to the conduct of states in matters of conflict or mutual interest, obligations and the making and breaking of treaties. There have been usages in various parts of the world, which have been overlooked more often than not and in all conflicts national interests have prevailed. "International Law, so called, is in reality national law regulating international relations of those states".

Islam has a complete Code of International Law. It, however, operates at the level of the *Millah* of Islam, on the principle that believers are an *Ummah* when considered with respect to the rest of humanity. If Muslim States, observe in their inter-state relations, the Commandments of the *Quran*, the super powers will find it difficult to drive humanity in World Wars, as they have done twice during twentieth century. These Quranic Injunctions dictate relations between Muslim states and also between Muslim states and others. Islamic Law is the only Law which forbids states to undertake aggression of any kind; not even for the spread of religion.

This document, apart from being the Constitutional Charter of the state of Yathrib was at the same time the document on the authority of which this state had come into existence. The person proclaiming the coming into being of this new state was Prophet Muhammad (PBUH), the last of the line of prophets, who had received Revealed Word of Allah. As a result of the contents of this document, the state of Yathrib received all those elements which add up to the formation of a state. "A state exists as soon as the four formal elements (a people, a territory, a government and the characteristics of sovereignty) can be found in it and that recognition by other states merely recognizes the social fact", and non-recognition does not alter its status. The newly created state of Yathrib was, however, recognized soon after its establishment. The Prophet (PBUH), immediately after the promulgation of this document went out of Yathrib, stayed with various tribes, each of which held sovereign status within its tribal territory, and executed friendly treaties with them. Apart from establishing treaty relations" with neighbouring tribes, these journeys of the Prophet (PBUH) fixed approximate limits of the territory of Yathrib. The boundaries of an Islamic State, cannot be a permanent feature. Islam cannot have and does not have fixed boundaries. Islam attracts people because of principles of justice and equality. It spreads and with its spreading are extended its boundaries. Islam has not remained static even during its days of political eclipse. The spread of Islam in Africa has been when a greater part of Africa had been occupied by European Colonial powers.

By Way of Persuation

In Malay Archipelliago Islam was spread by Muslim merchants at a time when Spain held sway over the area. "They did not come as conquerors, like the Spanish in the sixteenth century, or used the sword as an instrument of conversion; nor did they arrogate to themselves the privileges of a superior and dominant race so as to degrade and oppress the original inhabitants".

It is said of Al-Mamun that when a certain Yazdanbakht a leader of the Manichaean sect came on a visit to Baghdad and held a disputation with the Muslim theologians, in which he was utterly silenced, the caliph tried to induce him to embrace Islam. But Yazdanbakht refused saying, "commander of the faithful, your advice is heard and your words have been listened to but you are one of those who do not force people to abandon their religion".

It was the same in Eastern Europe where, "The Calvinists of Hungary and Transylvania, and the Unitarians of the latter country, long preferred to submit to the Turks rather than fall into the hands of the fanatical house of Hapsburg ; and the Protestants of Silesia looked with longing eyes towards Turkey ...," The writer speaks in the same vein of other countries and other lands. "Even in Italy there were men who turned longing eyes towards the Turks in the hope that as their subjects they might enjoy the freedom and the toleration they despaired of enjoying under a Christian government".

As said earlier, this toleration of Muslims, in all the then known lands of the Globe, was the result of magnanimity shown by the Prophet of Islam (PBUH) when dictating this document in Yathrib, at the time, when the first state of Yathrib was coming into existence. The Muslims have honoured the spirit of this document throughout these fourteen centuries, which is not a mean achievement. In spite of it, and may be because of it and the resulting popularity of Islam, it "Inspires perfidy of the Balkans, the hate of the Jews, the apprehension of the Hindus and the animosity of the Russians". The remarks of Abbas bin Ubada Ansari have been referred to above. His prediction continues to come true and may continue much longer. The basic reason for this opposition is the fear of loss of vested interests of the ruling classes and the religious heirarchy, of many faiths which upholds these classes and are a hindrance towards universal equality of man and the resultant justice and fairplay for the masses.

The tenacity with which Muslims have held on to the principle of equality is due to the fact that, they believe staunchly in the Sovereignty of Allah, which is the core and basis of all Islamic teachings. Islam stands for the Sovereignty of Allah alone and of none else. This, in practice, means that the Eternal Laws enjoined by Allah cannot be altered. If this principle was accepted by the ruling classes they would, after that, not be able to frame laws as and when it suited their vested interests. They desire to keep the framing of laws in their own hands and thus they and their institutions set aside for framing and promulgating laws retain Sovereignty in their own hands.

The law assures, that Parliament is omnipotent and paramount. It can make or unmake laws on any matter whatsoever.... The power and jurisdiction of parliaments, says Sir Edward Coke, is so transcendent and absolute, that it cannot be confined, either for causes or persons, within any bounds.... It hath sovereign and uncontrollable authority in making, confirming, enlarging, restraining, abrogating, repealing, reviving and expounding of laws, concerning matters of all possible denominations, ecclesiastical or temporal, civil or military, maritime or criminal. This fact is contained in their Constitutions, whether written or based on practice, precedence and legal judgements. Speaking of the Constitution of England (which included English possessions in Scotland, Ireland and Wales) Dicey, an eminent lawyer, has mentioned "three leading characteristics in the existing Constitution of England ; they are now generally designated as the Sovereignty of Parliament, the rule of law and the convention of the constitution". If a similar analysis was to be made of the Constitutional Charter of Madina, its leading characteristics, that would emerge would be firstly, the "Sovereignty of Allah and His Prophet (PBUH), secondly, 'The Rule of Law' and thirdly, 'The Equality of Man. As composed to the Sovereignty of Parliament which means sovereignty of man made laws, and Convention of the Constitution, these characteristics certainly carry more weight. Mankind has, time and again, failed to convince itself that it can successfully conduct its affairs, without Guidance from Allah. Mankind, in nearly every land, "has been the victim of disastrous illusion—the illusion of our ability to emancipate ourselves from natural laws". Whether we call them as Natural Laws, (Revealed to prophets of earlier eras) or openly admit that they are Laws given by Allah who alone is our Creator and Sustainer and Knows our needs far better than us, makes no difference. These are laws which are based on Truth from Him, who has set a destination for mankind which cannot be arrived at except by conducting ourselves in accordance with these Laws. Man has been given knowledge and intelligence, but both these qualities are limited as compared to the knowledge and Power of Allah. "It is evident that human intelligence has not increased simultaneously with the complexity of the problems involved." To-day, as much as in the past, civilized humanity has shown itself incapable of directing either its individual or collective affairs. The modern world, like the Quraysh of Mecca, needs to be bold and pay homage, to the basic principle of the acceptance of the Sovereignty of Allah.

This document, The Constitutional Charter of Madina, laid down, in no uncertain terms, that Allah alone wielded Supreme Power and that the method of invoking that power is Allah Himself and His Prophet (PBUH) is the interpreter of His Laws. This document also lays down priorities to be adopted for the security and defence of states established by Muslims. The test of Constitutions whether they are capable of meeting the needs of their respective states has been suggested by a modern American writer as follows:

> "How effective is the constitution in enabling us to come to grips with periodic crises? What are the

principle objectives of our national institutions? What service do they render? What are the rights and obligations of American citizenship"?

The Constitutional Charter of Madina, as a document, is fourteen hundred years old. If modern constitutions are examined in the light of the above mentioned questionnaire it would clearly come out that human mind has not made any perceivable advance in this respect. The history of events in Madina, subsequent to the issue of this Constitutional Charter, has been recorded in greatest possible detail. We can, as a result of its perusal, say that the periodic crises that occured in Madina, after the promulgation of this document, were conveniently solved through actions based on it.

Unanimous Acceptance

There is no doubt about the fact that at the time of its promulgation, the entire population of Yathrib had rejoiced about it and had unanimously accepted to live under its protection and abide by its laws.

This document, "brought into existence a voluntary association of all sections of Madinites—Muslims and non-Muslims, emigrants and locals, principals and clients,..." Aus and Khazraj, the two Arab tribes, were the only people who could claim that Yathrib belonged to them. They had been at war with one another, but had settled their differences, lately. An agreement had been reached tentatively that in order to give the place semblance of an organized community they should choose a king. Abdullah bin Ubbay the leader of Khazraj was being talked of as the future king of Yathrib when Bayate Aqba Thani took place. Soon after this, *Muhajirs* started arriving in Yathrib. They and the *Ansars* were a far more organized group, than any tribe could be, and Abdullah bin Ubbay's crowning ceremony was soon forgotten.

There were Jews also in Yathrib. They were all engaged in trade and commerce and being rich had built themselves strong forts outside the main city of Yathrib. The Jews, however, did not either own or belong to the place. A number of theories have been advanced, but the most plausible theory is that they were immigrants from Syria as a result of one of purges that used to be carried out from time to time, to rid the Holy Land of them.

They were living under the protection of various sub-tribes of Aus and Khazraj. They did not possess any right other than what the *Haleef*-protecting tribe—cared to allow them.

Status Changed

This document had completely altered their social and political status. They were being raised to the status of citizens of Yathrib like any other person from amongst the tribes of Aus and Khazraj. This was a great elevation in their status. They were no more aliens or emancipated slaves. They would, henceforth be able to speak up to the Arabs as equals and the word Jew would soon loose the sense of inferiority which it had, hitherto, carried all the world over. The Prophet (PBUH) was allowing them a further concession, which would soon make them a political force to be reckoned with. He was, on certain conditions, inviting them to become a part of the *Ummah* of believers. This invitation happened to be under Divine Guidance and was, therefore, all the more attractive. Although this invitation was also given to the Christians, but they were so few in Arabia that the Jews would have been certain to overshadow them always. This invitation, however, had one point which in the end was likely to be unacceptable to them. It was that they had first to accept the Sovereignty of Allah. The invitation being the result of an *Ayah* of Quran must have made them hesitate but they do not seem to have shown any such hesitation in the beginning. The Words of this *Ayah* of *Quran'*, are:

> "Say: O People of the Scripture! Come to an agreement between us and you: that we shall worship none but Allah, and we shall ascribe no partner unto Him, and that none of us shall take others for lords besides Allah. And if they turn away, then say: Bear witness that we are those who have surrendered (unto Him)". 3:64

The Prophet (PBUH) was trying to create a multi-national Ummah which was to form a coalition of all those who believed in Allah and thus were being asked to form a united front against the godless. He had advocated an idea, which the West have taken up lately, but not with the intention of finding a united platform for all religions, but, to find out means of accelerating Christian Missionary activities in Africa and South East Asia. What would have been the shape of a society, in which, all those who believed in Allah, were to form *One Ummah,* and yet continue calling themselves by their old denominations, would be difficult to imagine.

Hijrah of the Prophet (PBUH) had brought about a fundamental change in the society of Yathrib. There were, in Yathrib, Mushrikeen, who were pagan Arabs and did not follow any set rules, which could fall under the heading of Laws of a Religion. There were, as mentioned earlier, Jews, who, at least in principle, followed the law of Moses (May Allah's Blessings be on him). Because of being the followers of a Revealed religion, they considered themselves as superior to the pagan Arabs, although they lived under their protection. There were some Arabs who had adopted the law of Moses, but their position was strangely unidentifiable. They lived among their own families and observed Arab customary law, but considered themselves as possessing a higher intellectual creed. If they were asked to choose one of the two camps, in case of a quarrel, they would have joined their particular tribe and not gone to the Jewish camp.

The arrival of the Prophet (PBUH) altered the social structure of Yathrib completely. In fact, it had started undergoing a change since the Bayate Aqba Thani. The Prophet (PBUH) had appointed twelve leaders from among the Medinites who had come to Mecca to embrace Islam. The Prophet (PBUH) had told the gathering, "Bring out to me twelve leaders that they may take charge of their people's affairs.' They produced nine from Al-Khazraj and three from Al-Aus". This was the beginning of Muslims bringing into existence an organized Islamic Society. "With the appointment of these twelve leaders an organized Islamic Society came into being". On their return to Yathrib, these twelve leaders conducted the affairs of Medinite Muslims, until the arrival of the Prophet (PBUH).

The Jews had not been able to set up any communal life with the few Arabs who had accepted the *Shariah* of Prophet Moses. The Prophet of Islam was inviting not only Arabs but Jews, Christians and all others to share with the believers, higher values of the activities of a community organized on the basis of Sovereignty of Allah and equality of man-His most Balanced creation. The result was that, even when the believers were in a small minority, the social life of Yathrib, due to their presence, had started taking its direction from the Muslims and adopted Islamic values in an imperceptible way. The Prophet (PBUH) and the small band of his Companions set the pace and texture of social life and thus became the centre of all communal activities. Whenever any issue demanded Allah's commandment for its settlement or the prophet's own verdict in the matter, the Muslims did make all possible afforts to arrive at the authentic views of Islam on the basis of these two sources. The earlier Revelations of the *Quran* of Madina period are all relating to laws regarding various aspects of life. Many of them resulted from questions asked at these gatherings where the Prophet (PBUH) invited people to embrace Islam.

He is known to have gone to a Jewish school to preach Islam to them. If there passed a group of people, by the road, he would stop and join them to invite them to Islam, even though they disliked it.

New Social Structure

A new social structure based on the Sovereignty of Allah and equality of man was taking shape. A new culture was emerging out of this social structure. Man was being given, for the first time in his cultural life, the proper place in the scheme of things, and man's mind was awakening to his place in this universe. One can find no better key to the internal logic of a society than its conception of man and his place in nature. This high position had been bestowed upon man by Allah himself, in His Eternal Code of Life. The result was that the social and cultural trends of life in Yathrib, at a time when the believers were in a small minority, took a turn towards adoption of Islamic values, and life became centralised around the personality of the Prophet (PBUH) and his Companions.

As mentioned earlier the Constitutional Charter of Madina has importance for more than one reason. It is the earliest written document of the Government and State of Madina. Later documents like the Peace Treaty of Hudaybiya, the Victory Proclamation of Khayber, and the overlordship Gazette Notification of Aila granted to the Christian population of that place, were all of the nature of proclamation of cessation of hostilities due to one or the other reason. This document stands in a different position. It established a state and a government in order to meet aggression. Invasion by Quraysh of Mecca had to be stopped. Defence of a society cannot be assured without first organizing that society. When a society is organized it takes the shape of a state. The state must have law and it must also lay down as to what was the source of law and who in future would be entitled to amend or add to this law. All these steps were being finalised through the Constitutional Charter of Madina. This process has been explained in modern terminology in the following words. "Peace among men and a civilized society, which are one and the same thing, are imaginable only within a legal order equipped with institutions to give effect to principles and norms in the form of law..." The Prophet (PBUH) was laying down that the final authority in Islam would be Allah, through revelations to him. Arabian society was losely governed by custom. There was no written law. Absence of law was a great hindrance to the establishment of a progressive and stable society. The Charter was removing this imbalance. "Whenever men group together and approve of a given standard morality, they must speak finally in terms of a law. Law permits morality to grow and as it grows the standard of law is elevated and morality is further advanced, for the two have reciprocal influence".

In this case, although hostilities had not started, war had been declared and arrangements had to be made to face the enemy. Allah had also Commanded.

"O ye who believe! Take your precautions, then advance the proven ones, or advance all together". 4:71

It is beyond doubt that the document was promulgated to bring into existence the State of Madina so that it could be defended against the impending attack by the Quraysh of Mecca. Discussion leading to the declaration of its contents, if any, are conspicuously absent from both the *Seerah* and *Hadith* literature.

Totally Authentic

Its authenticity is, however, above doubt of any kind. It cannot be a spurious document. Once Islam and the Muslims had emerged as victorious, not only within Arabia, but had also liquidated the two strongest empires of the then civilized world, there was no need for them to concoct a document of the early period when Muslims were very few and not very strong. In actual fact once they stepped out of Arabia, they paid no particular attention to it. It is genuine both from external evidence and from the inner evidence of its contents. The idea that it is the sum total of a number of agreements arrived at on a number of occasions is so illogical that it should be ignored completely. As is well known, the events which took place after the promulgation of the Charter, developed with such rapidity, and in such an unforeseen manner that a situation had arisen where there was no need of fresh terms being issued, or new agreements gone into with any party. The idea that the document in its present shape is the result of numerous agreements is the result of the basic misconception, that it was an agreement. One may ask "agreement between whom, because the document was being issued with the heading "From Muhammad, The Prophet of Allah." Its contents were Legal Orders and not paragraphs of an agreement. A charter from some one in Power can be amended or additions made to it by the authority issuing the original charter. From Badr onwards the Prophet (PBUH) did not have to issue new instructions to any one in Yathrib. The Jews were getting weaker every day and signs of rebellion on their part had developed immediately after Badr. They had not "followed the believers and not fought along with them." They had not, therefore, qualified for any of the concessions granted to them through the Charter. If anything, any fresh document, would have curtailed concessions granted to them from the incidence of rebellious behaviour of the Jewish tribe, Banu Qainuqua, immediately after Badr, the Jews were not in a position to request for a reappraisal of their relations with the ruling party.

The arrival of ultimatum from the Quraysh of Mecca was a serious affair. They were a powerful tribe and had the influence which leaders of thought possess in a society. They exercised the sole authority of laying down the religious ceremonies and the

Arab Way of Life. They held the monopoly of carrier trade between southern Arabia and the flourishing market of Middle East, and were very rich as Compared to the rest of Arabia. An attack by them, against Yathrib, would wipe out this small agricultural town of Najd. War in any case, "is not a pass time. It is a serious means for a serious object". The Meccan object was very serious. Muhammad (PBUH) had "mocked their Way of Life," and taken refuge in Yathrib. To save their Way of Life they had to destroy him completely. They had awoken to the danger from the time of the second Bayah of Aqba. As already mentioned when some of the Companions started migrating to Yathrib they, "assembled in their council chamber, the house of Qusayy bin Kilab, where all their important business was conducted, to take council what they should do in regard to the Prophet (PBUH), for they were now in fear of him." It was suggested that "they should put him in irons behind bars." This was objected "on the ground that news would leak out that he was imprisoned, and immediately his followers would attack and snatch him away: then their numbers would so grow that they would destroy the authority of the Quraysh altogther".

After some further discussion Abu Jehl came out with a new plan. This was "that each clan should provide a young, powerful, well born, aristocratic warrior ; that each of these should be provided with a sharp sword ; then that each of them should strike at him and kill him. The Banu Abdu Manaf could not fight them all and would have to accept money which they would all contribute". Having failed to kill him they were not able to liquidate Islam in Mecca. They could not, however, let it prosper in Yathrib. They were afraid, as they said, that "Their numbers would so grow that they would destroy the authority of Quraysh altogether". They decided not to permit their numbers to grow and decided to act quickly. They knew of the disappointment of Abdullah bin Ubbay. His people had made a sort of jewelled diadem to crown him and make him their king, when Allah sent His Prophet (PBUH) to them; so when his people forsook him in favour of Islam he was filled with enmity realizing, that the Prophet (PBUH) had deprived him of his kingship. However, when he realised, that his people were determined to go over to Islam, he went too, but unwillingly, retaining his enmity and dissimulating".

Declaration of War

The Quraysh sent a letter to the people of Yathrib, but addressing it to Abdullah bin Ubbay. The letter was, in fact, a declaration of war. It said, "you have given protection with you, to our men. You should kill these people or turn them out of Yathrib. We swear by Allah, that if you do not do that, we will all attack you and having destroyed you, will capture your womenfolk". This was a very good excuse for him to use force and turn the Prophet (PBUH) and his *Muhajir* Companions from Yathrib. He was the head of a very powerful tribe, which appears to have been numerically stronger than others. Its members were alive to the needs of religious revival. Out of twelve leaders chosen to look after the affairs of Muslims of Yathrib, nine belonged to his tribe. He decided to use force if the occasion demanded to kill the Prophet (PBUH) and the few Muhajir Companions.

The Prophet (PBUH) heard of his decision and went to him. Very little of the conversation between them is recorded. Abdullah bin Ubbay was confronted with a new reality. Islam, although a religion of peace, denoted complete submission to the Will of Allah. It meant the acceptance of the Sovereignty of Allah which in practical life was demonstrated by obeying the Laws of Allah. This is what is meant by:

> "I created the Jinn and humankind only that they might worship me". 51:56

And one of the Commands of Allah is that He has Ordained righting for the believers.

> "Warfare is ordained for you". 2:216

The occasion for which this Commandment has been primarily Ordained is when some other group fights against you. It says:

> "Fight in the Way of Allah against those who fight against you, but begin not hostilities". 2:190

It has to be remembered that this *Ummah* is One:

> "Verily this Ummah of yours is One Ummah". 23:52

The Prophet (PBUH) brought home to Abdullah bin Ubbay in these words:

> Do you realise that if you use force the Muslims from Yathrib will fight alongside the *Muhajir* Muslims and you will be shedding blood of your tribe on both sides.

He realised the mistake he was making and decided not to use force against the Prophet (PBUH) and his companions. His change of attitude was the result of his fear of being defeated at the hands of determined fighters. History is replete with instances, where people have had recourse to peace for fear of being hurt, in the end. The philosophy of Ahimsa—non violence—is also the product of such logic, because the same people believe in Kali Devi, the goddess, which quenches its thurst from blood of gory murders. Peace accepted by him was of this kind. When we could not use force he resorted to mischief and remained a hypocrite and a tool of the Jews until his death.

History books are silent on further details of the conversations, that took place between the Prophet (PBUH) and Abdullah bin Ubbay, it would be correct to assume that the latter must have asked the Prophet (PBUH) the way Yathrib was to be defended against the Meccans. The details of the Charter lead us to the conclusion that the Prophet (PBUH) must have replied that the Muslims would defend Yathrib and if the others would like to share that responsibility the believers would permit them to join in this great honour. It could also be said that, as a result of the urgent need to defend Yathrib, the Prophet (PBUH) formulated the plan of establishing the state of Yathrib, giving it a Constitution, and laying down the responsibility of defence on believers. Abdullah bin Ubbay could not help accepting this plan. The next event mentioned in history books is the Constitutional Charter itself.

Shadow of War

The Charter was dictated under the shadow of an impending war of extreme intensity. Its defence paragraphs must belong to the same period. The concessions granted to the Jews are linked with defence paragraphs and must belong to the same period. The paragraphs covering general administration were also the demand of the time. There are no further events in the history of Yathrib, which could have resulted in the issue of further documents. The division of the document of Professor Sergeant in A, B, X, Y, etc, amounting to eight different documents can certainly be called a futile effort, made merely to create doubts and with no fruitful object. The war that was visualised when dictating this document lasted for nine years and had, before ending, embroiled the largest Empire of that period in it, thus initiaing the longest war of history—The war between the Crescent and Cross—which is raging even today, fourteen centuries after the Charter came into force, and is no where near its end as yet. Islam until then had laid greater stress on the building of character of individuals. The Charter ushered in the collective life of the *Ummah.* The principle that Muslims formed a nation by themselves even when they lived in surroundings, which were not purely Islamic, was given prominence by the Charter. The contents of the Charter make it clear that even when living as a numerical minority, believers take over the administration of the society on condition, that the principle of the Sovereignty of Allah is being acted upon. As mentioned earlier, as far as details are concerned, when dictating the Charter, greater emphasis has been paid to matters relating to the defence of the state, than to other matters. The Prophet (PBUH) as a result of the wisdom and insight granted to him by Allah, kept his mind centered on the period after the war, when need would arise for rehabilitation of people. In the words of a modern military thinker, "The true national objective in war lies in the 'after war'. If the civilized world is to be saved from collapse, there is urgent need to produce true grand strategists to replace the blind exponents of mass destruction". He argues that "If you concentrate exclusively on victory, with no thought for the after effect, you may be too exhausted to be profited by the peace, while it is certain that the peace will be a bad one, containing the germs of another war". The author is speaking from experience of two World Wars. Britain won both of them but lost the peace that followed.

The experience of modern world over the last two centuries has shown that the war to end war has yet to be fought, unless laws of war laid down by Allah are observed in total. The war that was initiated by the Quraysh of Mecca and won by the Prophet (PBUH) ended, as far Arabia was concerned, because the Prophet (PBUH) keeping the after-war period in view had done nothing, during and at the end of war, which could keep alive the hatred generated by war. Modern wars have tended to increase hatred to a point, when, a rapprochement becomes impossible. We need, therefore, to study his life, his teachings, his foreign policy and the manner in which he fought his war and then magnanimously pardoned his enemies. It will show a pattern of human behaviour unparalleled in the annals of human history.

The Prophet (PBUH) had accepted the responsibility of defending Yathrib against the threatened attack, when Yathrib had yet no state, no government and no army. He and his Companions were the total force available for this onerous task. There were no armaments, no provisions, no transport animals and no finances to provide all these instruments of war. He had, however, men, who were prepared to lay down their lives in the Path of Allah. He had trained them to such unchartered heights of Belief in Allah, that no weapon could force them to abandon their positions.

He also knew his enemies. They were resourceful. They were rich merchants and could furnish their army with the most sophisticated weapons. They also had the means to last them during a long drawn war. They had friends among Arab tribes.

They could, as a result widen the zone of war and have him surrounded and they had the means and facilities to make the blockade permanent, but his Belief in Allah outweighed those considerations. It is true that "once war begins, no one can tell how it will go. There are some who urge, that we should abolish all armaments, and refuse to fight on any pretext. If this view is put forward on religious grounds, I will not deal with it beyond saying, that it does not seem to me in accordance with the Bible... If on the other hand its advocates believe that it would make for peace, it is inconsistent with recent events. China offered little or no resistance to Japan, yet that did not save her from the loss of territories as large as Europe, and the slaughter of some thousands of her citizens" .

The position of believers, at the time of declaration of war by Mecca, was far more precarious than any community of peaceful and peace-loving people, who are threatened by a neighbour, who does not approve of their Ideology and their Way of Life. The enemy was the same, who had persecuted them in Mecca, ignoring relation of blood and friendship. A small number, a little over seventy had migrated to Habsha, and now less than fifty males had reached Yathrib and found a place, where they hoped to live according to Allah's given Way of Life, and they were being threatened with war and possible extermination. They had no alterative but to accept war. If they decided to avoid war, where could they go. They would have become stateless. The result would have been that the Islamic Society, which was visualised by the Prophet (PBUH) as a result of Revelations to him, from Allah, would not have been possible to be established. Allah's Promise was, that they would be uppermost if they were believers, was enough for them:

> "It is a promise from Allah in truth; and who can be more truthful than Allah in utterance"? 4:122

And:

> "(It is) a Promise of Allah. Allah faileth not His Promise". 39:20

And Allah has promised that:

> "Faint not nor grieve, for ye will overcome them if ye are (indeed) believers". 3:139
>
> "And verily Our word went forth of old unto Our bondmen sent (to warn) that they varily would be helped, And that Our host, they verily would be the victors". 37:171-173

They were indeed believers in its fullest meaning. No group of any *Ummah,* of days gone by, had reached heights, of belief in Allah, which they had proved to have reached, and were yet to prove on many an occasion.

Not in Vacuum

Documents of this nature are not issued in a vacuum. There is always a background and a pressing need for them. In fact, pressing necessity, for the execution and enforcement of such documents alone made them acceptable to people. Such documents, whether they are named as agreements, treaties, charters or constitutions, are promulgated because the very existence of those societies depends on bringing into existence means of laying down the pattern of communal life, and such documents provide and guarantee a disciplined life of the-community. Apart from rights and duties of individuals and groups such documents lay down restrictions and penalties for the breach of rules of conduct, expected of those for whose guidance they are issued. Preparations to meet the threat of war are taken in hand, when the danger is real and the entire society recognises it. War cannot be taken lightly because it "is a social phenomenon too complex to be governed by any simple formula". Except the Prophet (PBUH) himself no one was either qualified nor was there anybody who had the moral strength to accept the responsibility of making the decision to defend Yathrib or when the decision had been taken to take defensive preparations in hand and then conduct the war.

To accept the duty of defending a state and its people is a decision of great moral character. An ill prepared nation is in serious danger of losing its war. To lose a war means to surrender the "right of freedom of thought" and to lose freedom of thought means to lose the right to live according to one's chosen Way of Life, which includes one's mode of worship. The Muslims could not afford to lose the war. They had chosen the Islamic Way of Life of their free will. It was being challenged by the people, who had persecuted them for nearly thirteen years. They were determined, that if they could not win the war they would fight to the last man. The battles fought by the believers for the defence of Yathrib were all fought with the determination, that they would fight until each one of them had achieved Shahadah. The Prophet (PBUH) had trained his Companions to wish for Shahadah, and he was certain, that they will come up to his expectations. His historic words, just before the attack of Meccan Army started at the battlefield of Badr are a testimony of the believers having absorbed this philosophy. He had said:

O Lord!

If this little band of believers

Is wiped out to-day
There shall be none left
To obey your Commandments
Until the Day of Judgement.

There had been wars before and there were to be wars in future as well, but this war was different both in conception and the manner in which it was expected to terminate. Both sides were fighting to defend their respective Way of Life. It could end in not only the defeat of one army or the nation it belonged to, but it was to end with the end of the Way of Life to which the loser belonged. It was a war aimed at the extermination of the Muslim's Ideology and Way of Life. The idea, that all wars are fought for differences, which can be solved peacefully, does not appear to be applicable to this war. Normally it can be said that, "Just how senseless and futile an expedient it really is, can usually best be judged by those who lose rather than by those who have won". In this case it was not applicable because the losers were to forego the freedom of living in accordance with their chosen Way of Life.

Sovereignty of Allah

This document had been dictated keeping in mind this Philosophy of War, that to remain a believer in Allah was only possible when Sovereignty of Allah could be proclaimed and life was led in accordance with His Commandments. To achieve that it was essential, that land occupied by believers had to be defended to the last. It was, therefore, necessary, that Yathrib had its Basic Law—its Constitution—promulgated in a manner that its defence preparations could be taken in hand legally and constitutionally. Hence the correct heading of the document can be "The Constitutional Charter of Yathrib... Madina".

It was not an agreement with the Jews as Allama Shibli Noamani calls it. He says "The Prophet (PBUH) sent for *Ansars* and Jews and dictated an agreement which was accepted by both parties". Another eminent writer Jalal-ud-Din Jaffery writes, "When the Prophet (PBUH) arrived in Madina, he had an agreement written between the *Ansars* and the Jews". Naeem Siddiqui, the only one out of all Urdu writers, has shown a different approach to the problem. He writes, "The Prophet (PBUH) created an organization for the arming of the State of Madina, through which he integrated the Muslims, the Jews and the un-believers, into a new society. He had a written document of the nature of an agreement, prepared. The nature of this document was of a proper constitution and it can be correctly called as the first written constitution".

Nearly all writers of *Seerah* in Urdu have called the "Charter" as an "Agreement," between either the Prophet (PBUH) and the Jews, or between the believers and the Jews. An eminent learned man like Syed Abul Hassan Nadvi has termed it as an agreement of peace with the Jews. Having correctly said that, "The Prophet (PBUH) on this occasion gave a writing to the *Muhajirs* and *Ansars,* "he adds "which contained an agreement of peace with the Jews". Another eminent historian writes, "On arrival at Madina, the Prophet (PBUH) during the very first year of Hijrah considered it appropriate to execute an agreement with all nationalities on the principle of internationalism so that a national solidarity should continue in spite of the ethnic and religious differences". Khalid Alvi, referring to the Jews writes, "He (the Prophet (PBUH) made an agreement with them".

It could be that the word agreement has crept in because of absence of a proper equivalent of the term "Charter," in Urdu. The mistake dates back to Ibne Hisham, due to absence of a technical term for "Charter" in that age. He has used the word *Aahadahum* which has been translated as "covenant." The sentence as a result reads " the covenant between the Muslims and the Madinans and with the Jews".

Muslim and non-Muslim writers of *Seerah* in English, who belong to the present age, have also relied on Ibne-Ishaq, in more or less the same manner as Urdu writers. Abu Bakr Sirajuddin (Martin Ling) who has written with great devotion says, "and the prophet (PBUH) now made a covenant of mutual obligations between his followers and the Jews of the Oasis".

A non-Muslim writer of Pakistan origin says that before the signing of the agreement a thorough exchange of views had taken place. This may be correct, but no work of early period seems to mention a thorough exchange of views. He writes, "After a thorough exchange of views, an agreement was reached and was reduced to writing".

Muir while translating the document uses the words "Charter of Muhammad the Prophet" instead of "Charter from Muhammad," but in introducing it writes, "It was natural that Muhammad, holding these sentiments should desire to enter into a close and binding union with the Jews, and this he did in a formal manner shortly after reaching Madina. He associated them with himself by a treaty of mutual obligation drawn up in writing,...".

The Distinction

The difference between an agreement and a Charter is very vast. An agreement is between two equals and a Charter is given from one to others. An agreement can be rescinded by either party. A Charter can be altered, amended or cancelled only by the authority which promulgated it. Apart from the heading given to the document its contents alone can guide later researchers to give their verdict on it, whether it was a treaty, an agreement or a Charter.

Treaties are between states and usually the heading says so. For instance, "Security Treaty between Australia, New Zealand and United States of America". Similarly Pacts are between independent sovereign states. For instance, "Pact of Mutual Cooperation (CENTO)" was signed between a number of states including Pakistan, Turkey and Iran. Recently a new name for mutual treaties has appeared. This is called a "Convention." For instance, "Convention regarding the Regime of the Straits".

Let us, once again, look at Meethaq-e-Madina in a little greater detail, particularly its heading. It says:

> "This document (writing) is from Muhammad, The Prophet of Allah (PBUH.)."

It is clear that it is neither an agreement nor a treaty because it is not between Muhammad (PBUH) and some others. It is from him and he is the Prophet (PBUH) of Allah. Those receiving the document are being told that the person issuing this document is doing so in his capacity as the Prophet of Allah. Then it goes on to say that it is being given "To Quraysh and Yathribite believers."

Believers whether from Mecca or from Yathrib were all his followers known as his Companions. No group of people in the history of mankind have shown their devotion to their leader as was shown by his Companions to Muhammad (PBUH) the Prophet of Allah. When marching out to the battlefield of Badr, the leader of Ansars of Yathrib, Saad bin Muadh said, "We believe in you, we declare your truth, and we witness, that what you have brought is truth, and we have given you our word and agreement to hear and to obey; so go forth where you wish, we are with you; and by Allah, if you were to ask us to cross the sea and you plunged into it, we would plunge into it with you; not a man would stay behind. We do not dislike the idea of meeting your enemy tomorrow. We are experienced in war, trustworthy in combat."

Whatever else description or name may be given to this document it cannot be called an agreement between the Prophet (PBUH) and his followers. It was being given by him to them and they were all included in it, both the *Muhajirs* from Mecca and the *Ansars* of Yathrib.

There were others as well. They were:

"those who will follow them and fight alongside them."

It would be applicable to others as well, provided these others followed the lead of his followers, the believers, from Mecca and Yathrib. Apart from following the believers they had to take part in fighting alongside the believers to qualify themselves as recipients of this august document.

This heading ends with a brief last remark, "They will form *One Ummah* to the exclusion of others." It means that if the others qualified as recipients of the document, then they and the believers, the Companions of the Last Prophet of Allah, will form an Ummah, apart from the rest of humanity. It was a great honour, that was being bestowed on them, but the price was also very high. They had to accept the believers as their leaders and continue to follow them by joining in war with them against their enemies.

Thus the document was primarily issued as the Basic or Fundamental Law, The Constitution of Yathrib, so that defence arrangements could be taken in hand, on behalf of the entire population. The believers, being the group which had sworn allegience to him as a result of the *Bayah* formed the manpower of his army. The march to the battlefield of Badr proved this fact. None others were prepared to sacrifice themselves for a cause, in which they did not believe.

One More Charter

History has recorded one more Charter given by the head of a state. This was King John of England. This Charter, however, was taken by force by the barons of the realm, because, "King John was very unwilling to grant it. This was on the 15th of June 1215 A.C., that the Great Charter was sealed with the king's great seal. He agreed that 24 barons shall be appointed to see that he kept the promises which it contained. He agreed only because he was compelled.... He never meant to keep the promises that it contained, and he did not keep them. He sent to France for soldiers and when they came he made war on his own people. He asked his friend the Pope for help and the Pope helped him by ex-communicating all barons, by London under Interdict, and by telling John that he had no need to keep his promises". The surprising part of the whole story is, that, there was not much in the Charter, which an honest ruler of an average society need to have objected to.

It may seem strange that the Pope of all the people, should have advised a Christian ruler to go back on his promises. It was, however, not the first time, nor the last time, that the head of Church had advised a prince to go back on his promises. In one case, "the Pope, who PBUH his plans being nullified, by this (peace treaty) initiated the Magyars to break the peace; oaths sworn to infidels not being binding".

The Charter given at Yathrib was in the spirit of Islam, the New Way of Life. It had to be in accordance with all ethical, moral and legal principles laid down by Allah, for believers in Him and His Prophet (PBUH). The time of its issue was the most critical period in the history of Islam—a time when the threat against Islam and Muslims was the greatest. This fact must be kept in mind while studying the Clauses of the Charter.

The position in which the Muslims were placed at this time has been misrepresented by some Western writers. Preparations for defence of Yathrib have been interpreted as aggressive designs against the Meccans. A well known British historian writes that "Muhammad had now, as it were, thrown down the gauntlet, which the Meccans could not but pick it up. He had effectively challenged them to a full scale trial of strength". It appears that after writing a few more sentences he remembered that it was the Meccans who had declared war. He adds; "The Meccan belief Muhammad would avoid them rested on a mis appraisal of the relative strength and fighting qualities of the two parties". He has avoided to give the source on which he has based the superior strength of the Muslim Army.

General Directions

Clause 6.

"All parties will redeem their prisoners with kindness and justice according to practice among believers".

We have already looked at this Clause under Laws pertaining to defence matters. It would not be out of place to examine it under Laws or Directions of general nature. The matter deals with humane treatment of members of the Armed Forces. It would, therefore, clarify matters, if it was examined from the point of view of the individual in a Muslim society.

Islam, complete submission to the Will of Most Kind and Benevolent Allah, enjoins kindness amongst its members and expects mutual help and consideration between groups, which comprise the *Ummah.* When war takes place through the invasion of any part of the *Ummah, Jehad* becomes a Duty of all groups:

> "Warfare is ordained for you, though it is hateful unto you". 2:216

Even when the persecuted happen to be unbelievers Allah expects, that believers in His Benevolent Sovereignty, must go to their help:

> "How should ye not fight for the cause of Allah and of the feeble among men and of women and the children who are crying: Our Lord! Bring us forth

> from out this town of which the people are opporessors! Oh give us from Thy presence some protecting friend". 4:75

When war takes place, some achieve the highest honour of becoming martyrs, some get wounded and there is a possibility that some may be taken prisoners by the enemy. They had gone to war for the common cause of the *Ummah*. Therefore, it is the collective duty of the *Ummah*, that these prisoners are redeemed with Islamic kindness, which means, as early as possible and without any thought of how high the cost may be. Until the advent of Islam, and particularly until this Constitutional Charter was dictated by the Prophet (PBUH) of Islam, the redeeming of prisoners was not a statuary obligation in any known law of either any civilised society or of barbarians. In it the believers were ordered to redeem their prisoners with kindness and justice, which is the hall mark of believers. The others, which meant the Jews and idolators, were given a chance to live under the guidance of believers and to fight alongside them, in the Path of Allah. If they availed of this option, they were expected to show the same kindness to their brothers and to come up to the same standard of justice, which was common among the believers. They were, therefore, bound by law to redeem their prisoners, under this Clause. If this is the standard expected of allies of a Muslim state, it would be correct to assume, that a, "Muslim state has of necessity to be a welfare state .... particularly with reference to economic justice."

Man seems to have had a rebellious trait, developed in him, as a result of the persuations of Satan, which he, at times, is unable to control. Prophets sent by Allah have tried and have achieved varying results, but those who are disposed to rebellion, have reverted to the path of selfish and shortsighted policies. These rebellious elements, who on most occasions are only a small minority, create enough mischief to upset the general peace of society. Men of influence in all denominations have warned mankind of the dangers hidden in following the path of mischief with different results. A modern writer has sounded warning of the same nature by saying, "I feel sure that man faces the worst half millennium in his terrifying history. For man, today, must quickly learn who and what he is and how he is governed in nature, or else bring upon himself wars rebellions." Another writer has warned that science has, so far, failed to give directions, leading to peaceful communal life, "The tragedy of our times is that the science of destruction has run amock. And the problem is how to synchronize the science of life with the science of death."

The Prophet (PBUH) was teaching mankind the way to a communal life of peace, love and justice. He knew that mankind would not give up war unless and until Islam had become the Universal Way of Life. Until then war had to be discouraged, but steps had to be taken that the miseries of war were minimised as much as possible. He was leading mankind to that Way of Life which would eventually lead to the synchronization of the science of life and science of death.

Clause 18.

"The enemies of Jews will not be helped."

We have touched on this question, under Laws governing Jews only. We would like to add a few words here that this neutrality between the enemies of Jews and the state of Yathrib was to be resorted to in case the Jews did not accept the leadership of believers and did not take part in war alongside with them. If, however the Jews followed the believers and fought alongside with them, then, they were to become a part of the *Ummah* and enemies of Jews were to be enemies of believers. In case the Jews did not desire to become a part of the *Ummah* then a neutral position was to be maintained with the enemies of Jews. This appears to be the beginning of Laws of Neutrality. Modern writers call it the theory of "Neutral Law." It has been said that, "Modern theory has paid tribute to the doctrine of neutral law for their contribution to the so-called "modern system of International Law."

This Clause and a few others, establish the fact that this was the first document in the legal history of human efforts in the International Field. It must be remembered that the directions contained in this Charter, under general rules, are meant for the Guidance of entire mankind. Minorities will exist, among all nations, for a long time to come. There must, therefore, by some universal understanding with regard to the treatment to be meted out to minorities. This Charter shows a way towards those basic concessions to be provided to minorities.

Today, fourteen centuries after the dictation of this Charter by an unlettered Prophet of Allah (PBUH), we notice that there are still people in this world who refuse to their minorities the right to exist. This only happens in those countries, where the Sovereignty of Allah is being denied.

Clause 27.

"If any unbeliever, kills a believer, without good cause, he shall be killed in return, unless the next of kin are satisfied. All believers shall be against such a wrong-doer. No believer, if he believes in Allah and the Last Day, will be allowed to shelter such a man. Who ever shelters such a man, on him will be punishment of Allah on the Day of Judgement."

Law and order had to be maintained in this newly established state. Severest punishment was being declared for breaking a Fundamental Law of the land. Believers were the party, which was running the state as the Government Party, which had accepted the responsibility of the defence of the territories of the state of Yathrib. If a member of the ruling party was murdered without good cause it was important that the culprit should be punished. It was, however, laid down that if the next of kin desire to pardon the culprit no punishment will be meted out to him. The society being a mixed society, it was possible that the culprit was a close relative or a friend of one of the believers.

The state was new and young. It did not have time to lay down procedures of litigation. In any case this Charter was the Fundamental Law and procedural rules are not included in such documents. Hence no punishment was specified for this crime.

Clause 28.

"When you differ on anything the matter shall be referred to Allah and Muhammad (PBUH)".

The point to note is that in *multi-Ummah* society the highest authority to arbitrate is being named Allah and His Prophet

Muhammad (PBUH). The Jews were to remain as Jews and the *Mushrikeen*, though not specifically mentioned, were to continue in their belief as before. In spite of it Allah was being accepted the final authority, which meant that His Laws as conveyed to them by Muhammad (PBUH) was being accepted as the Law of the Land. It speaks volumes about the manner in which the Prophet (PBUH) and his few Companions must have conducted themselves, during the very short time, that they had been living among Yathribites since Hijrah. The conduct of *Ansar* Muslims, who had invited the Prophet (PBUH) and the change brought in their conduct and character since becoming Muslims, must have had a tremendous influence on the others. The spread of Islam in Indonesia and various parts of Africa has been the result of similar influence of Muslims penetrating into the interior.

This Clause leads to the conclusion that the Prophet (PBUH) ws able to impress on Yathribite non-Muslims, that what was being revealed to him, was from Allah and in exactly the same manner as had been revealed before him to other Prophets like Ibrahim and Moosa. In other words, they had accepted Sovereignty of Allah to be exercised through him.

This meant that Laws of Islam were to be the Law of the state of Yathrib, and all customs and traditions in operation were to become ineffective and illegal, if they contravened any Laws Revealed to Muhammad (PBUH).

The final authority in a state, whether it is a monarch or a house of representatives is the authority which has the right and prerogative to make law. Hence it is called the sovereign authority. Acceptance of Laws Revealed to the Prophet (PBUH) by Allah, amounted to the acceptance of Sovereignty of Allah in practice, but without acknowledging it in verbally.

Clause 32.

"Loyalty gives protection against treachery."

The declaration of war by the Quraysh of Mecca had made it essential, that every body should be warned against treachery at this time of grave danger to the entire population of Yathrib. We have dealt with this Clause under Laws pertaining to Defence, but, being a Law of general nature affecting the very existence of the realm and of such a nature that it will affect Muslim countries for ever it must be studied in greater detail keeping in view conditions faced by Muslim *Ummah* today and are likely to continue to affect for a considerable period in the near future.

The greatest danger to Muslim lands from treacherous activities is from the followers of pseudo-prophets, produced by European influence, during the nineteenth century. The followers of these new religions claim to be Muslims, while holding beliefs contrary to Islam. These non-Muslims going about with Muslim names and observing some of the practices of Islam will act as secret agents on behalf of foreign powers. They will play the part of Kaab-bin-Ashraf and Abdullah bin Ubbay without a moments hesitation.

It so happens that these non-Muslims, happen to be nationals of a number of Muslim countries, which, until some years ago, happened to be British colonies. The governments of these countries have to be vigilant. They must pay special attention to the security of their plans particularly in matters of defence. They have been directed not to employ such people in appointments of trust. Allah has Ordained:

"Do not take in trust accept yourselves." 3:118

The military position of Yathrib, as compared to Mecca was even worse than a small Muslim country of today, when compared to one of the super powers. The effort to defend against Mecca could not be given up. The consequences of defeat could not be imagined. It meant complete annihilation. Consideration of terms for existence at the end of an unsuccessful battle was out of question. It is an old axiom that, "Similarity between opponents creates laws of warfare, while dissimilarity leads to unlimited or absolute warfare,"which in the sixth century meant complete annihilation. Normal rules of warfare are not observed, where the weaker side is so weak that it cannot proclaim its opposition openly. The Prophet (PBUH) had decided that Yathrib should have no weak spot on the home front. Only then could he hope to face the enemy with all available strength.

Loyalty is a quality which has in itself the quality to furnish defence against treachery. None dare accuse a loyal person of a crime connected with or the result of treachery. The loyalty of Companions of the Prophet (PBUH) was above suspicion. It was this loyalty of theirs, which kept the internal cohesion of Yathrib intact. The first successor of the Prophet (PBUH), Abu Bakr was known for his loyalty to the Prophet. It has been said that, "The secret of Abu Bakr's strength was his faith in Muhammad (PBUH) Abu Bakr had no thought of self aggrandisement. Endowed with sovereign and absolute power, he used it simply for the interest of Islam and the people's good. He was too shrewd to be himself deceived, and too honest to himself to act the part of a deceiver. To the last moment of his life he had the betterment, contentment and freedom of the population, uppermost in his mind, who had entrusted themselves into his hands. His will was symbolic of the manner he looked at his responsibilities. "To him who shall succeed, give it as my dying request, that he be kind to the men of this city, which gave a house to us and to the faith. And the Jews and Christians, let him faithfully fulfil the covenant of the Prophet (PBUH) with them." Muir, like other writers, refers to the Charter a covenant. With Companions like Abu Bakr and Omar there could not flourish many disloyal men around.

Clause 33.

"The freedmen of *Thaalba* will be afforded the same status as *Thaalba* themselves."

This decision was in conformity with the spirit of Islam. Islam encourages people to set free their slaves, so that a free society comes into existence. A slave, is no better than an animal. He has no stakes in the preservation of the society in which he lives. A free citizen of a society of equals does not surrender, because, surrender makes him slave of the victor. Nations who lost their battles two hundred years ago remained slaves for two centuries. Even when they gained political freedom they continued to be economic slaves of the erstwhile masters. They have suffered becuase their grand parents surrendered to foreigners. This Clause shows the path to equality and freedom of man and was dictated to make certain that those who were freed and were slaves no more should be really free and prove themselves as honourable asset to the society in which they lived.

Clause 36.

"Anyone who kills another without warning amounts to his slaying himself and his household, unless the killing was done due to a wrong, being done to him."

Murders and killings upset and unbalance the smooth running of a society. Killings without warning possess an element of deceit and treachery, particularly when the killing is not to avenge a wrong already done by the culprit.

The warning, that such a killing amounts on the part of the murderer make to himself liable to killing and other members of his household were appropriate to the times. To avenge one murder, people of that age, were apt to kill entire family of the culprit. Murders are the worst of crimes in any society, and when their numbers increase the sense of security, and living among reliable human beings disappears.

"Clause 41.

"A man will not be made liable for the misdeeds of his ally."

It had been said in Clause 3 and 5 that prisoners will be redeemed with kindness and justice was common among believers. This was a clause which proved, that justice was kept uppermost in the Laws promulgated in a society, led by believers. Clause 34 had referred to alliances but no person could be made responsible for the misdeeds of his ally. This Law appears to be the fore-runner of the following *Ayah* of *Quran:*

> "And no burdened soul can bear another's burden". 35:18

The allies of Jews had been given the same status as the Jews themselves, but this could not make them liable for the misdeeds of their allies.

Clause 42.

"Anyone, who is wronged must be helped."

Kindness and justice had been declared as the common practice among believers. The Basic Law being given to believers had to come upto the standard of justice expected of believers. If a wronged person was not aided by the Law itself and law enforcing authorities, in a society composed of believers, then it could be said, that justice was a common practice among believers.

Clause 45.

"A stranger, who has been given protection will be treated as his host, while doing no harm and is not committing any crime."

Protection could be given by any one of the nationals of Yathrib. It was, however, being assured, that the protected will be treated at par with his host. He could not expect a higher reward than the person who gave him protection. It was the right of the host, that his guest received the same treatment, which he was entitled to.

This protection, however, became null and void if he committed a crime. The case of Kaab bin Ashraf should be examined keeping this Clause, as well, in view.

Clause 46.

"Woman will be given protection only with the consent of her family"

This was a social matter, but if handled carelessly it could develop in a long drawn war. Women are considered a protected trust to be honoured by men of that family or tribe. If a woman is forcibly carried away or given protection against the permission of her family, the act will amount to destroying honour, prestige and respectability of that family and tribe. To avoid any such trouble with the neighbouring tribes, a law was enacted that no one will give protection to a woman, unless the family of that woman had given permission to her to seek protection in Yathrib. Women of all tribes, inside and outside the state of Yathrib, were being given the honour they deserved.

Clause 47.

"In case of any dispute or controversy, which may result in trouble the matter must be referred to Allah and Muhammad (PBUH). Allah will accept any thing in this document, which is for bringing piety and goodness."

This Clause declares in no uncertain terms, the place where power rested in this newly established state of Yathrib. It means that the Fundamental Law of the land revolved around the belief in the Sovereignty of Allah. This Clause further reiterates this belief. It means that differences and disputes must be resolved in the light of *Shariah.* As *Shariah* is the result of interpretation of revelations from Allah, the decision, therefore, rested with the Prophet (PBUH).

All those present in the assembly were recognizing the Sovereignty of Allah and His Prophet (PBUH) even though they may not have accepted Islam in Total. They were thus, Constitutional Muslims for having accepted the Constitution based on *Shariah*—which gave the last Way of Life—Islam.

Clause 51.

"Every one, will have his share, in accordance with which party he belongs to."

As it happens in the case of political parties, the individual member, in case he differs with the official views of the party, cannot evade responsibility for the decision of the party. It was the same in tribal system. The views of the individual carried weight until such time as the decision was made. Once the decision had been taken by the tribe or the sub-tribe, all individuals had to abide by it. Their rewards or responsibilities had to be decided in relation to the party, to which the individual belonged.

It was only fair that individual's responsibility should be in accordance with that of his tribe. To avoid future complications, it was best to have the principle accepted and announced through the Charter.

Clause 53.

"Anyone who acts loyally or otherwise does it for his own good."

People knew of the impending war. They knew, that it would be a fight to the end. If the invasion came all were likely to suffer equally. The Meccans were not likely to show compassion to those, who did not take part in fighting. When a place is destroyed or looted the invader does not look round for those, whom he would like to spare or those who would like to be spared. The decision to follow the leadership of believers was being taken up voluntarily and after consideration of the result of accepting the responsibility or evading it. It was neither a favour nor act of grace towards the believers. Loyalty to this cause, in future, was also to be for their own good.

Clause 54.

"Allah approves this document."

This Clause has to be viewed keeping the occasion, of the dictation of the document in view. The background, in which the dictation was being made, has been surveyed in earlier pages. The Hijrah, the construction of the mosque, the declaration of war by Mecca, the decision to defend Yathrib, were all incidents connected with the purpose of the dictation of this Constitutional Charter.

The contents of the Charter studied so far have also to be borne in mind. The document opened with the words "From Muhammad, Prophet of Allah (PBUH)" This was accepted by all those present including the Jews and unbelievers. The superior status of believers had been established. The Sovereignty of Allah and His Prophet had been categorically explained and accepted. In matters of dispute the final arbitrator was to be the Prophet himself. Now finally the seal of Allah's approval was being put on to the document. It was not a part of the *Quran* — not a clear Revelation — but a document issued by Muhammad (PBUH) His Messenger — to which His consent had been obtained, and this Consent of the Almighty was being announced in open Court.

From Hijrah to the dictation of the Charter, the Prophet (PBUH) had given guidance and conveyed his decisions in the light of the Training and Guidance received by him from Allah. He does not appear to have received any clear cut Ordnance from Allah as to the nature of the State and Government of Yathrib. He had to establish the Deen — Way of Life — of Islam, which was based on the full, complete and unadulterated Sovereignty of Allah, but the details of his Constitutional Charter were to be filled in by Muhammad himself. As Hafiz Ghulam Sarwar has said, "Although Muhammad (PBUH) was inspired, as to what Allah wished him to do, the ways and means of carrying out His Message were left to Muhammad (PBUH). This was his part of the work. Allah would show him the path, but Muhammad (PBUH) himself had to walk it."

His was a great responsibility. There was a time, when he did not know, what were the responsibilities of a prophet of Allah. He had been "Quite unaware of the fact that he was to be Commissioned by Allah as the Last of the Prophets. We do not find any hint, direct or indirect, that his mind was preparing blue prints of any religious adventure." We have, therefore, to be content with the exact situation. The document was from him and not a Revelation from Allah, but it had His Approval.

Allah's approval was given, because it was for the good of humanity. It laid down, that matters were to be conducted in accordance with kindness and justice of the highest standard — the standard which had been placed before the best *Ummah* so far created amongst mankind (3:110). It has been unfortunate, in fact a tragedy, that this document has been overlooked by statesmen, both Muslim and non-Muslims, of the past centuries. As a result the world has drifted towards man made totalitarianism, which is the product of human mind in its totality. Its authors have also realised the dangers to which it is leading humanity. "It is only now, when Western humanity is faced with the apalling result of its work of destruction, that it is beginning to realise, what has happened and to look back on the road it has travelled. Yet it has not reached the point of admitting, that this totalitarian state is not the invention of a handful of criminals in the grand style, but its own product, the incalculable consequence of its own positivism, a position void of faith and inimical to metaphysics and religion. It will not yet believe, that it is the incontrolable result of man's loss of faith in the Divine Law, in an Eternal justice," justice which is the main theme of Islam, justice which alone can keep society free from internal intransigencies.

Clause 55.

"This document will not protect anyone, who is unjust or commits a crime."

Defence of the realm is a commendable action. To have joined the defenders of Yathrib and agreed to abide by the contents of this Constitutional document was an honourable undertaking, but it did not give a license to commit injustice or any act contrary to Law. On the contrary it demanded greater care to behave in an honourable manner and administer justice of the standard Commanded by Allah.

The king can commit no crime. It may be justifiable in societies, where the king is the source of Law. In Islam the source and fountain of law is Allah himself. No man, therefore, can be above law and as such membership of this document also carried added responsibilities, but no immunity.

Clause 57.

"Allah is the protector of the good people and those who fear Allah; and Muhammad (PBUH) is the messenger of Allah."

This is a statement of fact, an annunciation of the after tried and experienced Omnipotent Protection of the Most Merciful Allah. Allah is Good and protects His good servants, who fear Him and abide by His Laws. These Laws have been Revealed by Him to His Prophet and Messenger Muhammad (PBUH).

This document laid the Foundations of Revealed Law of Allah. This document at the same time Commissions Muhammad (PBUH) to interpret, explain, promulgate, administer and live according to the Law of Allah, so that his action can serve as the practical demonstrations of His Law until Time comes to an end.

"And in the day when the Hour riseth the unrighteous will despair". 30:12

8

Ethics of Administration

In an imperfect world, it has been man's eternal yearning to create perfect institutions. The ideal of the Caliph-Imam as a vice regent of the Prophet, and the head of the newly formed community of believers, was one of such efforts. It was meant to create a political institution, which would be free from moral bankruptcies commonly associated with politics. The institution in its original spirit did not last for long time. Its failure could be attributed to the fact that the Arabs before the inception of Islam had very little experience in the political organization of a large community. Tribal organization to which they had been accustomed from times immemorial was not suited to the centralized governmental machinery of a territorially integrated state. But even a bigger cause could be that the moral ideals, which supported the Caliphal edifice were difficult to attain in practical politics. The result was the office of the Caliph became a subject of acute controversy, and Muslim scholars of various schools of thought wrote almost a library of literature on the subject. The hold of the ideal over the popular imagination was however such, that in spite of repeated setbacks, people's faith in it was never shaken. This glaring incompatibility between the ideal and the reality kept gnawing at the soul of the Muslim community. Muslims in many lands suffered from the crisis of the conscience throughout their history.

Recession of Ideals

After the Pious Caliphate, the ideal receded from the field of practical politics, and the Muslim state was modeled on the pre-Islamic political and administrative practices of the newly conquered non-Arab lands. Religious and moral aspects of the Caliphate were reduced merely to a superficial embelishment, and political and administrative behaviour of the Muslim rulers was completely denuded of the spirit which had motivated the immediate successors of the Prophet on the seat of Caliphat-Imamate. In every Muslim dynasty, with a few exceptions, majority of the rulers were corrupt and incompetent. Most of them were guilty of moral turpitude, and under their rule public life in a Muslim community was thoroughly contaminated with vices of despotism, oppression and ethical irregularities. Widespread exploitation of the masses was a common feature, monarchs and state functionaries indulged in ethical lawlessness without any compunction of the soul. There were some great rulers, no doubt, who lived up to the great religious ideals of Islam, but such periods in Islamic history were always shortlived. The general tenor of the government and administration in a Muslim state remained far removed from the pristine values and beliefs of the doctrine. Sharia was the law of the land, but the functionaries who administered it were so utterly subservient to the will of the rulers that no independent judgement or interpretation could be expected of them. Ulemas (religious scholar) who in theory were the custodians of the high ethical standards in public life, were corrupted and majority of them lived as spineless minions of the state. The Caliphate was changed into sultanate, which was another name for military dictatorship. The society became a loose confederation of feudal estates, wherein the feudal lord and the tax collector were always on the rampage. So far as welfare of the masses was concerned, the spectacle of government and administration was depressing and disheartening.

It was in these circumstances that Muslim statesmen and scholars turned to "wisdom literature" and wrote some of the classics, which have enthralled students of Islamic studies for centuries. That most of the writers were statesmen and administrators should not surprise anybody, because the cream of talent in a Muslim kingdom always gravitated towards the court of the ruling prince. Attachment to the retinue of the ruler of the day was the highest certificate of merit that a scholar or a professional in any trade could have. Their primary responsibility was to ensure the welfare of the prince in all walks of life. The court was the nerve center of the realm and for an observant eye there was enough material to draw a comprehensive picture of the prevalent moral and political climate in the kingdom. Not all, but some of them used this accumulated knowledge to compile books on counsels for the kings, or general dissertations on the art of governing men. Some of these works have won permanent place in Islamic culture and literature. There is always something refreshing in them, although the expression might not be so absorbing and cultivated. According to Reuben Levy, these works constituted the Islamic version of the Eastern tradition of "wisdom literature manifested in such scriptural books as Job, and Proverbs, and frequently also in Sanskrit literature."

Wide Canvass

These statesmen-scholars used a very wide canvas to portray the dynamics of socio-political and religious issues with which they wrestled their mind and soul. Their approach was both diagnostic and prescriptive. They explored in depth the causes of the malaise, which had hit the Islamic civilization, and then in the light of precepts enunciated by the Quran, the Traditions of the Prophet, and the lives of great kings of the past, they drew certain guidelines which in their opinion could open vistas of rectitude for a world which had been so badly corrupted and demoralized. To explain their point of view they also made extensive use of anecdotal literature of many cultures. Each one of these works is a harmonious blend of facts and fables, out of which the authors have drawn shrewd and insightful conclusions. To dispel the tedium and monotony of their ethical sermons, they also make a frequent use of Persian and Arabic verses which are relevant to a principle or situation being examined. Stylistically these books lack the elegance and beauty of a good prose work, but they are remarkable for the breadth of wisdom, and depth of human insight. But more than anything else they provide a lucid account of the religio-political conditions of the Muslim society in which their authors lived. Moral and political failures of the rulers, and the inertia and helplessness of the people are depicted in a frank and candid manner. The range of topics discussed is also very wide. Justice, probity, duties and responsibilities of kingship, public morality, princely manners, statescraft, religious sects, political factions, dynastic squabbles, administrative failures, social foibles, economic problems, military matters, are all fit subjects for such works. Very often authors unroll detailed exposition of human nature, and relate it to the discrepencies and fallacies they notice in social life and political organization. They are also an immeasurable storeshouse of wit and wisdom. Their pages glitter with social maxims, spicy half-truths, and brilliantly spun anecdotes. At appropriate occasion people's habits, customs and eccentricities are also uncovered with great perspicasity. In short, everything which has bearing on human behaviour is examined in one form or another.

In spite of the exhuberance of their wisdom, however, note of caution is warranted for a student who approaches them for critical appreciation. Firstly it is to be understood that these works were not written by historians with a keen and anxious eye on the authenticity of fact. They were written by statesmen and administrators, out of their life long experiences, observations and hearsay, and very little care was expended to verify the historicity of the details. One has to be particularly careful about the anecdotes attributed to great personages of the past, because most of them seem to have been derived from untrustworthy sources. The integration of the materials also at various points is unscientific, and a reader tends to feel the strain of monotony as he goes through certain portions. But these deficiencies do not delete anything from the tremendous value they have for a student of government and administration in Islam, and the amount of pleasure they have afforded generation after generation of readers in many Muslim lands. They are free from rhetoric and abstruse constructions, commonly associated with Arabic or Persian prose. The beauty of diction is not there, but the style is simple and direct.

In this book nine classic books of the Islamic wisdom literature have been reviewed, but only those portions have been subjected to review which specifically pertain to the issues relating to ethical behaviour in politics and administration of a Muslim state. As mentioned earlier these works, though small, have an encyclopaedic range of subjects. But for our purpose only those elements have been skimmed which either portray the degeneration in which the Muslim society had sunk, or provide guidelines to understand the ethical contours of administrative machinery in a Muslim state.

Civility and Morality

There are two treatises with the same title written by two different scholars. The first was written by Ibn Adi (d 976 A.D.) a Syrian Christian scholar. Ibn Adi's book is basically a collection of ideas borrowed from the Greek ethical thought. There is nothing specific relating to rulers and administrators, but from his narrative an impressive list can be prepared to indicate virtues of good disposition and vices of corrupt behaviour. The list is as follows:

I. Virtues of Good Dispositions

1. Continence
2. Self-control
3. Dignity
4. Mercy
5. Trustworthiness
6. Humility
7. Truth of speech
8. Generosity
9. Aspiration
10. Steadfastness in adversity
11. Frugality
12. Tranquility
13. Love
14. Fulfillment of promise
15. Keeping a secret
16. Cheerfulness
17. Good intention
18. Courage
19. Great ambition

II. Vices in Corrupt Behaviour

1. Dissoluteness
2. Greediness
3. Shabbiness
4. Levity
5. Awkwardness
6. Excessive love
7. Pitilessness
11. Secret hate
12. Avarice
13. Cowardice
14. Envy
15. Treachery
16. Perfidy
17. Divulging a secret

8. Sternness
9. Falsehood
10. Deceit
18. Impatience in misfortune
19. Smallness of ambition
20. Injustice

The virtues listed above according to Ibn Adi are essential for the perfection of human character. They are cultivated by rigorous training of mind and soul and depend to a large extent on the depth and comprehension, that one possesses about the world. Self-discipline and abstenence from harmful pleasures of life are advocated as instruments of moral rectitude.

The second treatise was written by Abu Ali Ahmad Ibn Muhammed ibn Maskawaiha (d. 1030 A.D.). The author of this treatise lived during the military dictatorahip of the Buwaihid who had put Abbaside Caliphs under their forced protection. They captured Baghdad in 945 A.D. and remained the indisputable rulers of the Eastern Caliphate for 110 years. Ibn Maskawaiha was secretary of Al-Muhallabi, the Prime Minister of Muizz-al-Dawla the Buwaihid prince who conquered Baghdad. *Tahzih-al-Akhlaq* (The Correction of Disposition) is considered to be an outstanding work on the philosophy of ethics in Islam. The author believed that human conduct is built by restraint, courage and judiciousness. The fruit of righteousness stems out of integrity.

In other words, integrity connotes translation of worthiness, truth, and goodness into human action. They constitute a moral conquest over falsehood and evil. At another place Ibn Maskawaiha has listed four fundamental qualities which are vital for higher ethical standards and has contrasted them with four evils which constitute the bane of morality.

(i) wisdom —— ignorance
(ii) purity —— greed
(iii) courage —— cowardice
(iv) righteousness —— violence

Wisdom, a Virtue

Wisdom is a virtue of human soul by which men comprehend the existing things in the light of the words of God. It is a quality by which distinction is made between desirable and undesirable actions. Purity is an instrument of self-discipline. It is a thoughtful use of human desires and soundness of judgment. Righteousness is a sense of justice by which excesses and deficiencies are eliminated and a fair course of action is adopted. Anger, conceit, vanity, jesting, boastfulness, perfidy, unfairness, laying up treasures, are counted among the diseases of the human soul. Courage and judiciousness are advocated as antidotes to these evils. He pleads for restraint on desires and appetites. Courage is not merely a weapon to defend one's body and material possession, it is also a strength of mind by which evil propensities of self have to be conquered. Judiciousness stems out of wisdom cultivated through study and reflection. It is therefore incumbent upon all right-thinking people and seekers of truth and righteousness to search for knowledge in all directions. A person who has decided to discipline his soul, and wishes to avoid risks of moral defilement must, according to Ibn Maskawaiha, set before himself the following objectives :

1. He had striven to maintain what we would call personal integrity. This he defined as the preference (ithar) for what is worthy (al-haqq) over what is futile in beliefs; for what is true (al-sidq) over what is false in statements; and for what is good (al-khair) over what is evil (al-sharr) in actions.
2. He had emphasized the continuous struggle that he needed to keep up between his essential manhood (al-mar) and his animal nature.
3. He had felt the importance of adhering to the Law (al-sharia) and of recognizing the necessity of its functions.
4. He had endeavoured to remember agreements and to fulfill them, particularly any agreement that he had made with Allah.
5. He had shown little confidence in men, and this he accomplished by avoiding familiarity with them.
6. He had cultivated the love of the beautiful for its own sake and for no other reason.
7. He had appreciated the value of silence in times of agitation, until reason would direct him.

8. He had striven to continue any state of mind that was beneficial until it would become a habit.
9. He had approved taking the initiative in things that were creditable.
10. He had found that whole-hearted sympathy was necessary in order to work on any important undertaking without distraction.
11. He had felt that the fear of death and of poverty could be counteracted by doing what was still possible and by not being indolent.
12. He had casted out from his mind such anxieties as were aroused by sayings of the base, and he had tried to suppress his desire at night to plan something against them.
13. He had come to realize that he must be inured to wealth or to poverty, and to liberality or to contempt.
14. He had tried to remember times of sickness when he was in health, and occasions of joy and pleasure when anger was apt to arise, so that there might be less injustice and transgression.
15. He had rejoiced in times of trust, appreciating the goodness of hope and confidence in Allah, turning his whole heart to him.

He further points out that greatest happiness of man depends on the manifestation of the innate excellences of the human soul. The happiness of one man is linked with the happiness of the rest. Mutual assistance in other words is the essence of social health and stability. In pursuit of happiness, each individual should be a torch-bearer for the perfection of others. It is for this reason that Ibn Maskawiha points out that virtue cannot be practiced in isolation. Asceticism, in his opinion is wrong and inimical to individual and social happiness. In essence ethics is an instrument of self-discipline and a method for character-building.

Books for Counselling

Qabusnamh (Book of Qabus) or Andarz-nama (Book of Counsel)

It was composed by Kay Ka-us ibn Iskandar ibn Qabus in 375/ 1082 A.D. The author was the Ziyarid ruler of Tabristan. He was endowed with profound wisdom and literary attainments which are amply manifested in the said treatise. At the age of sixty-three Kay Ka-us thought to capture in book form his life-long experiences as a ruler and administrator for the guidance of his son Gilanshah. The purpose was to outline eventualities which are likely to befall rulers of men, and to suggest ways and means to tide over difficulties which so often crop up due to the chronic uncertainty of political conditions. John Alden Williams has given the following sketch of the purpose with which Kay Ka-us decided to write his experiences in the form of a book of counsel for the rulers.

In the advice of Kay Ka-us ibn Iskandar the Ziyari ruler of a little kingdom in the Caspian provinces of Persia, to his son, Gilanshah, we have a valuable insight into Islamic kingship as it appeared to a Muslim king in the eleventh century. Kay Ka-us is a professional member of the ruling class, and an affectionate father, who wishes to pass his knowledge to his sons. He is very conscious that even if a king cannot have lordly morals, he must appear to have them. He knows that a king must sometimes tell lies and kill, but it is not expedient to get a name for it. Virtue, or its appearance, is useful; it is one of the means by which a king in his civilization must try to secure his power.

Kay Ka-us had the ability to wield sword and pen with equal dexterity. The book has enjoyed great popularity in the annals of Persian literature. Wit, wisdom, frankness, conviction, directness of expression, and richness of experience constitute the highlights of the work.

The Qabus-nama consists of forty-four chapters and a preface. The contents of the book provide ample evidence that the royal author was deeply concerned about the growing malpractices in the administration of the country. The first thirty-four chapters are related to the general principles of moral life. They range from obedience to God to the uses of astrology, mathematics, and poetic arts. It is in the later chapters that Kay Ka-us turns his attention to the affairs of kingship and administration. Chapter thirty seven deals with services of the kings. Thirty eight is on the qualities of the courtier, the thirty ninth deals with the secretaries of the state and secretarial art; the fortieth chapter is on the qualities of the wazir ; the forty first on the duties and responsibilities of generals;

the forty second on the qualifications and duties of the king; forty third deals with farmers and agriculture, and forty fourth discusses generosity. The pervading spirit of all his analyses is emphasis on the cultivation of virtues and excellences which have been preached by Islam, Kay Ka-us is of the opinion that rational and practical side of religion should be a vital element in understanding Islam. Browne remarks :

> "The author's ideas display a curious mixture of craft and simplicity, of scepticism and piety. Thus he dwells on the ethical, as apart from the spiritual value of prayer, fasting, and other religious exercises as means to cleanliness, humility, and temperance; and advocates conformity with the laws of Islam, because there is no stronger bond than the Commonwealth of Islam."

The whole of the work is replete with worldly wisdom some of which at least has great relevence even to our own times. The book throws a flood of light on the state of affairs in the Muslim civilization as it existed during the Middle Ages. It advocates lofty ethical principles, which would be above greed and expediency. He is convinced that human society cannot exist without some kind of governmental organization, because man's bewildering propensities for evil need an effective machinery of control. "Now man has need of government and regulation; without direction he is brutal (uncivilized)." Government in turn depends upon authority, the way it is organized, the manner in which it is used in decision-making, and the image which people hold about it. Kay Ka-us has laid down certain principles which must be strictly adhered to if authority has to make any impact on affairs of men. A person making authoritative decisions should "be neither harsh, nor sharp tempered, nor devoid of clemency (yet be not so entirely yielding as to be swallowed upon on account of your softness) and never be so morose that you are not to be won over."

Worldly Wisdom

Browne has summarized the worldly wisdom of Qabus-nama in these words:

> His worldly maxims are shrewd, and wonderfully modern at times. He expatiates on the advantages of

> a smooth tongue, bids his son learn wisdom from fools, and cautions him against over-modesty, "for," says he 'many men fail of their objects through bashfulness.' His remarks on truthfulness are delightful. But do thou, O son, says he, 'be specious, but not a liar: make thyself famous as a speaker of truth, so that if at some time thou shoudst tell a lie, men may accept it as true from thee.' He also cautions his son against making statements which, though true, are likely to be disbelieved, and cannot be easily proved; for, says he, 'why should one make a statement, even if it be true, which it needs four months and the testimony of two hundred respectable witnesses to prove?

He is also of the opinion that in adopting a particular course of action, a man on the seat of authority should not act arbitrarily. Even with the maximum of learning and knowledge, it is always desirable to consult someone. Over-confidence in one's own abilities and judgment is symptomatic of arrogance, a quality quite unbecoming of those who have been entrusted with authority to preside over the destiny of human organizations. He says :

> Therefore, be not puffed up with your own learning, however learned you may be. And if any task befalls you, even if you have the capacity to perform it, do not rely entirely on your own judgment, for he who relies entirely on his own judgment ever regrets it. Never be ashamed of asking advice, consulting old men of understanding and well-disposed friends. Even Muhammad despite his wisdom and his prophethood, after becoming the examplifier and agent of God's work was told by him 'Consult them in the matter, O Muhammad' (Quran 3, V, 153).

He further adds that it does not behoove a man in authority to be "any degree careless over the duties of justice and governmental control and from treating overlightly anything essential to these matters." One must also be watchful that offices are not bestowed on "impecunious or impoverished men," and he compares such appointments to a dry canal which will not water fields and gardens until it is saturated with moisture. Meaning that a poverty-stricken man, if installed to a position of power, is most susceptible to dishonest dealings. Probably knowing that such a rule cannot be meticulously followed, Kai Ka-us mentions that authority should be maintained with firmness and spiteful disregard of it, should not be tolerated. Those who willfully disobey legitimate commands deserve exemplary punishment. But in order to avoid an ugly situation, those who wield authority have certain professional and ethical obligations. Their commands should be precise, clear and decisive. Their tone and intention should be firm and unambiguous. Their reputation should be such that people will not hesitate to repose confidence in their decision. Men of authority are custodians of the realm and it would be ridiculous to have someone take custody of the custodians or to have a guard for the guardians. He says :

> "The orders, then, of both kings and viziers must be unequivocal and their commands decisive, if their authority is to remain firmly established and their interest to prosper. Next, drink no intoxicant liquor, out of such drinking there arise carelessness, laxity and injustice Allah protect us from a wine-bibling vizier and wanton governor ! If it is the king who indulges in wine, decay soon pervades the realm. Therefore keep a watch on yourself and conform to what I have told you ; the vizier is the custodian of realm and it would be a very ugly matter if the custodian should need another to have a custody of him."

Kai Ka-us, in order to substantiate his contention narrates an anecdote, relating to a confrontation between an old woman and King Masud of Ghazni. The woman had lodged a complaint against a governor, who had refused to pay heed to the King's letter, which the woman had taken to him. The King decided to write a second letter, but the woman refused to carry it saying that such a letter had already been taken to the governor which had failed to redress her grievance. The King said "What am I to do?" The woman replied, "Your course of action here is simple. Maintain your authority in such a fashion that your instructions will be acted upon or else resign your authority and let another possess it leaving you to occupy yourself with your pleasures. Thus mankind will cease to be held fettered in the miseries of tyranny." In other words, an ineffectual authority is a gateway to tyranny, and a state where authority fails to get compliance forfeits its right to exist. Therefore authority requires strict control and vigilance from one who holds it. In other words an authority which is not used effectively is worse than anarchy because under cover of law officers will indulge in illegal extortions and the time would come when the country would be depopulated. An oppressive authority leads to decay and desolation and it is therefore extremely inexpedient to show any negligence in this matter.

Political Authority

After having established the necessity of political and administrative authority, our author goes on to elucidate ethical equipment of those who govern men. These ethical principles are spread over all the forty four chapters of the book. They are more or less the ones which have universally been applauded as pertinent guidelines for righteous action. In his opinion wisdom and virtue should be in inseparable partnership in life. If a person is wise, but the moral side of his character is tainted, he cannot be a success in life. He says :

> If you have wisdom, therefore acquire virtue for wisdom without virtue is like a man without clothes or a person without a face or a body without a soul. Indeed there is a proverb to the effect that 'virtue is the visage of the mind.'

The world is not meant for fools although they are in abundance, but nor are the wise of any good if their wisdom is denuded of ethical lustre and dignity. Kai Ka-us gives primacy to wisdom and virtue, because both are qualities, which are acquired and not inherited. He quotes an Arabic proverb which says, "Honour lies in the mind and in acquired worth, not in origin and noble birth," and then mentions Socrates, who in his opinion, once said "that there is no treasure better than virtue, no honour more glorious than knowledge, no ornament more beautiful than modesty and no enemy worse than an evil disposition."

An accomplished person is judged by his frank and fair disposition. Duplicity destroys trust, and if trust is gone other qualities can be of no avail. Profession, must synchronize with action. Any incongruity between the two can have a damaging effect on individual's integrity. Kai Ka-us says :

> "Once having made a profession of your beneficence, however, let not your actions contradict it. Do not say one thing with your tongue and harbor a contrary thought in your heart, lest you reveal yourself to be one who displays wheat but sells barley."

He maintains that it is a great virtue to be generous and benevolent, and believes that malice is a bane of the human soul, and it leads to spiritual impoverishment and social humiliation. He is however not very sure about modesty which according to an Arabic saying is bracketed with faith. He believes that modesty may be good, but "yet it may frequently happen that bashfulness is a misfortune to men. Do not therefore be so shamefaced as to cause failure or injury to your own interests. There are many occasions when boldness must be exercised to ensure that your purposes may be achieved."

It is through speech that most of the qualities of human character are manifested for the rest of the world. It behooves, therefore of those who make public policies and issue statements to be watchful of what they say. Language helps understanding, facilitates communication, and is the one and only effective carrier of information. Wrong choice of words can infuriate another person, inflict unnecessary humiliation, and damage human relations. Command over words is a powerful weapon, but one ought to be discrete in their use. Kai Ka-us has divided words and their uses into the following four categories: those neither to be understood nor uttered, those to be both understood and uttered, those to be understood though not uttered. Those which are neither to be uttered nor understood are they that contain some peril to the faith.

Noblest Category

The noblest category from the point of view of our author is the one "which contains those words which can be both understood and uttered." It is a matter of common knowledge that loose or sharp-tongued persons could be a source of great social and organizational tensions. They can breed resentment, and considerable apprehension and dissatisfaction both for superordinates and subordinates. Therefore one who is discrete in the choice of words is ethically fortified against many evils. Words should not be used for uttering falsehood, because lying according to our author "is a form of madness."

Another quality which can morally strengthen a decision-maker is to abstain from action unless the matter has been subjected to reflection and deliberation. Haste breeds waste—wastage of time, wastage of energies and wastage of resources. For some ignorant persons haste is synonymous with efficiency. This in reality is a sign of imprudence and irrationality. Many ills have befallen administrators and men of authority, who pronounced their judgements in haste. More often than not it can lead to injustice and tyranny. Anything which is done in a hurry carries an element of uncertainty; it reduces precision and determination which give authority in a state its effectiveness. He says :

"Both in speech and action, be weighty and deliberate."

According to Kai-Ka-us, quarrelsome and contentious persons are also ethically weak. They are mostly stubborn and irreconcilable in their attitudes. No group or organization can tolerate such members for a long time. It is extremely unbecoming of a man of authority shouldering vast responsibilities for decision-making to quarrel frequently. In this way he will not only lose respect, but become a source of many petty squabbles which lead to stress and tension. Quarrelsomeness very often stems from arrogance, which as all accounts agree, is a reprehensible quality from any ethical standard. He has depicted the evil consequences of such an attitude as follows : quarrelling is not indulged in by men of dignity, but rather by women and children. If a quarrel should on any occasion break out between you and another, do not utter all that you could say, but so conduct your quarrel as to leave a loophole for reconciliation. Don't be completely irreconciliable and stubborn; considering stubbornness and irreconcilability as the characteristics of persons of little worth. Realize that humility is the best of qualities, one of God's blesssing which no one envies. Do not with every word you address to others say 'O man'; this repetition of 'O Man without reason detracts from a person's dignity as a man, Extravagance and excess have also been listed as evils which ruin the moral fiber of human beings. According to Kai Ka-us, extravagance is the cause of poverty and all misguided persons, who tread this path have suffered in the long run. Anybody indulging in it is an enemy of his own interests. He uses the term with its widest connotations. Extravagance in his opinion does not merely mean indiscrete spending and thoughtless disbursement of funds. Excess in all spheres—eating, drinking, speaking and working—is bad because it makes one deviate from the path of moderation and rectitude. In his opinion one who indulges in excess "harms the spirit and deadens the living mind." He says :

> "You observe that the life of a lamp is generated by oil; if you pour oil into the lamp without measure and limit, so that it overflows the spout of the container and passes beyond the tip of the wick, it immediately extinguishes the lamp. Oil itself then becomes the cause of lamp's extinction, although had it been present in moderate quantity it would have been the means of keeping it alight once there was an excess of it, it became the means of lamp's extinction.

Man in charge of public affairs is supposed to have a good reputation. According to our author ill-repute begets shame, disgust and frustration. One should not be swearer of oath because people tend to lose faith in a person, who takes oath frequently. Riches and power cannot safeguard an incumbent of high office from evils of bad reputation. The best course is to create an image of trustworthiness because all right-thinking people shun the company of a liar. One should abstain from misleading others, and also be watchful that he himself is not misled. A person who has acquired this characteristic is certainly going to win the trust and confidence of those around him. A good reputation, particularly for trustworthiness is the Philosopher's Stone, which would make an individual an embodiment of sterling qualities. Unbridled appetites also spoil reputation.

Generosity of Mind

Generosity of mind is a quality, which mitigates the rigidities of law. It is true that without law political systems and administrative organizations cannot exist. But obsessively legalistic views could also be extremely detrimental to peace and harmony in the affairs of men. One should be an administrator of law and not its captive, and in administering rules, according to Kai-Ka-us, the most dignified thing is not to punish people for trivial mistakes, and if a petitioner comes the best course would be to forgive him. If at all a persen is to be punished and there is no escape from it, the penalty should be strictly in proportion to the gravity of the offense, and if possible may be a little less than what is entailed by law. Clemency and mercy are virtues of high merit. An officer who is not generous in his attitude creates tension and ill-feelings among persons subjected to his jurisdiction. A person who holds money higher than honour is doomed to ignominy. Avarice and insatiable lust for wealth are enemies of honourable conduct, and one who indulges in dishonourable deeds brings destruction on those who are held in esteem and honour.

It is a common characteristic of men working in governmental hierarchies, or may be it is a common feature of human endeavors in all avenues of life, that they want to have acclerated promotions. They want to attain highest rank overnight, and impatience is writ large over all their activities. Subordination is galling to them, and by swiftest means they want to get the highest position available. Kai Ka-us thinks it is unethical and he says : "Until you have borne the drudgery of subordinate position, you will never attain to the comforts of high ranks." There is considerable truth in the remarks of our author because many ills in human organizations stem from ambivalent behaviour of over-ambitious persons. They make life for others irksome, have no peace and equanimity in their own lives, and very often intrigues and frictions which lead to the disenchantment of the participants can easily be attributed to them.

In Chapter VIII, Kai Ka-us has listed forty two counsels which Nushirwan (the just) gave to his son. Some of those which are relevant for men in authority and who hold in custody the welfare of the people can be listed as follows :

1. The great man who looks upon himself as small is the great man of the age.
2. There is no meaner person in the world than he to whom appeal is made for help and though able to grant it refuses.
3. If you desire to remain free of unhappiness be not envious.
4. If you desire to command men's respect then exercise justice.
5. If you want not to be disillusioned, do not regard an undone task as having been done.
6. If you do not wish to be stricken with shame do not remove what you have not yourself deposited; and if you desire not to be mocked behind your back, respect them that are subordinate to you.
7. If you desire to be included in the numbers of honourable men, give covetousness no place in your heart.
8. If you desire to be a man of justice be generous as far as lies in your power towards them that are subordinate to you; and if you desire your heart never to be stricken a blow which no remedy can heal, never engage in agreement with fools.
9. If you wish to retain men's esteem, learn how to esteem other men.
10. If you wish for effectiveness in your tongue then restrain the rapacity of your hand.

The Qabus-nama was written at a time when the political authority of the Abbaside Caliphate had almost been extinguished. The Commanders of the faithful still wielded a supra-national spiritual authority, but it was facing growing challenges from new sects and heretical cults. The author makes a strong and stirring advocacy of Sunni Islam. Therefore there are a wide ranging discussions on theological matters which point out that a ruler in order to cultivate wisdom must follow the word of God meticulously. He made a fervent plea for effective governmental authority, but at the same time pointed out that it could only be established if the people living under its jurisdiction were happy and prosperous. Extortion and recklessness in his opinion perpetuate tyranny, seal the well-springs of justice and would ultimately spell ruin and desolation for the kingdom. Authority should not be an intoxicant, and rulers of men should be equipped with six qualities, "awesomeness, justice, generosity, respect for law, gravity and truthfulness" The four basic factors which maintain peace, order and stability in a kingdom, according to Kai Ka-us are authority, army, finance, and prosperity, and they are all interdependent.

Tradition Politics

Siyasat-nama : Nizam-al-Mulk (d. 685/1090), the author of this treatise was Prime Minister for more than thirty years of two Seljuq monarchs, Alp Arslan (d, A.D.-1072) and Malikshah (d. A.D.-1092). This was a period of acute ideological stress and political lawlessness in the Muslim world. In this stormy climate the Seljuqs had been able to establish a stable kingdom by conquering Khwarizm, Tabaristan and Persian Iraq. Their rule touched the highest watermark of economic prosperity, political stability, and intellectual development during the reign of Nizam-al-Mulk. He enjoyed unlimited power and through his prudence, sagacity and diplomacy was able to maintain peace and tranquility in the kingdom. His role as a statesman and administrator in one of the most critical periods of Islamic history has been summed up as follows :

> "As a great Iranian Vizir he conspicuously exemplifies the chief minister's role of mediator between a despot, in this instance, an alien Turk and his Persian subjects— he enhanced the dignity and prestige of the Seljuqs by inculcating canons of royal behaviour and etiquette, and he tempered military harshness with lessons in judicious clemency and conciliation. He built up Seljuq powers with the Sultan as the keystone in an integrated administration."

Hitti calls him "one of the ornaments of the political history of Islam. His political and administrative achievements were great, no doubt, but in Islamic history his reputation primarily rests' on scholarship and his generous patronage of art and letters. He was particularly anxious to encourage scholars and theologians, for whom he established *madrassahs* (Institutes of Studies) in all the major cities of the kingdom. Nizamiyah colleges, named after him were built in Nishapur and Baghdad between 1065-67. At these institutions instruction was imparted by leading intellectual and religious luminaries of the day. Al-Ghazali, one of the greatest theological thinkers of Islam, taught at both the academies. The Nizamiyah college in Baghdad was a rendezvous for famous preachers; for nearly two centuries, and disappeared only when it was merged in a new college founded by Caliph Mustansir (A.D. 1226-62). According to Goldziher the foundation of Nizamiyah college was an "epoch-making advance" in the development of higher learning in Islam. Nizam-al-Mulk was not only a patron of scholars, he was himself endowed with scholarly qualities of very high order which have earned for his Siyasatnama a place of eminence among the great prose works of Persian literature. E. G. Browne has summed up the significance of this book in the following words:

> The Siyasat-nama is, in my opinion, one of the most valuable and interesting prose works which exist in Persia, both because of the quantity of historical anecdotes which it contains, and because it embodies the views on government of one of the greatest Prime Ministers whom the East has produced—a Minister whose strength and wisdom is no way better proved than by the chaos and internecine strife which succeeded his death."

The work was written at the behest of Malikshah. It is divided into fifty chapters, thirty nine of which were completed at the time of its original submission to the king, but later eleven more chapters were added on subjects relating to government and religious controversies, which were threatening the unity and solidarity of Islam. The declining years of the great statesmen when he made up his mind to revise and enlarge his work were beclouded with gloom and distress. He had become a victim of court and *harem* intrigues, which ultimately cost him his life. John Alden Williams has depicted the last years of the aged and shaken Prime Minister in the following words:

> About 1091 the aged minister began to write again, and now his words had an urgent note. Times had changed. Much of his earlier advice had not been heeded, and Malikshah's favourite wife was his enemy. The Sultan was engaged in a quarrel with the Caliph, and had also come under the influence of adventurers and heretics. The elder statesman outlined the dangers that particularly threatened the Seljuq empire, and the states like it. Before the addition to his book could be presented to Malikshah, however, Nizam-al-Mulk was dismissed from office. In A.H. 485/A.D. 1092 he was murdered by Ismaili assassins in circumstances suggesting that they may have been sent with the knowledge of the Sultan or his queen.

The author's main purpose was to write a basic source book on the art of governing men. It was an effort to examine the political and administrative dimensions of a despotic form of government, a system which was extremely susceptible to abuse of authority and corruption.

Rich Scholarship

Muslim scholarship has always been very rich in religious literature and history. Scholars have always found in religion and history an immeasurable reservoir of wisdom and human experience. Religion was the revealed word of God, while history was a resplendent stockroom of events which if intelligently and objectively analyzed could be a tremendous source of guidance and enlightenment. Nizam-al-Mulk's knowledge of both these sources was deep and profound and in collecting the substance of Siyasat-nama, he relied heavily upon them. At the conclusion of his work he has made the following remark:

> So ends this book of the Rules for Kings. Your humble servant was previously commanded to compile a volume on this subject, and he carried out the command. At the time he composed thirty nine chapters extempore, and submitted them to the Lofty

> Throne (may Allah exalt it.) They were found acceptable. However, that was merely an epitome. Later he expounded at his leisure, and wrote chapters and related stories on a variety of subjects, expounding everything in the clearest and simplist language. Let him not listen to what others say, but read this book constantly; he will never be wearied by reading this book, for it contains advice, wisdom, proverbs, interpretation of the Quran, tradition of the Prophet (upon him be peace; stories of prophets, memoirs of saints, and tales of just kings, it tells of the lives of the departed and deeds of the living.

The instrument of instructions from the king which commanded the author to compile this work pointed out that the administration of the kingdom was decaying, and that he should find out reasons for that sorry state of affairs, and search out remedies against evils which had destroyed peace and harmony in the working of the government.

The purpose of commissioning the seasoned statesman to write such a treatise was that out of his long administrative experience and knowledge of history and religion he should produce a manual, which would ensure stability in politics and honesty in administration. In short, the book was to be a digest of political wisdom and knowledge about administration so that decision-makers in both fields could make ethical and rational judgments. As he proceeded with his compilation, Nizam-al-Mulk widened the scope of his assignment, and made frequent comments on the state of affairs of Muslim societies in his own time. Whenever opportunity arose he unhesitatingly uncovered the evils of contemporary government and administration. There is, however, a basic deficiency in the book that it only makes comments, but does not give any clue about the actual machinery of the government. The book also gives an impression of having been written in a hurry. As the author himself confesses, the first thirty nine chapters were written extempore, as such, in spite of his experience, wisdom and breadth of comprehension, which are abundantly reflected in every chapter, they lack the depth and authenticity of historical research. Pieces of advice and anecdotes relating to noble qualities of the past rulers have not been coherently organized. The scope of the book, however, is fairly wide. The writer has collected large numbers of maxims on good government, and discusses in reasonable detail duties and responsibilities of state functionaries, both at the center and in the field. In analyzing various issues he draws extensively on the storehouse of experiences, which he had accumulated during thirty years of service as a leading administrator of the Muslim world. In his opinion a Muslim ruler should be physically handsome, his character good and untainted, courage undiminished, justice perenial, and warlike qualities unquestioned. Nizam-al-Mulk's advocacy of absolute monarchical rule is understandable, because that was the accepted ideology of the day, but he repeatedly insists that all authority should be exercised within the boundaries of Sharia (religion). He firmly believes that religion is a powerful antidote against those corrupting elements which are rooted in human nature. Since the rule in most cases are not conversant with religious law, he insists that while making public policies they should show special deference to the opinions of the doctors of law. Companionship of the learned assures sound judgment and rulers can fulfil their religious, moral and temporal obligations effectively. He says:

> It is incumbent upon the king to inquire into religious matters, to be acquainted with the divine precepts and prohibitions and put them into practice, and to obey the commands of God (be he exalted) ; it is his duty to respect doctors of religion and pay their salaries out of the treasury, and he should honour pious and abstentious men. Furthermore, it is fitting that once or twice a week he should invite religious elders to his presence and hear from them the commands of the Truth, he should listen for the interpretations of the Quran and traditions of the Prophet (may Allah pray for him and give him peace) and he should hear stories about just kings and tales of the Prophets (upon them be peace). During that time he should free his mind from wordly cares and give his ears and attention to them . . . then the way of prudence and rectitude in both spiritual and temporal affairs will be opened to him.

Knowledge of Religion

Knowledge of religion has always been considered an essential quality for rulers in Islam. It is deemed to be a remedy against vanity, jealousy and numerous other kinds of evil. It insures equity, probity, and justice. Nizam-al-Mulk had to insist more on religion because he lived during one of the most critical periods of the religious history of Islam. All kinds of heretical doctrines were trying to sap the original simplicity and purity of Islam. In Siyasat-nama he has devoted six chapters to these heretical doctrines. He examines their origin, principles, practices, and undesirable consequences, which result from them in the body politic. He had deep-seated hatred for Ismailes, and Batnis, and bitterly opposed the employment of Jews, Christians, and Zoroastrians in government service. He argues, representatives of these communities, because of their affluence formed a great source of corruption in the realm. In his opinion, since the non-Muslim minorities were rich, they could easily buy public offices. Probably the chain of his famous Nizamiya colleges in the kingdom was meant to remedy this defect. Graduates of these institutions were religious scholars, but they were primarily trained to fill administrative positions in the government. They were expected to keep the people on the "Straight Path" Vladimir Minorsky says:

> In the *Siyasat-nama* of Nizam-al-Mulk we have a document of first importance setting forth the program which combined the force of the Turks with the administrative methods of the Sassanids and the great Abbasid Caliphs. The system of spies, of messengers, and of troops skilfully assorted from different elements was harmonized with the founding of the religious colleges, those nurseries of administrators who were to watch over the rectitude of the path followed by their flocks.

He was convinced that if the rulers and officials do not conform to the same religion, administration suffers from chronic distrust and unrest.

Heavy Responsibility

Nizam-al-Mulk feels that governing of men is a very heavy responsibility ; particularly personal rule of despotic kings entails special obligation. Any ruler who has usurped despotic powers must exercise constant vigilance over the conduct of his functionaries otherwise the state would be under permanent threat of dissolution. Rulers must have proper machinery to collect information about the activities of public officials and they should have the courage and honesty to punish them for all omissions and abuse of authority. He recommends an effective network of central intelligence, which would keep a watch over the actions and affairs of all senior officers. He relates a story of Nushirwan (The Just) the pre-Islamic Iranian king, who attributed financial and moral degeneration of his kingdom to the negligence of his father who had failed to keep himself well-informed about the shameless embezzlements of his civil servants. A king should appoint informers in every part of the country, because that is the only way to safeguard people against oppression. Information received from such sources should reach the king directly. The author is fully aware of the delicate nature of such spying and reporting on public officials and would therefore advise the rulers that agents of central intelligence should be persons of unimpeachable integrity and honesty so that what they report is not subject to any suspicion. An arrangement of this kind would enable the king "to know every event that takes place and will be able to give his orders as appropriate, meeting out unexpected reward, punishment or commendation to the persons concerned." Nizam-al-Mulk is of the opinion however, that information culled out of the secret reports of the informants should be anxiously examined, before any decision is based on it. Every report needs to be dissected with patience and understood with care. The Quran says : "O you who believe, if a wicked man brings you tidings, verify it lest you smite some people in ignorance and then repent of what you did.'

After giving the above citation from the Holy Book, Nizam-al-Mulk says:

> "So one should not be precipitate for precipitancy brings regret, and regret is of no avail. . . . Elders of religion have said, 'Haste is from Satan, deliberation is from the Merciful. Works undone can be done, but that which is done cannot be retrieved."

Like other writers on ethics and administration, Nizam-al-Mulk has emphasized justice, honesty, accessibility to complainants and generosity of mind as the best moral equipment for rulers of men. Justice in his opinion is the corner-stone of political and administrative stability. Injustice wrecks state and ruins peace and prosperity of the people. He deems that it is the personal responsibility of the head of the government to see that the legal institutions are strong and not discriminatory in the administration of justice. Law should not make any distinction between high and low, and the entire official world should give ungrudging support to judges in their daily work. If anything contrary to this principle happens it is symptomatic of decadence. He says :

Dignity of Judiciary

All other officers must strengthen the hand of the judge and uphold the dignity of the courts. If anyone makes excesses and fails to appear in court, however exalted he may be, he must be forcibly compelled to be present. For in the time of The Companions of the Prophet (upon him be peace and blessings) justice was dispensed in person and not delegated to anyone else, so that there could be no scope for injustice. In every age from the time of Adam (peace be upon him) until now, in every nation and every country men have practiced equity, justice and striven after righteousness, and when this has been so, dynasties have endured the generations.

Justice bridles the evil intentions of the oppressors, and protects and preserves the rights of the oppressed. Governments are judged by the means they adopt to eradicate evildoers and the remedies they provide to victims of injustice. He believes that "sound judgment is a better thing to have than a powerful army."

Honesty is universally recognized as a vital requirement for good, effective and efficient administration. Corruption has been a cause of ruin of many establishments. Nizam-al-Mulk has not made a scientific or psychological inquiry into its causes, but he emphatically points out that unchecked corruption is a sign of political ailment. In a climate of distrust; effective implementation of public policy is simply impossible. Nizam-al-Mulk has suggested special watchfulness on tax collectors, who in his opinion are the biggest source of corruption. Every tax collector who is in charge of a revenue district should be given strict instructions not to harass the peasantry by untimely demands and additional extortions. In his dealings with the public he should be guided by civility and courtesy. If a tax collector has taken a bribe, the best course would be to reclaim the money from him, deprive him of his office and ban all future government employments to him. In view of the universality of corruption, he recommends exemplary punishment for the culprits. He narrates the story of an officer who was beheaded by King Altiginm because he took some hay and a chicken from a peasant. Honesty among senior officers is of particular significance because juniors are very likely to be influenced by their behavior. He points out that if an officer of the rank of wazir is corrupt, the other officials will behave likewise or may be worse.

Accessibility of common people to the chambers of administrative decision-making to complain against wrongs suffered at the hand of public servants has been acclaimed as one of the cardinal characteristics of Islamic code of ethics for administrators. It is a virtue which insures rectitude in administration, and generates popular trust and confidence in government. Even the most despotic governments require the cooperation of the people, but if the latter do not have the right to complain against administrative decisions, no cooperation will be forthcoming. It is for this reason that Nizam-al-Mulk at several places in his treatise has warned the rulers against inaccessibility of government functionaries to aggrieved persons. He says:

> "It is absolutely necessary that on two days in the week the king should sit for the redress of wrongs, to extract recompense from the oppressor, to give justice and to listen to the words of the subjects with his own ears, without any intermediary. ... I have read in the books of the ancients the most of the non-Arab (Persian) kings used to put up a high platform and sit up there on horseback so that they could see all the complainants gathered about, and they would redress the grievances of everyone. The reason for this was that where the king sits in a place protected by gates,

locks, vestibules and screens, self-interested and oppressive persons can keep people back and not let them go before the King."

He cites the example of Nushirwan, who, in order to save the people from palace guards and other officers had hung a chain with bells, which any complainant could pull and seek redress of grievances. If the people have no access to the rulers, the only other alternative under despotic rule for people to undo wrongs is to strive through conspiracies and revolts.

Generosity and large-heartedness are also advocated as essential characteristics for those who wield political or administrative authority in a state. They eliminate fear from the mind of a common man and enable him to give maximum compliance and loyalty to the state.

Significant Features

Nizam-al-Mulk has listed certain other features of good administration, which in his opinion, ensure peace and stability in a kingdom. He feels that collectors and other field officers should be transferred every two or three years. He does not want officers to be entrenched at one place for a long time, because the longer they stay at one place, greater the chances of their becoming a source of tyranny and maladministration. They are likely to become corrupt and indifferent to the interest of the masses. He further recommends that the King should not appoint his personal friends as officials of the state, nor should the officers be included in the circle of his intimate friends. By virtue of their closeness and friendship with the ruler, they become arrogant and practice oppression and high-handedness. He also believes that the best way to avoid abuse of administrative authority is to introduce participative approach in decision-making.

Holding consultations on affairs is a sign of sound judgment, high intelligence, and foresight. Every person has some knowledge and in every branch of knowledge one knows more and others less. One may have knowledge and never have put it into practice or tested it. Everybody in the world agrees that there has never been any mortal wiser than the Prophet . . . and Gabriel (upon him be peace) often used to visit him, bringing inspiration and giving news of things past and things to come ... in spite of all this perfection, in spite of all his miracles, God (be He exalted) said to him (in the Quran 3:153) (Consult them in affairs) 'O Muhammad, where you do any work, or when you are confronted with an important matter, confer with your companions.'

Some Advices

At another place he has mentioned that it is very unbecoming of seniors to reprimand their juniors publicly. Loss of honour leaves a dent in one's ego and an individual with a damaged self-respect can never be honest and efficient. It diminishes goodwill in organizations; as such the best course according to our author is to overlook a mistake, if it is committed for the first time. Administration is an onerous job. It taxes all human faculties, therefore, those who are involved in it deserve every possible encouragement. Their achievements and services should be properly rewarded. A disgruntled bureaucracy can do a lot of damage to the peace and security of a country. There should be no wastage of talent in society. Each capable person has a right to ask for appointment according to his abilities, so that he could earn his livelihood. Another fallacy which continuously erodes administration, is lopsided distribution of work. He warns against assignment of two or more positions to one person or one position to two persons. In both cases performance is bound to be faulty and inefficient. He says :

> Enlightened monarchs and clever ministers have never in any age given two appointments to one man or one appointment to two men, with the result that their affairs were always conducted with efficiency and lustre. When two appointments are given to one man, one of the tasks is always inefficiently and faultily performed; and in fact, you will usually find that the man who has two functions fails in both of them, and is constantly suffering censure and uneasiness on account of his shortcomings. And further, whenever two men are given a single post each transfers (his responsibility) to the other and the work remains for forever undone.

Counselling the Rulers

Kitab Nasihat-al-Muluk : This book was written by Abu Hamid Muhammad-al-Ghazzali (d. 505/1111) who ranks among the greatest theologians of Islamic history. The work was originally composed in Persian and later translated into Arabic. Scholars have claimed that several popular writings attributed to Ghazzali are spurious, but none has contested the authenticity of Nasihat-al-Muluk. The treatise was written at the behest of Sultan ibn Malikshah sometime between 499/1105 and 505/1111. Ghazzali lived during he Seljuq period and his thought and mind were greatly influenced by the state of affairs prevailing at that time in the Muslim world. After complete mastery of the canon law theology, and mysticism, Ghazzali studied critically the writings of those, who vehemently opposed the orthodox view of Islam. He also read Batinite and rationalist philosophers with special interest and anxiety. In this way he kept the spectrum of his philosophical and spiritual inquiries very wide and whatever he wrote or discussed was always imbued with precision and profundity. He considered *aql* (intelligence or reason) as one of the supreme graces of man and included it among the greatest gifts of God. It was his belief that all religious doctrines except the fundamentals like the existence of God, revelation and prophethood could be substantiated through basic reason. In religion his greatest work was *Ihya Ulum al Din.* (Revivification of the Sciences of Religion). In 1106 he was asked by Sultan Sanjar of Khuransan to resume teaching in the Nizamiyah College at Nishapur. In 1109 he retired to Tus and spent the rest of his life as a mystic. He died on the 18th of December 1111 at the age of 53. It is said that *Nasihat-al-Muluk* was compiled during his retirement shortly before death.

In all his ethical writings, al Ghazzali preaches that men become perfect only by emulating attributes of God in their character. He wrote:

> "The perfection of the worshipper as well as his happiness lies in imitating the qualities of Allah the Most High and in adorning himself with the meanings of His attributes and of His names ... in that measure of course that may be considered within his right."

He contends that there are all kinds of failures and frailties associated with human character, but most evils result when ambition and anger dominate man's disposition. Ambition in his opinion is a source of "shamelessness, wickedness, extravagance, stinginess, hypocrisy, defamation, impudence, folly, greed cupidity, flattery, envy, rancour, gluttony, and lewedness. Anger induces men to indulge in rashness, excessive spending, haughtiness, boasting, arrogance, self-admiration, derision, making light of others, disdain, mischief, abuse." In order to mitigate the effect of these vices, al Ghazzali has mentioned qualities like "chastity, contentment, abstinence, fear of God, piety cheerfulness, a comely appearance, modesty, ingenuity, courage, generosity, self-control, fortitude, clemency, endurance, forgiveness, stability, genius, bravery and gravity" which in his opinion if harmoniously blended can produce an ideal human character.

"Al-Ghazzali was a keen and anxious student of human behaviour and tried to explore psychological and social causes of men's actions in organized society. In his opinion each action is composed of four factors, i.e., *Khawatir* (affections of mind), *raghbia* (inclination), *itiqad* (intellectual conviction), and *irada* (will). In other words:

Khawatir, *Raghbia,*
(Affections of the mind) (inclination)

Itiqad, *Irada,* *Amal,*
(intellectual conviction) (will produce) (action)

In his Ihya-al-Ulum-al-Din, Al-Ghazzali compares human heart to a fortress, which has to be guarded against satanic intrusions. Anger, desire, envy, and greed are the the main gates through which Shaitan (Satan) leads his hordes of evil to attack this fortress. Religion and reason are the primary defences against such inroads. If they are weak, Satan and his evil forces have every chance of being triumphant in human life. So far as moral accomplishments are concerned, he has divided humanity into four groups :

(1) "The first are those who are heedless who do not distinguish truth, from folly and beautiful from the base."

(2) "Those who know well enough the baseness of what is base, but they do not become habituated to good conduct

because they consider that their evil conduct is something enjoyable."

(3) "Those (who) actually approve of base dispositions maintaining that they are necessary, right and beautifiul."

(4) "The fourth kind are those, who along with what accompanies corrupt belief and practise, see also a sort of virtue in their very excess of evil and the destruction of lives."

Moral Values and Precepts

Moral values and precepts constitute a universal antidote against error and evil, but men belonging to the fourth category are so wicked that no amount of persuasion could convince them about the aims and objectives of righteous action. Morality in his opinion is a skill or a habit of mind which can be cultivated only by conscious efforts. It consumes time, and requires absorbing interest, but once an aptitude for ethical conduct is developed then it flows effortlessly into all channels of human affairs. In his Ihya, Al-Ghazzali has made the following remarks:

> "This question of moral progress is precisely like progress in the arts, for if anyone wishes to acquire skill in caligraphy, for instance, he must exercise the necessary mental perseverance. He must engage in what the skillful writer gives him to do, which is the production of a well-written line. At first this will be a matter of requirement and of imitation. And afterwards he must not cease to give his attention to making this well-written line until his aptitude in doing so is established, and until his skill becomes actually a mental quality. In the end he will do naturally and easily what was at first an arduous effort. The time however, will be good which he had made good, first with conscious effort, but in the end quite naturally. This is all because of mental capacity to receive an impression"

Nasihat-al-Muluk, which is strictly a treatise on administrative ethics, is replete with Al-Ghazzali's depth of understanding about human character and behaviour. It also shows the sad spectacle of political lawlessness and administrative anarchy which was rampant all over the Muslim world at that time. There are nostalgic references to glories of Muslim and non-Muslim past when justice and equity reigned supreme in human affairs. He complained bitterly of the wickedness of the people and the luxuriant and comfort-seeking existence of rulers. He was convinced that Islamic society was unhinged because unethical character of politics and administration had destroyed its moral moorings. Another reason which in his opinion had wrecked peace and order was that political authority was either too weak or too lenient. He was convinced that wickedness could only be eradicated by firmness. He says:

> "The reason why we are saying so much on this subject is that our present age is an exceedingly wicked one. The people are wicked and the Sultans are preoccupied with the lower world. With wicked people things cannot be set right through tolerance and indulgence . . . power to inspire awe and maintain discipline are essential, if the individual is to be able to go about his business and if the people are to have security from one another, peoples' outlook has been corrupted and in which they have all grown wicked in both deed and intention."

Bitter Experience

The wickedness of the people, the torn fabric of once powerful caliphal authority of the Abbasides, deep ideological frictions which plagued the Muslim world, and worries of his declining years, made Al-Ghazzali a mystic during the last phase of his life. The *batinis* under the leadership of their teacher the Fatimide-al-Mustansir (1035-1094 A.D.) and Nazarites led by Hasan-al-Sabbah (d. 1129) with his spiritual and military headquarters at Almout, challenged the righteousness of Sunnite doctrine which was the official creed of the Abbasides and the Seljuks, and used all subversive means to dismantle their political hegemony. There was chronic insecurity of life and property, and anarchy and lawlessness were almost endemic. In such a socio-political climate, mysticism with its negative approach to wordly gains, and human ambitions, had every chance of capturing the imagination of scholars and intellectuals. Therefore it is not surprising that Al-Ghazzali in his retirement preached mystical ethics. Nasihat-al-Muluk is replete with admonitions, ancedotes, aphorisms, which furnish an eloquent testimony to the deep-seated mystical proclivities of its author. He believed that ghoulish enticements of the world hamper man's salvation. It was common among mystics to believe that lust for worldly gains and insatiable appetites grievously injure the welfare of mankind. Al-Ghazzali says :

> "You should understand that a stopping place is not a fixed abode, and that man is in this world in the role of a traveller, the mother's womb being his first stop and the grave his last stop."In order to substantiate his contention about the transitory nature of human life and treacherous ways of the world he has given ten analogies to create awareness about them :

1. This is to explain the spell of this World. God's Apostle said, "Hold aloof from the world for she is a worse spell-binder than Harut and Marut. The beginning of her spell is that appears to you in such a way that you suppose her to be stationary and fixed in relations to you; for you look at her, and she is the universe itself yet she is continually fleeting from you.
2. She resembles a worthless woman who is vicious and importuanate and lures men to her in order to make them her loves, then takes them to her house and destroys them.
3. She is like an ugly old hag who masks her face, but has put on fine clothes and done herself up ornately. Men see her from afar and are enchanted with her, but when they remove her veil they are dismayed to find such ugliness.
4. He will then understand that this world resembles the route of a traveller, starting from the cradle ending at the grave, and with a given number of stages in between.
5. You should understand that this world, in the pleasures which her sons get from her and again in the disgrace which in the after-life they suffer because of her, is like

a person who eats rich and sweet food in such excess as to ruin the stomach.

6. Jesus declared that the seeker of this world is like the drinker of sea-water, the more he consumes the thirstier he becomes and he will continue drinking until he perishes and he will never be cured of that thirst.
7. This is that a person who comes into this world resembles one who goes as a guest to a home of a host, whose custom is to keep his mansion always adorned for guests and to invite them in parties. The host places before them a tray of jewels and gold, and a silver censor with aloes wood and incense for giving fragrance, but they leave, the tray and censor for the next party when it arrives.
8. This world's inhabitants, in their preoccupation with its affairs and forgetfulness of the world to come, resemble a ship's passengers, who on reaching an island go ashore to perform the natural functions and rituals ablutions. The ship's officers call out "Let nobody take too long or get busy with anything except the ablutions as the ship is to sail soon."

Thoughts embodied in the above analogies form the crux of Iranian and Arabic mystical literature. Many of their connotations are inimical to the basic principles of Islam. Mystical ethics is vastly different from Islamic ethics in the sense that Islam insists on purity of thought and action, preaches that, life of sin and vice is destructive, enjoins virtue and righteousness, but does not advocate asceticism. Its approach is positive and activates the believers to appreciate and enjoy the fruits of this world, but in doing so they should abstain from excesses and injustice which lead to immoral acts. The frame of reference of Nasihat-al-Muluk is predominantly mystical. Moreover the treatise has focused most of its attention on the kings. There are only passing references to administrators and other state functionaries. Some pages have been devoted to the role and qualities of Wazirs (Prime Ministers) and Dabirs (Secretaries), but the author does not provide a comprehensive picture of the ethical basis of these offices.

For instance, in his chapter on secretaries, Al-Ghazzali has put more emphasis on the shape and form of a pen to be used by a secretary than on the qualities of head and heart which would mold his character as an administrator. The chapter on Wazirate, however, though short, has some references to the ethical foundation of this office. His exposition of the moral qualities of kingship are detailed and exhaustive and this has accorded the book a respectable place in Islamic literature. From this material a student of administrative ethics in Islam, can glean valuable guidelines to crystalize moral basis of government and administration in an Islamic society. The qualities depicted no doubt were meant for the princes, but they could be equally relevant to the character and behaviour of the functionaries who executed their policies.

Foundation Rock

According to Al-Ghazzali, authority is the foundation rock over which the super-structure of a politically organized society is built. Authority ensures stability and prosperity for the realm, but it is a delicate instrument. It is both a bane and a bliss. If exercised righteously and with care, wisdom and prudence it can be a source of eternal blessings, but abuse or misuse of authority can damage peace and order in a country. He says:

> "This is that (the ruler) should first of all understand the importance and also the danger of authority entrusted to him. In authority there is a great blessing, since he who "exercises it righteously obtains unsurpassed happiness, but if any (ruler) fails to do so he incurs torment unsurpassed only by the torment for unbelief, . . Such being the case there is no greater blessing than God's grant to a person of the office of ruler and Sultan, whereby an hour of his life is raised (to be equivalent) to the whole life of any other persons, but if he shows no appreciation of this blessing and gives himself over to tyranny and passion, there is a terrible wish that God on High will count him as an enemy."

He makes reference to the two traditions of the Holy Prophet in which a serious warning has been administered to those who have been given the responsibility to preside over the destiny of a Muslim community. The Prophet said "If any man is granted authority over the Muslims and does not look upon them as he would look upon members of his own household, tell him he will get his place in Hell." "Two persons in my community will be denied my intercession ; the tyrant and the innovator, who practices such exaggeration in religion that it goes beyond the limit." There is, however, a slight contradiction in Al-Ghazzali's approach to authority. He begins his analysis by pointing out that exercise of authority within the boundaries of ethics and religion is the greatest benediction of God. An hour spent in the righteous use of authority is equal to the whole life of other human beings, but a little later in the same chapter, he takes considerable pains to explain that all authority, just or unjust is subject to divine admonishment. He says:

> "Hudhayfah (ibu-al-Yaman) used to say: 'I never praise any holder of authority. Whether virtous or wicked. When asked why, he replied that it was because he had heard God's Apostle declare : "On the Resurrection Day, all holders of authority will be brought in: whether unjust or just. All will be stationed on the (bridge called) Sirat, and God on High will inspire the Sirat to shake them off in one sharp shake; for there will not be a single one among, them who has not judged unjustly taken a bribe when trying a case, or lent his ear overmuch to one contestant. All will fall off the Sirat, and all will go down the Hell for seventy years, at the end of which they will reach their final resting place."

Mystical Suspicion

Mystical suspicion and derision of wordly possessions could be the reason for this outright condemnation of all kinds of authority. Whatever might have been the reason, Al-Ghazzali's earlier statement that righteous use of authority brings unsurpassed happiness and ensures salvation hereafter is the true ethical basis of authority of Islam.

Justice and equity according to Al-Ghazzali constitute prominent branches of the true Faith. Injustice and inequity are vices for which there is no atonement. The unjust Sultan is warned against severe torments, and a prince who collects taxes from his subjects and does not practice impartiality between the strong and the weak, and is arbitrary in his judgments will have to pocket odium of God. Justice in his opinion entails strict adherence to the laws of God. A ruler, whether he inflicts punishment or shows compassion must exercise discretion. Excessive compassion is as bad as excessive punishment because both are contrary to principles of justice. He quotes the following tradition of the Holy Prophet:

> "God's Apostle stated that on the Resurrection Day, holders of authority will be brought in and told 'You were shepherds of my sheep', (One will be asked) 'Why did you award a penalty and inflict a punishment on so-and-so in excess of what I bade you?' He will reply: 'O Lord God, in wrath because they were offending against you and he will be told, Why should your wrath exceed Mine?' Another will be asked 'Why did you inflict a punishment falling short of what I bade you?' He will reply 'O Lord God I did so out of compassion' and he will be told 'Why should you be more compassionate than I am? Their God on High will order them to be shown the corners of Hell."

A ruler should refrain from injustice and it is incumbent upon him to exercise constant vigilence over the behaviour of his soldiers and civil servants. If he is just, and his employees are unjust, the conditions of society will never improve and he would be held responsible for their misdeeds. Justice becomes effective and meaningful only if the entire governmental machinery is pervaded with judiciousness and all state employees make justice a permanent feature of their professional ethics. Al-Ghazzali is of the opinion that if the chief holder of authority is just and endowed with excellences of character, there is every possibility that these traits will be emulated by his subordinates. He points out that Shaqiq-al-Balkhi, a learned ascetic once told Harun-al-Rashid the Abbaside Caliph, "You are a fountain and the other officials (who help you to govern) the world are the streams (which flow from it). If the fountain is clear, there can be no damage from silt in the channels; if the fountain is turbid, there will be no hope (of maintaining) the channels." Unjust officials have a tendency to hood-wink the rulers and more often than not they indulge in tactics and use strategies by which injustice is portrayed as justice. Such functionaries are the greatest enemies of state and their evil intentions spell destructions of the realm.

Passion and Anger

Passion and anger render the prospects of justice bleak, and it therefore befits a ruler who is in search of just laws to avoid them as much as he can. Intellect should be the guardian of those passions which blur human vision, and hamper perception of reality in its true perspective. Outward appearances are often deceptive and in order to do justice men are advised to comprehend things as they really are Al-Ghazzali sums up his views on this subject as follows :

> "To sum up (the ruler) must act justly towards his subjects and (at the same time) keep his staff, household, and sons on the path of justice. Nobody, however, can do this unless he first observes justice inside himself. Now justice consists of restraining tyrannous instincts, passions and anger in order to make them the prisoners of reason and religion, and not letting reason become the prisoner of tyrannous instincts, passions and anger .... reason is the army of God on High, and that passion and anger are the army of the Devil. How can a man who keeps God's army captive in the hands of the Devil's army act justly towards others .... you should understand and be assured of this, O Sultan, that justice springs from perfection of the intellect and that perfection of the intellect means that you see things as they really are and perceive the facts of their inner reality without being deceived by their outward appearance."

After justice Al-Ghazzali expects men of authority to be humble in disposition. He is conscious of the fact that authority has the tendency to become a narcotic of human mind. It makes people proud and arrogant and pride and arrogance impel holders of authority to become angry and revengeful very fast. These undesirable characteristics deprive human personality of that eternal lustre that stems out of humility and modesty. Anger which in his opinion is a manifestation of pride is a "blight of the intellect". As an antidote to the natural inclination of pride among men of authority, Al-Ghazzali advocates forgiveness, generosity and forbearance. These qualities in his opinion distinguish men from beasts. In this connection he makes a reference to the tradition of the Holy Prophet in which he mentioned three things for the perfection of faith. They are : "not to form a wrong intention when angered, not to set aside what is right when pleased, and not to take more than what is right when powerful." In order to further support his contention he mentions another saying of God's Apostle in which forbearance and forgiveness have been considered as good as fasting and prayer for the purity of human mind and soul.

Significant Principles

Redress of the grievances of the masses is another principle of governmental ethics, which has been emphasized by Al-Ghazzali in a great deal. He insists that if a ruler disregards public petitions; he is treading a dangerous path which can pose immeasureable hazards. He brackets redress of people's complaints with religious duties. For a healthy polity a ruler must have a network of effective espionage by which he can uncover people's reactions to governmental policies. Accessibility of officials to complainants has always been considered one of the fundamental principles of administrative ethics in Islam. Practically all writers on the subject have accorded this quality a high place in the professional and moral equipment of public officials, Al-Ghazzali says:

> "The Arabs (have a saying); that nothing is more damaging to the subjects and more prejudicial and sinister for the king than royal inacessibility and seclusion; and that nothing impresses the hearts of the subjects and officials more, than ease of access to the king. For when the subjects know that the king is easily approachable it will be impossible for the officials to oppress one another. Through making himself readily accessible, the king will acquire information about all the affairs of which he must

> never be heedless of the prestige of the monarchy is to be maintained and if he himself is to reign undisturbed."

Oppressive rule of inaccessible officials destroys peace and prosperity and ultimately political fabric is torn into shreds.

In Islam religion and politics are inseparably integrated. It is essential for a political authority to safeguard interests of religion from internal and external attacks, and watch the conduct of the subjects so that sanctity of religion is not tainted by eccentric distortions and heretical practices. As has been noticed earlier Al-Ghazzali lived at a time when Muslim lands were plagued with religious dissensions and established Suunite doctrine was being virulently questioned by many new sects in Islam. Therefore safety of religion was a matter of deep concern for Al-Ghazzali. In Nasihat-ul-Muluk he repeatedly emphasizes that kings must take special care to eradicate heresies from their jurisdictions. A ruler under all circumstances, in his opinion, should abide strictly to laws of *sharia,* and his image among masses should be that of a devout and conscientious adherent of religion. He must adopt stern measures against those, who deviate from the established order, because this is the only way by which he can acquire reputation as a defender of the faith. He says :

> "The quality which kings most need is correct religion because monarchy and religion are like brothers. (The king) needs it equally whether he be healthy or sick. He must be diligent in matters of religion, performing the duties at the proper times avoiding eccentricity and heretical innovation and shunning unjust and immoral actions. If he hears that any person in his territory is suspect as regards religion, he must summon him and interrogate him until he repents or else punish him or exile him from the territory; in this way the kingdom will be purged of eccentrics and heretical innovators, and Islam will be strong. He must keep the border lands populated by sending garrisons, strive to increase the power of Islam, and keep the Prophets Sunnah fresh and vigorous."

Evil Traits

All human beings have certain evil traits like envy, ambition, spite, cupidity, and love of pleasure and it is one of the primary duties of a ruler to adopt such effective measures by which these vices can be contained. This is a vital service which can be done by men presiding over socially organized entities for the cause of human welfare. A weak authority can as much be a cause of ruin as tyrannous authority, and a competent ruler always avoids both extremes from his actions. Piety, equity, and awareness of the interests of the people are advocated as essential characteristics of those who administer human affairs. Since rulers don't have divine vision, they are advised to exercise special vigilence over behaviour of their administrators. This would minimize chances of corruption and other baneful practices commonly associated with administration. Umar I, the Second Caliph after the Holy Prophet, in one of his sermons said :

> "O People! In the time of the Prophet the divine inspiration used to come down, and through that inspiration he used to know men's outward acts and inward thoughts, both good and bad. Now the inspiration has ceased and we view every person by his public behaviour; but God the Strong and Glorious is well aware of men's secret motives. I try to ensure that neither I nor my assistants and revenue officers ever take anything from the people (wrongfully) nor ever give (anything to anybody wrongfully)."

Al-Ghazzali is convinced that corruption, nepotism, and favouritism result from negligence, irrational mildness and constant slackness of rulers. If a ruler personally supervises administration and anxiously looks into affairs relating to the welfare of his people the impact of these vices could be reduced considerably. If the king is upright, his subjects and officials will be upright, but if he is dishonest, negligent and comfort-seeking, people living under his jurisdiction and officers implementing his policies will soon become slothful and corrupt.

Al-Ghazzali has devoted a separate chapter on magnanimity which in his opinion is a sterling quality for rulers and administrators. Magnanimity is an antithesis of low-mindedness. He defines the term as "self-restraint and courage and self-respect and self-knowledge, but the numerous anecdotes that follow these definitions, show that the term is used to connote large-heartedness and generosity. Particularly if a person is blessed with munificence, he should not hesitate to provide financial and material succour to others. He quotes the saying of Umar ibn al Khattab who said, "Take good care not to be mean-minded, for I have seen nothing more degrading in men than low-mindedness." Reference is also made to aphormism of a sage who said, "The essence of greatness is taking pains and the essence of error is haste ; the essence of depravity is miserliness". Another sage said, "If men open their hands to give generously their faces will shine luminously".

Divine Gift

According to Al-Ghazzali, political authority as embodied in kings and governors is a divine gift and a trust. Application of this gift for the general good requires cultivation of certain graces such as intelligence, knowledge, sharpness of mind, ability to perceive things, perfect physique, literary taste, horsemanship application to work and courage, together with boldness, deliberation, good temper, impartiality towards the weak and the strong, friendliness, magnanimity, maintaining toleration and moderation, judgement and, foresight in business, frequent reading of the reports of early Muslims, and constant attention to the biographies of the kings, and inquiry concerning the activities of the kings of old, because the present world is the continuation of the empire of the forerunners. He further refers to the letter which Yuman the Dastur wrote to Anushirvan in which he advised the king to promulgate justice, use intelligence, exercise patience, and practice modesty and to abstain from envy, arrogance, narrow-mindedness, and malice. At another place he mentions Sufyan (al-) Thawri who said that permanent happiness of men depends on intelligence and knowledge and cultivation of such excellences as "chastity, courtesy, absteniousness, honesty, truthfulness, modesty, compassion, kind-heartedness, fidelity, patience, tact and equanimity."

Divine Politics

Akhlaq-i-Nasiri : *Akhlaq-i-Nasiri.* Its author Nasir-uddin-Tusi (1201-1276 A.D.) was born ninety years after the death of Al-Ghazzali. He was attached to the court of Assasins Chief Ala-al-Din (1220-1255) at Alamut. Like the rest of the writers who preceded him, Tusi was convinced that salvation of mankind lies in establishing a political system which is divine in origin. He calls it Siyasat-i-Rabbani, (Divine Politics). He elaborated his views on this point as follows :

> "There is no state more ruinous than that which means the abandonment of the divine administration (siyasat-i-rabbani) and the wasting of his favours. That is the very essence of unrighteousness, for it is ingratitude for his benefits and a denial of which is the equivalent of unbelief. For the true content of oppression is the placing of things at wrong places. Thus the manager becomes the managed, the King becomes the subject and the lord becomes the slave."

Al-Tusi lists absent-mindedness, rashness, cupidity, and oppression as the bane of human conduct. In his opinion human soul is motivated in all actions by three faculties, i.e., reason, appetite, and temper. Reason distinguishes between good and evil, appetite helps acquisition of goods and physical pleasures and temper helps man to defend himself against injury. Man in his opinion can be reasonable, but he has also the tendency to succumb to a very low level of irrationality also. In order to attain high level of perfection, it is essential to curb appetite and discipline one's temper. Al-Tusi believes that men have many things in common with animals, and morality is meant to minimize the role of animality in human affairs. Lust and unbridled aspirations to satisfy bodily desires reduce man to the level of a beast. They hinder healthy development of human personality and as such it is essential to safeguard oneself against such a degradation. He says :

> "It may be said in regard to what man has in common with animals and other forms of life, that if his animal nature prevails over him and his inclination is in that direction, he will be degraded from his proper rank

> to that of the order of beasts or even lower. For the Quran says "They are like the brutes. Yea, they go more astray." (VII : 178). He reaches the place, for example, where he longs to gain the pleasures and the desires of the body, those for which the bodily sense and powers are eager and have a craving—such as things to eat, things to drink, things to wear, and marriages. The result is that the power of beast soon gets the upper hand. Or his development is similarly curtailed if he takes to violence and assault and vengeance, which are the fruits of anger having sway."

Sole Objective

Al-Tusi, following other moral philosophers in Islam insists that the sole objective of human existence is the perfection of man's soul. *Nafs-i-natiqa* (soul) in his opinion has two powers—the power of knowledge and the power of action. Knowledge entails comprehension of the known world and mastery of arts and sciences relating to it. Action relates to human capacity to harmonize— variegated powers of self in a manner that they do not try to dominate each other. Everything good or bad has been entrusted to the custody of man. Preferences are all his own, and if he is careful and vigilant he can control evil propensities, and through his watchfulness he can direct them for personal and social goodness. If his control is casual or relaxed, or his powers deficient, he will be left destitute of moral purpose in life. He has illustrated his point as follows :

> "Others said that the situation of mankind with reference to these selves is more like that of a man mounted on a powerful horse, when with a dog he goes out to hunt. If the authority is with the man he will employ his riding animal and his hunting animal with discretion. He will be attentive to what is necessary for the well-being of all of them in time of danger, and he will make arrangements for what food is needed for them all in just measure. Thus as companions in eating and drinking and in other matters of subsistence, they will be maintained

according to the needs of their respective natures. But if the riding beast has his own way and does not recognize the authority of the rider, then he will start to run wherever he sees the best grass. In roughness of gait, in straying from the road, and in making speed at the wrong place, he will give great annoyance to himself and his companions . . . Also if the hunting animal has its own way, at the time when it sees the prey it will lead the riding animal and its rider in that direction as fast as it can, with resultant hardship and fear of destruction, as has been mentioned. It is even probable that in the course of the encounter, when fighting with the animal that is hunted, it will itself be wounded and worn out that it will perish. But if the two beasts are subject to the rider who knows what is best and who has the right to command, they will be saved from these misfortunes and accidents."

Al-Tusi warns against excesses. In his opinion any deviation from accepted standard can unhinge a situation. Overdoing is one way of excess and neglecting the other. Men, in order to live a healthy, moral existence must avoid both. Virtue is moderation, while evil resides on both extremes. Wisdom, bravery, purity and righteousness are midway virtues in his opinion, and their extremes on both sides he has analyzed as follows :

"To be absent-minded is on the side of excess, for it is the employing of powers of thought on what is not necessary, or to a greater extent than is fitting. Some call this self-deception or being like a large over-ripe cucumber. To be ignorant or stupid is to err on the side of carelessness or neglect, in voluntarily failing to make use of the power of thought, not because of any physical limitation."

"Rashness, which is from excess, is always ready to start something which it is not seemly to start, whereas cowardice, which is on the side of insufficiency, is avoiding things which it is not commendable to avoid."

"Cupidity, which is on the side of excess, is greed for pleasures beyond measures that is proper, whereas the abating of passion which is on the side of deficiency, is lack of initiative in seeking necessary pleasures, or such as reason and law permit—when this indifference is voluntary and is not due to physical limitation."

"Oppression, which is on the side of excess, is the acquirement of the means of living by methods that are reprehensible, whereas living oppressed, which is on the side of deficiency, consists in affording opportunity to anyone who is seeking the means of living by methods of violence and plunder, i.e., in submitting to their being taken without justification and merely because they are themselves object."

Reputed Treatise

Al Fakhri : The author of the book Muhammad Ali son of Tabataba (Rapid Talker) wrote this book in 1302 A.D. in honour of Prince Fakhr-ad-din Isa son of Ibrahim. The treatise enjoyed wide reputation for authenticity and scholarship among the later Muslim scholars. It was first translated into French in 1910 and later the Arabic text was published in 1921. The English translation of the work was done by C.E.J. Whitting in 1947.

The author in his introduction has given reasons for the compilation of this book. His main purpose was to provide a compendium of knowledge for kings and rulers because their ignorance, lack of historical perspectives and indifference to the interest of the subjects, in his opinion, constituted one of the fundamental causes of the ruin of kingdoms. The ministers, he points out, always felt happy under a prince who was not knowledgeable, because that would facilitate their monopoly of power in the state. A monarch with knowledge and will of his own was always considered a threat to the prerogatives of a minister. The immediate cause for writing this treatise was the desire on the part of the author to furnish a manual of statecraft to his patron from whom he received kindness and hospitality.

Special Characteristics

The book has been divided into two parts. In the first part he has listed certain special characteristics which form an indisputable, moral and intellectual equipment of a ruler and establish his superiority over his subjects. The second part gives a chronological account of dynasties which ruled the Muslim empire during different periods of history. It is the first part of the book which is relevant for our purpose because in it the author has elucidated his ideals about the ethical foundations of a Muslim polity. The narrative, like other books on the same subject, is embellished with verses from the Quran. Traditions of the Holy Prophet, anecdotes from the lives of rulers, who were just and generous in their attitudes towards the subject. The author has abstained from theoretical discussions regarding the origin of power, and the nature of religious and temporal authority in Islam. He says, "it (book) has been composed only to deal with systems of government and conventions useful in current affairs and in conflicts which occur, in the rule of subjects, safety of the realm and improvement of manners and conduct."

First Set of Qualities

Knowledge, intelligence and justice are the first set of qualities which according to Al Fakhri, can help a ruler or administrator to escape from errors of judgment. To be governed by an ignorant ruler in his opinion is the worst tragedy that could happen in a society. Knowledge that he envisions for just and efficient and kind-hearted rulers is not a specialized knowledge of arts and sciences. What he expects of them is a general familiarity with different areas of learning, so that they can coordinate matters of public policy with insight. Specialization in his opinion leads to obscurity of thought and narrowness of mind, both of which are detrimental to efficiency and comprehension. They must have enough understanding so that they can enter into dialogue with experts. A ruler or administrator must have breadth of vision and sufficient understanding so that his subordinates will not be able to deceive him. Knowledge, however, in his view is culture-bound, because polities derive their strength or weakness from the socio-religious and philosophical climate in which they are nurtured. Knowledge imbibed by men in authority will also differ according to their personal proclivities, but the author of Al Fakhri believes that over a period of time each social system develops its own ethos and ethical principles which are always deemed to be essential for intelligent and effective administration of the realm. He says :

> "The studies of the rulers of Persia were laws, moral precepts, literature, history, geometry and the like. The studies of the rulers of Islam were philology, grammar, lexicography, poetry and history, so much so that an error in speech was one of the most objectionable faults in the royal dignity, and man's rank might be advanced with them by a single anecdote, a single verse of poetry nay a single idiomatic word. As for Mongols, all these studies were rejected and other studies were popular with them—economics, accountancy, for balancing the budget and the estimates of revenue and expenditure, medicines, and astrology to choose occasions."

Fear of God

Like other Muslim thinkers Al Fakhri advocates that fear of God is the foundation-rock for a stable moral character and most of the sterling qualities of human behaviour, and other ethical excellences stem from it. He believes that rulers tend to be irate and full of hatred. But in his opinion these are ignoble qualities which lead to moral degeneration. A ruler should show love and concern for his subjects rather than pity. If a ruler or administrator has nothing but pity for his people, the society will be full of disenchantment and bitterness. In a population which is alienated a ruler will, never be able to get proper affection and cooperation. He says :

> How can a ruler attain his desire in major affairs of state, and achieve his intended objects, save through the willing cooperation of his subjects? What wisdom is there in that ? Is there aught in it some embitterment of the ruler's life, the excerbating of his subjects against him and the estrangement of them from him ?

Feelings of Conciliation

Bonds of the rulers and the subjects have to be cemented by feelings of conciliation. These feelings in his opinion, are cultivated only through clemency and forgiving attitude of the administrators. Generosity of mind, spaciousness of thought are qualities which are of invaluable significance in winning the hearts of people. Al Fakhri has enumerated ten basic qualities which could insure peace, order, and prosperity of the kingdom. They are, (1) to spare bloodshed, (2) to guard property, (3) to protect morals, (4) to prevent disasters, (5) to restrain evil-doers and troublemakers, (6) to check the extortion which follows from civil war and unrest, (7) to study the affairs of the subjects in depth and detail, (8) to reward good and punish evil, (9) to exercise constant vigilence and (10) to manifest unending care. These prerequisites are vital determinants of legitimacy in a political system. A ruler who entirely relies on his independent judgment, will miss the depth of understanding and richness of information and alternatives which are produced by-consultation. The author mentions that if the Prophet used to consult his companions so often in handling the affairs of the community, he sees no reasons why the rest of the Muslim rulers should claim immunity from it. On the question of consultation enjoined upon the Prophet by God, Al Fakhri has summed up the views of the various schools of thought in Islam as follows:

> The theologians disagree as to whether God, Most High, commanded his messenger to seek advice despite the help and advice given to him by Him. On that there are four views. First, that he was ordered to consult the companions to win their loyalty and secure their willing cooperation. Secondly, that he was ordered to consult them in war, so that the correct view might be confirmed for him, and he act accordingly. Thirdly, that he was ordered to consult them because of the useful and advantageous (counsel) they possessed. Fourthly, that he was only ordered to consult them in order that people might copy him and this I hold, is the best view and the most correct.

Thus, according to Al Fakhri, consultation in decision-making creates confidence, disarms resistance, and once the people are convinced of the integrity of the ruler they develop the natural tendency to emulate him.

Impetuousity, and ennui are very unbecoming characteristics in a ruler. They bring nothing but humiliation. It is one of the supreme ethical responsibilities of the ruler to protect people from oppression and strengthen the hands of the weak so that he can fight battles of life with success. "Among the duties of a ruler to his subjects is restraining the stronger from (oppressing) the weaker, giving the lowly justice against the powerful, establishing the rule of law among them, maintaining their rights as they should be maintained, helping the dejected, answering any of them who cries for aid, and holding the scales of justice equal between the most distant of them and the nearest, the lowliest and the mightiest."

It is indisputable that the ethical standards of the government to a large extent depend on the moral values of the administrators who run the affairs of the state. As such recruitment should not be left to chance. It must be based on sound judgement. Al Fakhri mentions the practice of a ruler who used to publicize the name of a person who was a potential candidate for a position of responsibility. In this way he used to feel the pulse of popular reaction to the future appointee. In the light of information thus collected he used to finalize his decision. He had informers who used to mix with the common people in disguise and collect information on such matters.

Firmness and strength of character are qualities which are always applauded in the art of governing men. Firmness, however, has to be based on reason and compassion. Indiscriminate persecution or highhandedness would never be considered as signs of firmness. Such excesses should be distasteful to a ruler, unless they are necessitated by some unavoidable emergency. Obsessive firmness is symptomatic of arrogance which creates a climate of frustration in society. Pride in ones ancestory does not help in politics. One should feel proud of one's own attainments in civility, culture and knowledge.

Faulty View

People tend to take a simple but faulty view of administration. They categorize administration into five kinds: of the home, the village, the city, the army, and the state. They believe that "he who administers his home well, will administer his village well, he who administers his village well, will administer his city well, he who administers his city well, will administer an army well, and he who administers an army well, will administer a state well." Al Fakhri believes this oversimplified analysis deceptive because many whose domestic affairs are well administered are poor administrators of the affairs of the state, and those whose administration of public affairs is superb are weak and inefficient in administering domestic affairs. The role of sword and pen has been a subject of deep controversy among Muslim scholars on politics and administration. Sword symbolizes military establishment and coercive power of the state, while pen stands for civilian machinery which is created to administer affairs of kingdom in peace time. Al Fakhri has summed up this controversy as follows :

> The realm is guarded by the sword and administered with the pen. People disagree about the sword and the pen, as to which of the two is superior, and takes precedence. Some think that the pen has it over the sword, and urge in support of their view that the sword guards the pen, and so stands to it as a guardian and servant. Others think the sword superior, and urge that the pen serves the sword because it provides the soldiers with their pay, and so it is a servant to it. Others say that they are equal and that neither of them can function without the other. They say a realm is fertilized by generosity, populated by justice, secured by common sense, protected by courage, and administered by leadership.

The author of Al Fakhri is fully aware of the critical nature of power in politics. He thinks it is a delicate instrument which has to be wielded with care and utmost anxiety. He says that "the practice of power is more difficult than (to obtain) power itself." Power has to be exercised with patience and fortitude. If power passes into the hands of an impatient person, there is every possibility of its being abused and misused. A seeker of power must also have the ability to discriminate and should also be endowed with talent and insight to make sound judgement. It would be better if he is aware of the vicissitudes of life, and the ebb and flow of human fortunes during different eras of history. Power without tact and grace is a crude weapon which can be extremely dangerous for civilization. A person holding power must be able to cajole his enemy with tact and hide his secret with grace. Power corrupts where an individual becomes over-confident, and refuses to seek advise from others. One's own commonsense alone cannot resolve complexities of politics and administration. It requires constant reinforcement from the genius of others, in the form of consultation.

The most competent ruler according to Al Fakhri is one "whose work rules his play, and whose judgement overrides his desire, whose deeds express his intentions, whose will does not counter his luck, nor anger his cunning." One of the qualities of a competent ruler is, his ability for self-examination. It is a common fraility among rulers that they always try to camouflage their failures. A ruler with a high ethical standard would readily subject himself to public scrutiny and speedily accept his failures and deficiencies. Self-assessment and self-realization are characteristics which clarify vision. A ruler ought to be a personification of affability, his kindness proverbial and manners exemplary. If the attitude and habits of the governors and the governed synchronize, systems tend to be stable and prosperous. People cannot blame the acts of rulers if their own life and character are imbued with the same spirit. It is also essential for administrative efficiency that the decision-maker be in a position to anticipate dangers. An administrator who lacks these qualities is patently incompetent.

Another matter which requires special consideration of rulers is the verification of information received from government informants. It is a matter of common knowledge that kingdoms have suffered grievous wrongs at the hands of corrupt and selfish spies. Rulers have committed egregious blunders in relying for their judgements on wrong information.

For you have to judge that which appears (in the open) while God judges the hidden. Dislike on behalf of your subjects, what you dislike for yourself. Conceal the shame of others and God will conceal for you that which you wish concealed. Be not in a hurry to believe the informer, for he is dishonest even though he may give good advice.

Since there were long periods of anarchy in Islamic history Muslim political thinkers had always deep concerned about peace and stability. Many of them concluded that only a strong and powerful ruler could provide security of life and property to his people. They unhesitatingly acknowledged that even if the ruler was unjust, his rule should be preferred to one who was just but weak. The latter in their opinion was unable to protect the fundamental rights of his subjects because his weakness made him susceptible to exploitations by self-seeking nobles and other vested interests in the realm. People were victimized by overambitious and unscrupulous fortune-hunters, and instead of suffering the despotic rule of one they would be subjected to many despots. Al Fakhri has made the following remarks on this controversy:

> They have disagreed as to the unjust ruler and the weak just ruler. They (mostly) prefer the strong unjust, arguing that the unjust powerful (ruler) guards his subjects against "vested interests" (and protects them by his power) from others than himself. His pride preserves them from being damaged by others than himself. So his subjects are in the position of who one is spared damage by all men but suffer damage by one. The weak just (ruler) neglects (the interest of) his subjects, and everyone has authority over them, and every hoof tramples them, so that they are in the position of one who is spared damage by one and suffers damage by all.

Compendium of History, Philosophy and Sociology

Muqaddima : Ibn Khaldun, the author of the *Muqaddima,* ranks among the greatest historians of the world. The book is basically on the philosophy of history, and has never been included in the literature on political or administrative ethics. It is a compendium of history, philosophy and sociology, and unquestionably the greatest work of Muslim scholarship which has won universal recognition for depth, comprehension, and creative insight into all organized affairs of men. Ibn Khaldun dealt at length on all theoretical and practical aspects of government and administration, and in doing so he has not failed to uncover ethical dimensions of the art of governing men. He emphasized that human life is a playground of good and evil, and evil propensities in organized moral communities are manifested, in the form of aggression and injustice. Governmental authority, in his opinion, is the only force which can save social systems from evil consequences of injustice and aggression. He says :

> Mutual aggression of people in towns and cities is averted by the authorities and the government, which hold back the masses under their control from attacks and aggression upon each other. They are thus prevented by the influence of force and governmental authority from mutual injustice, save much injustice as comes from the ruler himself.

Ibn Khaldun is perceptive enough to know that governmental authority equipped with the coercive power of the state is necessary to ward off dangers of subversion from within and destruction from outside. But at the same time he is fully aware that all bureaucratic structures have a built-in tendency to abuse this authority. It is not uncommon for guardians of justice and equity to commit brazen acts of injustice and inequity. How to guard against the guardians is a prominent theme of Ibn Khaldun's great work, and it is in this connection that he has unrolled the discussion on administrative ethics. His feelings are that although evil is ingrained in human nature, but still more often than not, men prefer doing good than pursuing actions which are morally reprehensible. Politics and public morality in his opinion should be inseparable from the affairs of organized communities. He says :

> "The existence of (royal authority without the simultaneous existence of) the perfecting details would be like the existence of a person with his limbs cut off, or it would be like appearing naked before people."

The Perfection

The emphasis all along in his great work is on perfection of Islamic principles of ethics. Prudence, wisdom, kindness, justice, fortitude, and honesty are repeatedly mentioned as glories of human conduct which give continuity and stability to moral communities. They ensure peace and order in kingdoms and give moral legitimacy to governmental authority. He says that 'politics is concerned with the administration of home or city in accordance with ethical and philosophical requirements, for the purpose of directing the masses toward a behaviour that will result in the preservation and permanence of the human species.' He insists that lawgivers must live up to the spirit of the religious laws because they are good for both here and hereafter, and they are free from foibles and frailities so commonly associated, with man-made laws. To articulate his views still further Ibn Khaldun has reproduced a long letter written by an Abbaside general Tahir ibn-al Hussayan to his son Abdallah b. Tahir when the latter was appointed governor of ar-Raqqah Egypt by Al-Mamun. He speaks admiringly of the contents of this letter and mentions that Al-Mamun was so impressed by the depth and wisdom of the subject matter that he ordered that the letter be circulated among all officials stationed in various regions of the empire. Tahir starts this letter with usual exhortations of a devout Muslim, impressing upon his son the need to cultivate the fear of God and never to be forgetful of the fact that ultimately he would be accountable to Him for all his deeds and misdeeds, and one who holds authority over people, shoulders a grave responsibility. One of the primary duties of a God-fearing administrator is to preserve law and order, avoid brutality, protect the life and property of his subjects and to see that God's laws are not violated. It is also incumbent upon rulers of men not to allow their prejudices to interfere in the administration, and that they should set an example of moral rectitude so that people can repose confidence in their leadership. He says :

> "Do not be swayed from Justice according to your likes and dislikes, either on behalf of a person close to you or on behalf of one remote to you—In addition when people notice your (religious attitude) they will have respect for your rule and reverence for your government."

Those who are charged with the authority to govern men, have primary responsibility to exercise constant vigilance over the behaviour of their subordinates. A negligence in this direction has been the cause of ruin for many a ruler. It is a universal phenomenon that delegated authority, which is not investigated and supervised constantly, has a tendency to exploit people, and once a situation like that arises, kingdoms tumble very fast towards decadence. Tahir is unequivocal in his statement that this is the most important task of one who has been entrusted with the sole responsibility of governing and guiding the masses. This is the only way to preserve the spirit of the religion in the life and character of a polity. At the same time it is essential that the wrong-doers should not go without punishment which should be according to principles ordained by God. Rank and status of culprits should not interfere in the dispensation of justice. Even postponement of punishment can have an impairing effect on public opinion. Justice deferred is no justice. Anger, deceit and levity are some of the evils which administrators must avoid in their actions. Tahir makes significant remarks about arrogance which is common vice among those whose authority is unchecked. An authority which has no ethical base is unislamic. Authority according to Islam is only a means to an end and not an end in itself. The ultimate authority belongs to God. Human beings hold it only as a trust. This accountability to the ultimate source is a recognized principle of Quranic law. He says:

> Beware of saying: "I am in authority. I may do what I want to do. This soon reveals a lack of sense on your part and little certainty of the one and only God. Let your intention with regard to (God) and your certainty of Him be sincere. You should know that royal authority belongs to God. He gives it to whomever he wants to give, and takes it away from whomever he wants to take it away."

Divine Retribution

According to Tahir, men occupying high positions in government are subject to divine retribution more than anybody else, because their actions can make or mar the fortunes of millions living in their jurisdiction. They probably don't know that by not using authority in a righteous manner they are being guilty of stark ingratitude to God who confers power as a special privilege on a selected few. The only way one can repay this gratitude is by dispensing justice and working ceaselessly for the welfare of the subjects and curbing greed and lust which inhibit ethical performance. He administers a special note of warning against extravagance and ostentatious living of state functionaries. Avarice and insincerity of officers, always have a disenchanting effect on social life in a community. Generosity, he preaches, is a balmy quality and its constant practice ensures trust and confidence in administration. Tahir has depicted the relationship between the ruler and his subjects in the following words:

> "You should know that by your appointment, you were made treasurer, guardian and shepherd. The people under your jurisdiction are called subjects (raiyah flock) because you are their shepherd and overseer. Therefore accept from them what they give you of their affluence, and use it for the administration of their affairs, for their welfare and for providing for their needs. Employ for them understanding skilled and experienced men, who have theoretical knowledge of, and are able to act with, political wisdom and moderation. Give them good salaries. This is one of the duties incumbent upon you in connection with the task from which you have been entrusted."

The above remarks show that the writer was fully aware of the significant role which the selection of personnel plays in creating a healthy administrative climate. Understanding, experience, knowledge, political wisdom and moderation are some of the salient qualities, which he thinks are essential for good administrators. On the other hand it is the responsibility of the government to see that salary structure is rational so that administrators can have adequate income to maintain a certain respectable standard of living. Financially dissatisfied public service can play havoc with the fortunes of the people. Adequate salary is not an absolute safeguard against corruption or dishonesty, but it can certainly reduce its intensity considerably. Tahir also advocates effective intelligence service as another safeguard against excesses of officials. This would keep the government well-informed about the behaviour, style of life and other activities of officers working in the field.

Another theme which Tahir has developed at length is the accessibility of the ruler to his subjects, particularly the poor ones who don't have the means to find ready access to the regular law courts. If these simmering grievances of the people are not corrected, they can ruin the stability of the kingdom. He says :

> Devote yourself to looking after the affairs of the poor and indigent, those who are not able to bring before you complaints about injustices they have suffered, and other lowly persons, who do not know that they may ask for their rights. Inquire about these people in all secrecy, and put good men among your subjects in charge of them. Command them to report to you their needs and conditions, so that you will be able to look into the measures through which God might improve their affairs.

Even if officials are legally accessible to the public, many of them have the tendency to adopt such measures which would discourage a visitor from visiting public offices. Either there are restrictions on the number of interviews one can have with an official or there are so many barriers of security and secrecy, that petitioners have neither the courage nor the means to surmount them. In order to make accessibility meaningful Tahir suggests that, 'let people frequently come to see you and show them your face. Let not your guards hinder them. Be humble towards them. Show them your smiling countenance. 'Be lenient with them when (you put) questions and speak to them, Be benevolent to them in your generosity and bounty.' And lastly it is the duty of the government to keep a constant watch on the accumulation of wealth and property by state officers and no effort should be spared in exercising vigilance on their faithfulness, straightforwardness and support for the government. Very often, it also happens that one has an access to an officer, but the latter's attitude would be so scowling and arrogant,' that the complainant would never be able to unburden all his grievances. It is unbecoming of an officer to give an interview to an aggrieved person, and then to give such a shabby treatment, that he may not turn up again with any complaint.

Perfect Diplomacy

Akhlak-i-Jalali : Muhammad ibn Asad Jalal-al-Din-al-Bawwani (1627-1501 A. D.) the author of this book was attached to the court of Turkoman ruler Uzun Hassan, who at the meridian of his power, had diplomatic relations with Venice and Constantinople, in the West, and Samarqand and Herat in the East. The period of his rule was crowded with political turmoil and administrative anarchy. The character of the people had been adversely affected by lawlessness, and the ethical standards of the rulers and administrators were painfully low. The main purpose of the writer was to find causes of the prevelant stresses and tensions which had so completely polluted the moral climate in administration, Muhammad ibn Asad was a prolific writer and he wrote on variety of philosophical and mystical subjects in Arabic, but his most famous work is *Lawamie ai-Ishraq fi Makarim-al-Akhlaq* popularly known as Akhlaq-i-Jalali. The book has been frequently printed and widely read in Iran and Indo-Pakistan sub-continent. In 1839 it was translated in English by W. F. Thompson under the title *Practical Philosophy of the Muhammadan People.*

The author has made extensive use of the ethical writings of the Greek philosophers and Muslim scholars who preceeded him, but every discussion carries a deep stamp of his own genius. His analysis of human nature and character is unquestionably very rich and profound, and constitute a meaningful manifesto to guide men in sorting out issues which are morally right. He believes that man is a vice-regent of God on earth and emulation of divine attributes is his ultimate destiny. This is a difficult assignment and he points out that to fulfil the obligations of vice-regency "two things are necessary, (i) mature wisdom which means perfection in knowledge, (ii) and eminent ability which connotes perfection in practice." Muhammad ibn Asad had a firm conviction that knowledge is meant to serve mankind and unless it is put into practice, human affairs will never be smooth and harmonious. He said, "Knowledge without practice is a burden, and practice without knowledge is a mischief."

He has drawn a very comprehensive list of virtues which in his opinion make life socially and morally worth living. These characteristics lend luster, dignity and richness to human behavior and assist human organizations in the realization of their objectives. He has made four broad categories of virtues and labelled them as Wisdom, Courage, Temperance, and Equity, and then under each category he lists certain qualities which ensure the growth of a morally healthy personality.

***Wisdom* :** It means penetration, quickness of intellect, clearness of understanding, facility of acquirement, propriety of discrimination retention, recollection.

***Courage* :** It means magnanimity, collectedness, elevation of purpose, firmness, coolness, stateliness, boldness, endurance, condescension, zeal and mercy.

***Temperance Shame* :** (The author calls it soul's restraint upon itself when aware of intending to commit anything odious, that it may guard against deserving censure. One of the Prophets saying is this, *Shame,* is a compendium of every virtue). Good humour, righteousness, easiness, patience, content, steadiness, piety, regularity, integrity, and liberality.

***Equity* :** It consist of fidelity, union, exactitude, tenderness, brotherhood, gratitude, good fellowship, good faith, cordiality, submission, resignation and devotion.

The above virtues are not merely abstract ethical principles in the opinion of the author. They are meant to be operational instruments for conducting human affairs. For government and administration, Muhammad ibn Asad has added a few other moral responsibilities also. He points out that a free and frequent interaction between governors and governed is essential for justice and cooperation. Any government where people don't have access to rulers is a bureaucratic tyranny. The author of Akhlak-i-Jalali has expressed his opinion on this aspect as follows:

> For this reason intercourse with our fellow creatures in the way of cooperation is incumbent on us all, or else we deviate from the first principle of justice and fall into the path of inequity, like that class of persons who betake themselves to a savage retirement from mankind, and remain altogether aloof from cooperation with their fellow men, loading them however, with the burden of their support and then

> they call seclusion and consider meritorious in fact it is altogether a state of inequity.

The above statement testifies to the fact that Muhammad ibn Asad feels that meeting people and cooperating with them is an essential characteristic of a good government. In fact this is a quality which can infuse trust, confidence and cooperation in all areas of human relations. He has further clarified the distinction between the righteous and the unrighteous government by saying:

> "He who conducts the righteous government in his rigid adherence to the role of equity, considers his subjects as his children and his friends, placing all covetousness and love of money under the control of judgment. He that conducts the unrighteous government adheres to the principles of force, treats his subjects like beasts of burden, considers them as slaves, and is himself the slave of avarice and passion."

Like other Muslim writers on administrative ethics, Muhammad ibn Asad emphasized in unqualified terms that virtue and rectitude among rulers always have a widespread impact on the subjects. It is a natural tendency among people to emulate their governors. If a ruler is good, his goodness would be a source of inspiration, but if he is bad, the people unhesitatingly follow the same course. It is therefore vital for the moral uplift of society that administrators should set an example of honesty, justice and integrity. This will give dignity, poise, and solidity to the character of the masses. In Akhlak-i-Jalali this problem of the image of the ruler or administrator has been explained as follows:

> "We are told in holy writ, 'Men resemble their contemporaries even more than their progenitors', and 'Men are of the same religion as their princes.' Hence when the age's guidance is in the hands of a just king everyone directs his course towards equity and the attainment of virtue, on the contrary, the people likewise incline to falsehood, covetousness, and vice of every description."

The qualities which would endear the rulers to the subjects are, seriousness of purpose, rational decision, resolution, endurance, hardwork and incorruptibility. Moreover, authorities in a kingdom are expected to be anxiously concerned about three fundamental principles for the welfare of the state: (i) Financial stability, (ii) kindness and compassion to the people, (iii) and ability to keep away petty-minded people from government offices. Employment in a state, according to the author, should be reserved for people who are talented by nature, and prudent in thought and action. Ibn Asad compiled a code of ten articles, which in his opinion could ensure a sound moral base for administrative behaviour:

(1) Whatever he holds impossible toward himself he should hold inadmissible towards his people.

(2) Quick justice.

(3) Abstinence from licentious and sensual gratification.

(4) Courtesy and kindness in decision-making.

(5) Faith in the supremacy of the will of God.

(6) Nothing should be done in the opposition to the Message of God.

(7) Mercy and Indulgency.

(8) Should associate with men of righteousness.

(9) Maintaining everyone in the position he deserves.

(10) Officers, soldiers and the people in this relationship should be so balanced that they could not injure each other's interest.

There are many other discussions on morals and manners in Akhlak-i-Jalali, relating to individual and social life, but they don't have such relevance to government and administration. Friendship, family, property, rearing of children, rights and privileges of wives, education of women, rights of parents, meals, etc. are some of the subjects on which the author has dilated in depth. In short, the treatise is a valuable compendium of ethical values both Islamic and pre-Islamic which the author considers, provide richness and dignity to human character. He insists that without positive moral climate, and universal ethical standards social system decay and wither away. In short, the treatise is of indisputable significance for understanding the practical moral standards of the Muslim people and Thompson is right when on the title page of his translation he calls Akhlak-i-Jalali 'the most esteemed ethical work of Middle Asia'.

According to Erwin Rosenthal, *Jaial-al-Din-al-Dawwani* made extensive use of Nasir-al-Din Tusis *Akhlaq-i-Nasiri,* and to a large extent many of his concepts and discussions were only summaries of Tusi. Al-Dawwani, however, being a theologian, jurist and scholar, has put greater emphasis on traditional Islam. His narrative is free from Greek philosophical influences which so conspicuously dominate Tusi's analysis. His examination of ethical, economic and political problems in a Muslim polity is direct, precise and lucid. A ruler who isolates himself from his fellow men is unjust in his opinion. Rulers, he suggests are 'physicians to the temperament of the world' and their main responsibility is to inculcate righteous opinions, mold convictions of the people, and fashion their disposition in a manner so that good actions could be ensured. In his opinion people are divided into five categories, "good, with good influences on others, good in themselves without influence, bad without bad influence, and finally the opposite of the first group, the bad ones who exert a bad influence." A ruler's most onerous responsibility is to maintain an equilibrium among all these kinds. That in essence is the purpose of authority in a state and following other works on governmental ethics, he insists that those in authority should have kindness, and compassion and that in selecting state functionaries, rulers should not entrust offices to mean people. Moderation, respect for people's rights, devotion to their welfare, justice and close vigilence over the working of the government and fear of God are the other qualities which give strength and stability to kingdoms. Rosenthal has summed up Al-Dawwani's contributions as follows:

> These examples show how Al-Dawwani combines philosophy both ancient and modern with Quran, Hadith and tales as found in the 'Mirrors.' In this way he gives an interesting and colourful account of political thought which is intellectually satisfying and traditionally unobjectionable.

Counselling for Ministers

Nasaih ul-vuzera vel-Umera : *[The Book of Counsel for Vezirs (Ministers) and Umera (Governors)].*

This small treatise was written by an Ottoman statesman during the later half of the seventeenth century. It's author, Baqqal-Oghlu Sari Hajji Muhammad Pasha was born in Constantinople, but biographical details of his early life are missing from available historical records. In 1671, probably as a teenager, he became an apprentice in the office of the *ruznami je-i-evvel,* an important official of the Treasury department. By hard work, devotion, and knowledge of the financial problems he ultimately became the head of this department. In 1702 Rami Muhammad Pasha, the grand vezir appointed him chief defterdar (Treasurer of the Empire). This was the pinnacle of his professional attainments, but it made the last years of his life extremely uncomfortable. Ottoman administration during this period was a web of unending intrigues, in which all the senior officials of the realm, governors of provinces, courtiers, and members of the royal sergalio were deeply involved. Every senior public servant lived in a state of chronic insecurity. This can be illustrated by the fact that Muhammad Pasha was seven times in and out of his job as a *defterdar* of the empire. His ability and experience were of no consideration to his opponents. Ultimately he fell victim to their jealousy and enmity. By orders of Sultan Ahmad III he was dismissed and imprisoned in the castle of Qavla on the Aegean coast. After sometime in February 1717 he was executed, his head was sent to Constantinople where it was hung on the gate of the Imperial palace.

Writing in Exile

It is assumed that the Book of Counsel for Vezirs and Governors was written during one of the exiles of Muhammad Pasha. The main purpose of the scholar-statesman was to give a detailed account of the political and administrative vicisitudes which had engulfed the empire at that time. Ottoman bureaucracy has always been accorded a place of eminence among the great historical bureaucracies of the world. Its spirit was autocratic, but during the earlier period of the dynasty under capable rulers who presided over an unwieldly empire, which stretched from Constantinople to Egypt and from Algeria to the borders of Persia, it worked efficiently. But this era of territorial expansion and administrative efficiency, ended with the death of Suleyman the Magnificent. After him the fortunes of the empire were in the hands of harem-reared princes who were educated in the cloistered atmosphere of the palace through eunuchs, slave-girls and pages.

War State

The Ottoman empire in essence was a war state. It was one long crusade against the infidel world. As long as the rulers were busy conquering foreign lands administration was efficient and resourceful. Bat once the territorial expansion stopped, there was rapid deterioration in the efficiency and moral standards of the administrators. Revenues which used to flow from booty, ransom, and other spoils of war disappeared, and the empire entered into a period of financial decadence from which it could not recover. While revenues decreased, the luxuries of royalty and its sprawling circles of regal parasites kept on increasing. Ease-loving Sultans, luxuriating courtiers, disgruntled armies, rebellious governors and repacious bureaucracy completely wrecked the machinery of the government. Bernard Lewis says :

> "The breakdown in the apparatus of government affected not only the supreme instruments of sovereignly, but also the whole of the bureaucratic and religious institutions all over the Empire. These suffered a catastrophic fall in efficiency and integrity which was accentuated by the growing change in methods of recruitment, training, and promotion. This deterioration is clearly discernable in the Ottoman archives, which reflected vividly and precisely the change from the meticulous, conscientious, and strikingly efficient bureaucratic government of the sixteenth century to the neglect of the seventeenth and collapse of the eighteenth centuries."

Ottoman administration which under Murad II Muhammad the Conqueror and Salim I, was a source of strength and stability under later weak rulers became an instrument of corruption and exploitation. Sale of public offices became a common feature, and one who paid the highest price would immediately start using his official position unscrupulously for personal gains, because he was not sure when another bidder would replace him. A contemporary western observer of the time remarked that "the frequent changes of the principal ministers saps silently the foundation of the empire, and gives to the government terrible wounds. Those who are elevated to office, for seeing that this will not long be held, preferring their own enrichment to the interest of empire, let it perish in order to assuge their avarice, and being able to enrich themselves only by unjust means they make use of every means." Army, which was once one of the finest fighting machines, was reduced only to a pale shadow of its former strength and character. Janissaries which had played a significant role in the creation of the empire, taking advantage of the weakness of the ruling Sultans, had monopolized all positions of power in the state. Their devotion to the ruling Sultan was only a facade for self-aggrandizement and the non-payment of salaries by the government led them to pillage the land freely and indulge in illegal extortion from the peasantry. The commanders on the frontiers kept false registers to defraud the Treasury at Constantinople. Palace intrigues, corruption, deceit, jealousy and treachery were commonly noticed in every area of politics and administration. Gibb and Bowen have summed up this phase of the Ottoman history in the following words :

> "The ruling institution had thus by the eighteenth century, undergone as complete a transformation as was compatible with the maintenance of most of its original forms. Instead of inspiring its members to earn merit by the exercise of talent and virtue, it taught them they must look to corruption for advancement, and might safely neglect duties that should have been concomitant with their privileges. Finally, instead of providing the sultans with an efficient instrument for the preservation and extension of their power, it was now scarcely strong enough to maintain their authority at home, and become an engine of feeble tyranny over those of their subjects that were unable to continue against it."

It was in this depressing climate of moral and material decadence that Muhammad Pasha wrote his "The Book of Counsel". He admired the political wisdom and high moral standards of administration of Ottoman rule during the fifteenth and sixteenth century. But he felt that in his own time the empire had reached the nadir of its ethical standards. His analysis is illustrated with verses from the Quraṇ Traditions of the Prophet and relevent passages from earlier works on the subject. The narrative is an index of author's rich and vast experience which he had accumulated as a high-ranking administrator. As defterdar (Chief Treasurer) and as member of the Imperial Divan (Central Cabinet) he had ample opportunity to observe from very close quarters, every branch of administration. Although Muhammad Pasha's main focus was on the Ottoman administration, but in diagnosing the causes of its decline he has pointed out certain basic ethical principles, which can be relevent for administrators, holding positions of power and prestige in any society. In subject matter, Nasaihul-vuzera vel-umera, resembles a great deal with Siyaset Namah and Qabus-namah, although in breadth and depth of analysis it falls short of the earlier works. The treatise is divided into the following nine chapters :

(1) Explanation regarding the behaviour and habits of the Grand Vezir.

(2) Explanation regarding the official positions and the harmfulness of bribes.

(3) Explanation regarding the behaviour of the Secretary of the Treasury and holders of office.

(4) Explanation regarding the Bektashi Corps.

(5) Explanation regarding the condition of Rayas (the subject peasants and the harmfulness of tyranny and oppression of the poor.

(6) Explanation regarding the state of the Ever-Victorious Frontier and the qualities of commanders.

(7) Explanation concerning avarice and liberality, greed, covetousness, pride, and envy, humility and arrogance, good temper and bad temper and hypocrisy.

(8) Explanation regarding faithful friendship and the harmfulness of calumny and backbiting.

(9) Explanation regarding the state of the Ziamet and Timar (the two principal categories of fiefs in the Ottoman feudal system).

Absence of Facts

Muhammad Pasha, in his narrative does not mention anywhere the moral degeneration of the royal household, or the inexcusable negligence of the Sultans cowards the affairs of the state. As an employee of an autocratic ruler, he probably could not openly criticize the Sultans whose tyranny and pursuits of pleasures had changed the machinery of government into an engine of coercion and exploitation. He opens his first chapter with the following remarks :

> "Since the Lord without equal, who showers down abundant gifts (may His glory be exalted beyond the reach of imagination) has made that firmly founded dynasty, the surpassing Ottoman Sultanate, to be the refuge of the rulers of the times, and has made their court, which pours out on every hand favours from the ocean of abundance, to be distributor of the sustenance decreed by Providence to the people of the world, it has consequently become a necessary responsibility and obvious obligation of the padishah to fulfil the incumbant gratitude due for their Divine Grace in accordance with the precept." "Everyone of you is a shepherd and everyone is responsible for the flock, he should make affluent the condition of the governed and establish good order in the affairs of the citizens."

Muhammad Pasha advocates that officials occupying positions of authority must abstain from illegal practices, avoid injustice and remove weeds and thorns of tyranny and corruption. Administrators in his opinion should be free from the baneful attitude of discriminating among people. Rich and poor, high and low, friend and a stranger, all should be treated strictly according to the principles of law and ethics. They must have the moral courage to speak the truth, because truth alone ensures integrity and emancipates human thinking from deceit and suspicion. Hasty use of power is also detrimental to sound administration. In the application of his authority an officer has moral duty to weigh intelligently and rationally pros and cons of every bit of evidence and information. He says :

> "Throughout their period of authority let them treat with equality the humble and the noble, the wealthy and the poor, the learned and the unlearned, the one from far and the one from nearby, the visitor and the neighbour—let them not make use of their power until the evidence is complete—to the glorious padishah let them speak the word of truth without veiling and concealment. For the Prophet of God has said, "words of truth are the best alms."

Evils of Administration

The largest portion of the treatise, however, is devoted to the evils which are bred in administration by corruption and worldly greed of public servants. These evils had completely changed the life and character of Ottoman government. A bureaucracy with a legendary reputation for efficiency and uprightness became a playground of internal frictions and squabbles, and in their dealings with the public, its members were always busy in devising means by which they could further their worldly fortunes. The man in the street and the defenseless peasantry were completely disarmed against their deceitful manipulations. According to Muhammad Pasha, lust for wealth is a sign of unhealthy politics. It makes a holder of authority unscrupulous, time-server, haughty and disdainful. While giving advice to the grand vezir, he makes the following remarks :

> "The grand vezir especially must not be a time-server thinking of the benefits of money; let him shun the hope of gathering wealth and treasures and spend his ability in preparing a remedy for the weakness and languidness which prevent the good health of the country—nor let him become puffed up with his greatness and exhibit to the people an appearance of haughtiness and disdain—whatever appointed thou mayest receive from among the exalted offices be content with the designated salary and be on the guard against tyranny and cruelty and daring to cause harm to the people through greedy longing to amass wealth."

He has further castigated bribery in the following words :

> "Bribery is the beginning and root of all illegality and tyranny, the source and fountain of every sort of disturbance and sedition, the most vast of evils and the greatest of calamities. It is the ruin of corruption than which there is nothing whatever more calamitious to the people of Islam or more destructive to the foundations of religion and government. Than this there is no more powerful engine of injustice and cruelty, for bribery destroys both faith and state."

The menace of bribery in the seventeenth century Ottoman administration, had increased manifold because administrators were not only getting bribes and gifts from the people, but large scale bribery was practised within the ranks of bureaucracy for promotion, transfer and acquisition of new offices. Such a practice had such degenerating consequences for administration that Mohammad Pasha wrote "to give office to the unfit because of bribery is a very great sin." The virus of corruption had become so widespread, that even judges were not immune from it. They freely auction their judgments in favour of the highest bidder. He sums up his discussion about the harmful implications of bribery with the remarks that "to government officials the disease of bribery is one whose cure is hard to determine. Perhaps it has no cure, yet there is no disease without remedy. This must be considered in all its aspects and absolutely eschewed and avoided." He is particularly insistent that officials of the treasury who hold in custody the wealth of the state should have an untarnished record of honesty and integrity. They should be men who have full comprehension of the affairs of the realm, and complete awareness of all the dynamics which are shaping the character of a polity at a particular time. They should be men, who are experienced, righteous and religious. They should be watchful of the 'trustworthiness or contemtibleness of those who follow the rocky and unrighteous road of teachery', because that is the only way to save the country from frauds and misappropriations. Revenue officials, are very susceptible to calumny and derision from jealous persons. This further necessitates that they should be honest and upright. He says that 'those who are defterdars (Treasury Chiefs) should be extremely circumspect in behaviour, upright and devout, devoid of avarice and spite. They should be satisfied with the revenues assigned to them by the Exalted Government and should not desire bribes from anyone or be greedy of amassing wealth and profits.

Army's Responsibility

According to Muhammad Pasha, the responsibility of the army, particularly its commanders, in creating higher standards of public morality is equally important for the health of body politics. The Ottoman army had become one of the most corrupting influences in the state. On the frontiers, commanders used to draw salaries for soldiers who did not exist. Knowing the power and prestige of Janisseries, all kinds of people had joined their ranks either through intercession or bribery. The result was that corps which was once the pride of Ottoman army became an asylum for good-for-nothing fortune-hunters. Many who had never budged out of Istanbul, had not rendered any service in a campaign, were drawing salaries of soldiers, or pensioners.

If the above mentioned evils emerge in a political system the greatest sufferers, according to our author, are the poor raya (subjects). A tradition of the Prophet compares oppression to darkness, and another one says "Guard yourself against the prayer of the poor man, even though he be an unbeliever." After quoting these sayings Muhammad Pasha goes on to prove that in the last analysis, it is the people who are the real benefactors of the rulers. It is through their sweat and blood that nations attain their greatness. Therefore anyone who neglects their comfort and interest is in reality an enemy of the state. He says:

> "The rayas (subjects) are a trust from the Creator of man and Universe. The state exists through them and treasure produced by them. If the subjects be always protected they become not wretched, but increase. Kindness to them and protection of their affairs from the hands of tyrannical oppression is a form of worship."

In support of his contention he quotes a famous Arabic maxim of statecraft which reads as follows :

> "Without men of consequence there is no ruler, and without property there are no men of consequence, and without prosperity there is no wealth, and without justice and good administration there is no prosperity."

Ethical Characteristics

Over and above the qualities of honesty, trustworthiness and integrity, Muhammad Pasha has listed certain other ethical characteristics which he deems essential for men, who have been given the charge of public affairs in a state. Irritable and bad-tempered person can never make a good officer. An officer should be free from jealousy and hypocrisy, and in dealing with people he should avoid pride and arrogance. Generosity of heart and liberality of attitude will strengthen his position, and people will not hesitate to repose confidence in his decisions. Avarice is a positive disqualification because it is a manifestation of man's unregenerate nature. Passion without reason and ill-humor are also accounted as major evils of administrative behaviour. Wrath in the opinion of the author spoils belief just as aloes (a plant which has bitter juice) spoils honey. Humility gives richness and dignity to human character, while haughtiness is a moral debasement. He quotes a tradition of the Prophet in this respect which says "He who has in his heart an atom's weight of arrogance enters not into Heaven."

Vicious Intrigues

The Ottoman governmental machinery during the sixteenth century was crowded with vicious intrigues. Faith and fidelity were conspicuous by their absence from human relations. Our author had full share of this intrabureacratic deciet and treachery which ultimately cost him his life. Therefore, one is not surprised that he has introduced a special chapter on friendship to prove that human interaction should be free from flattery, and it should be based on mutal sympathy, trust and confidence. It should not be an hypocritical facade to hide spite and hatred. A friend should be one to whom you can entrust your secrets and who has the ability to live up to his promises, whose affections are not fleeting and who loves truth. Men have a tendency to gravitate towards and cluster around rulers and men of authority. Not all who do so are trustworthy. Large numbers of them have always some personal axe to grind. The character of such persons has been portrayed by the author in the following words :

> "They desire amicable relations and double-faced friendship in order, purely for their own advantage, to dupe with all sorts of tricks and wiles someone of eminence for a great personage of government and to cause him to commit sins. In the end they become the cause of his suffering. If diligent inquiry be made, they are found to be sinners and wine bibbers. How can good come from such as these ? Such men are boaster and braggarts, liars and bringers of false accusation, contemptible in nature and abominable in character. They are unmixed evil, obstacles to good, exaggerators, flatterers and time servers."

Men in authority are also warned against 'talebearers and backbiters', because they have the evil habit of adding uncalled for comments to information passed on to them. In his opinion, "rulers must expel and drive away such persons from their councils and give them neither pleasantry nor license." And in the end the author advises all men of rank and status in government to be at guard against calumnous persons, because the Quran itself has said, "Slander not one another. Would any of you like to eat the flesh of his dead brother ? If so you would despise him."

9

Behavioural Ethics

The character of the Muslim community is not determined by the acceptance of the rituals alone. Acceptance has to be translated into action. All acts of devotion manifested in Salat (Prayer), Som (Fasting), Zakat (Charity), and Haj (Pilgrimage) are rigid and compulsory, not so much because they ensure a better place in heaven, but because they provide social harmony in the society and engender self-discipline. They give to the community an ethical 'steel frame' within which it can earn rewards on this earth. The ethics in Islam, however, is revealed. It is not the product of philosophical speculations or rational interpretation of the events resulting from man's social and political life. It has its counterpart in Christianity in the form of Protestant Ethics, but the religious ethics in Islam is more compulsive and comprehensive, and there is greater emphasis on the revelational aspect. Gibb has expressed the following views on the religious nature of Islamic ethics.

Source of Ethics

"The fact that the source of Muslim ethics was religious intuition transmitting a divine revelation to mankind, was important also for the structure of Muslim society. Viewed in the light of the ultimate principle which regulates human existence, all human institutions take a new significance. They are not immaterial to the religious life; they either express or do not-express the Will of God for men, and they either conduce or do not conduce to a life of true submission to God."

To fortify the ethical basis of a Muslim society, Hadith (the tradition of the Prophet) has been made the most important supplementary force with the Quran. The Prophet in his life articulated moral connotations of a variety of human situation's. The Traditions of the Prophet constitute a massive and valuable store house of ethical principles, which can make Quranic precepts and ideals more realistic. Even the vast compendium of Islamic law is deeply rooted in ethics. There is no such thing called the dichotomy of law and morality In Islam. The Quran, the Traditions of the Prophet, and Fiqh (Jurisprudence) form an ethical reservoir for all occasions which saves the Muslim community from dwindling into moral anarchy.

For acts of omission or commission, there are certain specified penalities, which cannot be increased, decreased or cancelled by any state authority. Taking into consideration the inherent foibles of human character, and permanent moral infirmities, which crowd the life of an average man. Muslim thinkers have insisted that state is an indispensable institution, obedience to its commands is essential for the peace and prosperity of the community, but the state is also under eternal obligation to provide its citizens with an ethical climate, which would enable them to realize the moral purpose of human existence.

The Quran and the history of Islam furnish an eloquent testimony that right action is the only yardstick by which value or worth of human character could be judged. The Quran says:

> "And those who strive in our (cause) we will certainly guide them to our Paths: for verily God is with those who do right."

Constant Struggle

Life in Islam is a constant struggle to overcome satanic propensities which run in human blood. Believers have been instructed to keep a strict watch over their thoughts and actions. Inner purity of soul is as important as the external manifestation of rites and rituals. It is also laid down that every possible step should be taken to make human life in an organization positive and constructive. In other words, mystical morality of self-abnegation, penance and seclusion is against the spirit of Islam. Goodness is valuable only if it is practiced in society and is used as an instrument for the welfare of the community as a whole. In order to perform a righteous action, and acquire eligibility for membership in the commonwealth of believers, one is expected to practice certain fundamentals in the form of *Ibadat* (prayers). These prayers are basically meant to purify the heart and soul of man, but their true meanings are realized only when this purity in the form of goodness and virtue is reflected in the social interaction among the members of the Muslim community. T. J. DeBoer has summed up the nature of Islamic ethics as follows:

> "The ethics of the Quran might be summed up in the trite formula: 'Believe and do right.' Belief of course is the primary obligation, since without belief all works are vain—a mere mirage in the waste."

In other words religion is the basic source of social ethics. Belief takes precedence over actions, no doubt, but if it is only an embellishment of soul, and actions of men do not synchronize with its substance, it becomes only a hollow spiritual exercise.

Thus in every code of ethics in Islam, belief and action must always go together. According to an authentic religious text *hadith* (saying of the Prophet), morally rewarding works or actions are as follows:

(1) Honour towards parents.

(2) Not to take a niece in marriage against her will.

(3) To pay one's day-laborers well.

A tradition of quite another cast, which had its source among the devout gives the following list of precepts:

(1) Love the poor, and be accessible to them.

(2) Look always at those who are beneath you and gaze not at those who are above you.

(3) Never solicit anything from anyone.

(4) Be loyal to thy kinsfolk, even if they should vex you.

(5) Always speak the truth, even when it is unpalatable.

(6) Be not overawed in the paths of Allah by the reviling of the reviler.

(7) Frequently cry aloud, "There is no might or power save by Allah," for this comes forth from the treasure which is hidden under God's throne."

The Pragmatism

Islamic ethics is pragmatic and is an integral part of the faith. The spread of Islam, however, beyond the frontiers of Arabian peninsula brought it into contact with other ethical disciplines, and in due course, comparative study of different ethical systems became a very important part of the traditional philosophy of education in Islam. Later, out of this synthesis, a science of morals, called Ilm al-Akhlaq was developed, which attracted the attention of some of the greatest scholars in Islam. But in spite of countless alien influences, in essence, the ethics in Islam remained Quranic. As long as the Muslims were firmly anchored to this morality, Islam remained a dynamic and forward-looking movement. It opened flood-gates of revolutionary forces, and Muslims became the torch-bearers of civilization in every land they inhabited. But the moment they disengaged themselves from the moral moorings of the Quran, their civilization collapsed like a house of cards. To attribute the downfall of Islamic civilization to a single factor would be a sacriligious oversimplification, but this much is certain that lack of ethical basis in politics and administration was one of the major causes of the downfall of Muslim kingdoms. Corruption, tyranny, backwardness and exploitation completely eroded their foundations. Political and administrative life of the community became a playground for the neferious activities of self-seekers and king-makers. Most of the cherished excellences were sacrificed at the altar of expediency and self-interest. Therefore, it should be a matter of serious interest for a student of Islamic civilization to assess those moral qualities of administration, which constituted the basis of its earlier glories and achievements.

The Honesty

This is a moral quality which refrains individuals from inflicting injury on others by way of cheating, or misappropriation of their possessions. Dishonesty breeds aversion, pollutes social life, degenerates politics, and corrupts administration. All religious and ethical philosophies have emphasized that, honesty ensures stability and happiness for mankind, while dishonesty, they point out, is a sign of moral decadence. Honesty safeguards men against temptations which one finds at every step and gives richness and dignity to human character. Dishonesty, on the other hand, denigrates character, multiplies distrust and suspicion. It is baneful in all areas of life, but its impact is particularly ruinous if a dishonest person happens to occupy a position of authority. As such, honesty has deep relevence to administration, where most of the authority of the state is concentrated.

According to Islam, corruption is a sin for which there is no atonement. The Quran has clearly pointed out, that corrupters will be subjected to divine chastisement. It is an irreligious act which deserves severe condemnation. It says :

> "Not to consume each other's wealth unjustly, nor offer it to judges as a bribe, so that, with their aid you might seize other men's property dishonestly."

> "Give just measure and be not of those who diminish and weigh (things) with an exact and right balance. And defraud not the substance of any people, and do not act corruptly in the earth making mischief. And guard yourself against the punishment of God for all sorts of corruption."

Another verse of the Quran says:

> "But seek the abode of the Hereafter in that which Allah hath given thee and neglect not thy portion of the world, and be thou kind even as Allah hath been kind to thee and seek not corruption in the earth lo ! Allah loveth not corrupters."

It is a matter of common knowledge that corruption is universal in human life. In every period of history, sages and reformers have waged unending crusades against tendencies, which produce corruption. The Holy Prophet in his administrative reforms gave highest priority to honesty and moral integrity of officers. His instrument of instructions to officers always highlighted right action and honest conduct in unmistakable terms. Officers were disallowed to have anything beyond their salaries and allowances, and even gifts of all kinds were forbidden. Omar A. Farrukh has summed up the Prophet's views on nepotism or favouritism in the following words :

> "If the man in authority left the better and the fitter (Man) in favour of another because of relationship between them, or because the other man happened to have emancipated him from slavery or because of friendship or of being from the same locality, the same nationality, Arab, Persian, Turk, or Greek, or because of a bribe received in kind or service or for any other cause, or because of a grudge against the more capable man or of an animosity between them; he who does this is a cheater of Allah of His Messenger and of the Faithful (Muslims)."

Accumulation of worldly riches for ostentatious living or for the benefit of one's children are common and universal foibles of human character. Men tend to fall victims to these temptations very easily. Men who are susceptible to these foibles do not deserve any public office. The Quran says, "And know that your wealth and your children are a temptation and that Allah is He with whom there is a mighty reward." The Prophet took special care in allocating offices of the state. A tradition has been narrated by Bukhari from Huraira in which the Prophet pointed out that if the offices were assigned to unworthy people that would mean the end of this world.

The principles of honesty enunciated by the Prophet were strictly adhered to by his four successors in organizing and administering the affairs of the Pious Caliphate. Although historical evidence is meagre, but whatever is left of their official correspondence, is an eloquent testimony that honesty was insisted and advocated for all administrators in all areas of governmental activity. Officers were repeatedly reminded of their duty to God and the people, and anybody found corrupt or dishonest was promptly reprimanded and punished. Umar I, under whom the city state of Medina became a vast empire, is credited with the creation of an effective and efficient machinery of government in Islamic history. The organization of administration was simple, but he set very high ethical standards for public servants of the state. Civil and military officers found guilty of corruption were always subjected to severe reprimand, and very often they were given exemplary punishment. In 17 A.H., Umar I dismissed Khalid-bin-Walid on charges of bribery. In his dismissal order he wrote that corruption in any form was a naked tyranny. In another letter to Umaro-bin-As, the governor of Egypt, the Caliph made serious inquiries about the ways and means, by which he had accumulated wealth and property, which he did not possess before his appointment as governor. This is a clear indication, that in Islam, rank, status or services to the state would not help an administrator to escape the punishment, which he deserves for his dishonest deeds. In an official circular addressed to the governors of the provinces, Umar I forbade acceptance of even gifts, which in his opinion were also a form of corruption.

Imperishable Impact

Hazrat Ali, the last of the Pious Caliphs, has left an imperishable impact on Islamic thought. Among the companions of the Holy Prophet he was known for his courage, foresight and prudence. He ruled during one of the most stormy periods of early Muslim history, but he did not allow the moral climate of his administration to deteriorate. Even in the midst of growing political restlessness in the realm, he maintained high ethical ideals of Islamic administration. A letter written to Malik-bin-Ashtar, when he was appointed governor of Egypt, has been considered by historians as Hazrat Ali's great contribution to the growth of administrative ethics in Islam. The document is of immeasurable significance. The caliph expressed his views on official honesty in the following words: "Then come officers of your state. You must supervise their work. They must be appointed after a careful scrutiny of their capabilities and characters. These appointments must be made originally on probation without any kind of favouritism being shown or influence being accepted. Otherwise tyranny, corruption and misrule will reign in your state. While selecting your officers, take care to select experienced and honourable persons, members of respectable families who had served Islam during its early days, because these are usually of noble character and good repute. They are not greedy and cannot be easily corrupted. They mostly have before them the ultimate result of their thoughts and their deeds. Keep them also well paid, so that they may not be tempted to lower their standards of morality and may not misappropriate the cash of the state which they hold in their trust; and even if after being paid handsomely they prove dishonest, then you will be right to punish them. Therefore, keep a careful watch over their system of work and rule. You may also appoint trustworthy and honest men to watch over the activities of these officers. The knowledge that they are being watched secretly will keep them from dishonesty, misrule, malpractices and tyrannizing the subject. Protect your government from dishonest officers. If you find any of them dishonest and your confidential intelligence service submits acceptable proofs of his dishonesty then you must punish him. This may be physical punishment, dismissal from service and taking back from him all, which he has dishonestly collected. He must be humiliated and must be made to realize the infamy of his crooked deeds. His humiliation and punishment must be given publicity so that it may act as a lesson and a deterrent example to ot.ers."

In another letter, Hazrat Ali condemned officers, who had the habit of attending parties arranged in their honour by interested people. This he thought was also corruption, though of a subtle nature. The letter was addressed to Osman-ibn-Haneef, the governor of Basra and read as follows :

> "Ibne-Haneef! I have received information that a person of Basra invited you to a dinner and you immediately accepted the invitation. And very sumptuous meals were served there, finest varieties of viands were placed before you—I am sorry to hear the news. I never expected that you would accept invitation of person who invite big officers and rich

> people and from whose doors people and hungry paupers are turned away rudely."

Similarly, in another letter to a collector of taxes, Hazrat Ali condemned misappropriation of government money. In his opinion, it was a disgrace of the highest order and should not be tolerated. He pointed out that an officer, who was guilty of such an act had sold his conscience to the devil. He said :

> "Be it known to you that the person who misappropriates the poor rate fund, who fills his stomach with such amounts and who harms his religion and injures his conscience with such deeds will be punished and disgraced in this world as well as the next. The worst form of dishonesty is the breach of trust of the public funds and the despicable example of maladministration is that the Imam (ruler) should tolerate such forms of dishonesty."

The perusal of the official correspondence of the pious Caliphs shows that acts of dishonesty were not tolerated in administration, and complaints against dishonest officers were handled speedily. They believed that if the rulers want to retain the confidence of the people they must check dishonesty promptly. In order to eliminate nepotism they made every possible effort to curb clanish affinities among administrators; Nepotism in their opinion forbids the available talent in the community to fructify in its fullness. People will not repose confidence in a government where jobs and positions are distributed through favouritism. They emphasized that faith and trust of the masses is the best guarantee against maladministration and political insecurity. Hazrat Ali in one of his letters said :

> "Let your attitude be such that they do not lose faith in you because a good faith on their part will reduce many troubles of administration and will relieve you of many worries and anxieties."

To further ensure honesty in administration, officers were debarred from pursuing other vocations in life. Moreover, several other practical steps were taken to inculcate propriety and honesty among officers. They were provided all possible amenities and comforts, because it was believed that inadequate salaries and absence of reasonable facilities could be one of the factors, which compel public servants to be corrupt. The Holy Prophet felt that if the officers are debarred from sources of additional income, justice demands that they should be provided with enough funds, so that they could lead a respectable existence. He had laid down special instruction for their salaries, and housing accommodations. But at the same time he insisted that an officer, who seeks more than what is legally sanctioned for him is guilty of the breach of trust. In Abu Saad a tradition of the Holy Prophet has been recorded as follows :

> "Mustaored bin Shaddud reported : I heard the messenger of Allah say who is an officer of ours, let him take a wife, and if he has got no servant let him take a servant and if he has got no house let him take a house; who so takes besides that is one who commits breach of trust."

Corrupt officers have a tendency to be secretive about their ill-gotten fortunes. In Islam this is a sinful act. All employees of the state are obliged by religion to give an honest account of their possessions to the public. Each official is accountable to God and the people. The Prophet once said :

> "O you men! who ever of you is appointed to work for us and then conceals from us even a needle there from or what is above it, is a treacherous man."

In short, Islam has condemned dishonesty in public affairs in the strongest possible terms. A dishonest official has been warned against all kinds of evil consequences, the greatest of them being the chagrin of God.

State-crafts

Later Muslim writers on political ethics and states-craft have also emphasized honesty in government in unequivocal terms. Kaikaus, the author of *Qabus Nama,* has pointed out that bribery is as bad as usury. He has expressed his opinion on the dishonesty of the officials in the following words:

> "Money gained from office under the sultan resembles roses and jasmine, which in a single day make themselves beautiful, sweet-scented and highly

> reputed. But also it is as ephemeral as the flowers, and like them the profits derived from office cannot be hidden away. Money acquired in the service of the sultan is more easily dissipated than the dust on the surface of the world, and although the honour of service of royal masters is the best form of capital, the money which accrues from it is no better than usury."

Emphasis on honesty in administration increased in later Islamic history because unfettered personal rule of despots in various dynasties had made administration in a Muslim kingdom extremely susceptible to corruption. The original concept that all functionaries including the Head of State were servants of God, holding authority from Him to serve the common good of mankind, had disappeared from the practical politics of Islam. The result was that greed, avarice, and dishonesty had become common features of Muslim administration. Lust for power, and desire to amass worldly fortunes were noticeable in all areas of administrative activity.

Despotic rulers and unscrupulous civil servants, free from the fear of God and the Day of Judgment, completely wrecked the spirit of Islamic administration. Ibn-e-Taimiyya has summed up their characteristics as follows :

> "A class dominated by desire for power and doing mischief having no consideration whatsoever of the Day of Judgment. They realize that they can only attain domination with (various kinds of) payments, and these are not possible except by extorting money illegally. Consequently they become plunderers (from some people, conferrers of favours on some other people). Those say, no one can obtain to domination unless he be one, who eats and lets others eat. If an upright man, who neither eats nor lets others eat, attained to power, the higher officials would detest him and finish by deposing him. Sometimes they are not satisfied with that; they may cause him bodily and financial harm. Those people consider only their immediate (interests) in this world and neglect the future good of this life and the life to come."

Piety, the Yardstick

Ibn Taimiyya insists that in Islam piety is the only yardstick to determine the competence of an individual to hold a seat of authority in government and administration. Any other criteria of personnel recruitment is a stark dishonesty. In his opinion assigning positions in government on the basis of caste, cult or kinship, denigrates the very mission of Islam. He says :

> "It is the duty for any one, who directs any part of the public affairs of the Muslims—to employ the most suitable person he can find in each position, which is under his control—if he rejects the worthiest and most proper candidate in favour of another, because the other is his relation, friend, or freedman, or because they belong to the same country, legal sect, religious order, or ethnic group—Arab, Persian Turkish, Anatolian — or because he has accepted a bribe or service for this man, or for other reason, or because of some personal animosity towards the worthier candidate or some enmity between them, he cheats God and His Prophet and the Faithful."

The reason for which piety is advocated as a measure of honesty is that there is no other way of determining precisely the honest intentions of an individual. Rigorous psychological tests and written examination of modern times can uncover instincts like aggression, sentimentality, and sobriety to some extent, but they fail to provide reliable indicators regarding qualities such as honesty, sympathy and a sense of justice. Piety which means fear of God, simple and austere life, and purity of thought and action, was therefore considered a better touchstone for honesty. Later in Islamic history as piety declined among the Muslims, writers on politics and administrative ethics started suggesting other means for scouting honest people for government service. Family, wealth, and sectarian affiliations were advocated as pertinent instruments to determine ability of an individual to be honest. The philosophy behind this approach was that people with pecuniary conditions should not be elevated to positions of authority in government, because poverty of the position holder could be a factor in making corrupt.

Kaikaus has made the following remarks :

> "Never grant office to impecunious or impoverished men, especially if it is important office, because they will not concern themselves with provision for you until they have provided for themselves. Those on the other hand, who have means and possessions of their own, will not immediately busy themselves on their own account. It is like the irrigation of fields and gardens. If the canal supplying the field or garden is moist and well-soaked, it conveys water quickly to field and garden; but if the earth in the canal is dry, and water has not for a long time passed through it, then when water is admitted, until it itself is saturated with moisture, it will not deliver water to the field or garden. The impecunious tax-gatherer resembles the dry canal, in first satisfying his own needs and then turning to yours."

Ibn Taimiyya says that in popular Arabic vocabulary bribery is also called *bartil* which originally meant that the mouth of the briber is closed from the truth. A tradition of the Prophet has highlighted this fact by pointing out that "when the bribes enter through the door, honesty flies through the skylight."

In pursuit of honesty, however officers are not allowed to become insufferably arrogant. Honesty should be supplemented with graces like civility and courtesy. Particularly officers, who have constant public dealings—like tax or revenue collectors—are instructed to be honest as well as accommodating and courteous. Without these additional qualities honesty cannot make any significant contribution to public good. Ibn Khaldun has added austerity as another factor to strengthen honesty in human character. Luxuriant living makes an individual indolent and increases his chances of becoming corrupt or dishonest. In his opinion, if public officials are habituated to ease and luxury, the social system as a whole will fall on evil days.

Ibn Khaldun, in his discussion of the rise and fall of a sedentary culture, has given an insightful account of the causes which in his opinion lead to corruption of civilized communities. Sedentary culture he believes originates in cities and adversely affects all areas of social and economic life. Addiction to elegance and pageantry become common. Fads and fashions, the natural accompaniments of luxuriant existence, consume most of the creative energies of the people. Limited means, high taxes, and extravagant living compel people to indulge in immoral practices. Cheating, fraud, theft, perjury, and usury paralyze the framework of social life. Nobody remains immune from this morally polluted climate and even esteemed persons and members of noble families are corrupted, and this ultimately is the sign of degeneration and disappearance of civilization.

The Justice

In religion and philosophy, justice has been emphasised as one of the greatest manifestations of nobility. It gives luster, richness, and dignity to affairs of men, and saves humanity from the evil consequences of force, fraud and aggression. Justice has two distinct meanings. Firstly, it is a quality of the human mind, which helps an individual to distinguish between right and wrong in life.

Secondly, it is an administration of codified legal rules and procedures in a regular law court. Impartiality, objectivity, and rigidity are the chief characteristics of formal legal codes, while graciousness, ability to curb ambitions, and desire to control appetites are the properties of justice, when it is understood as an ethical quality.

Islam has made provision for both kinds of justice. An administrator in a Muslim state is subject to both kinds of regimentation. In the religious literature, and the books on law and administration, however, justice is emphasized as a quality which mostly pertains to mind and thought. The Quran has elucidated the importance of justice as follows:

> "O ye who believe: Be steadfast witness for Allah in equity, and let not enmity of any people seduce you that ye deal not justly. Deal justly— that is nearer to your duty. Observe your duty to Allah."
>
> "O ye who believe: Be ye staunch in justice witness for Allah even though it be against your ownselves, or your parents or your kindred."

A socio-political climate, in which sense of justice is high among people, is most conducive to ethical development. The Holy Prophet laid great emphasis on this quality. Books of Hadith are replete with traditions of the Prophet indicating his deep and serious concern regarding injustice in life. In his opinion, justice is all-pervading and no area of human existence should be free from its impact. Some of the traditions of the Holy Prophet have been recorded as follows:

> "Abdullah ben Amr reported that the Messenger of Allah said: Verily the just persons near Allah will be upon pulpits of light on the right side of Merciful and both His hands are right hands of those who are just in their orders and in their family and what they are given to rule."
>
> "Abu Sayeed reported that the Prophet said: Verily the dearest of men near Allah on the Resurrection Day and the nearest of them before Him for company will be a just ruler."
>
> "Ibn Omar reported that the Messenger of Allah said: Verily the Sultan is a shade of Allah on earth. Every oppressed man out of His servants takes shelter to him. When he administers justice, there is reward for him and their gratitude on the part of the subjects."

Quality of Justice

There is a saying, "government will continue with unbelief, but not with injustice." According to Ghazzali, the success of any political authority depends on the quality of justice in its jurisdiction. In Islam, an unjust governor of men is threatened with torments reserved for infidels, while a just and righteous ruler has been ensured of unending blessings. According to Ghazzali the Prophet once said, "One day of just rule by an equitable Sultan is more meritorious than sixty years of continual worship." Justice, from the Islamic point of view is a powerful safeguard against arbitrary action. Excessive punishment and excessive compassion, both have been labelled as arbitrary. Writers on administrative ethics in Islam have further elucidated the concept of justice by saying that it entails regimentation of passion and control of aggressive instincts in man.

In another work of outstanding merit called Kimiya-i-Saadat, Gazzali has given further elucidation of his concept of justice and gives certain definite characteristics which he says can give stability and peace to society. The qualities enumerated are meant for the ruler, but it is understood that they are equally applicable to the rest of the administrators, who are actually governing the people. These characteristics are as follows:

(i) In every case the ruler should mentally put himself in the position of the contending parties.

(ii) He should fulfill the desire of those, who have come to him for justice.

(iii) Justice is possible only when the ruler does not indulge in luxurious food and clothing.

(iv) He should practice leniency, not harshness in his official dealings.

(v) He should try that the subjects should be content with the rule of law.

(vi) He should not attempt any conciliation at the expense of law.

(vii) He should supervise the affairs of the people in the same way as if he were to supervise his own household affairs and should deal with the powerful and the inferior in the same manner.

(viii) He should try to meet the learned as often as he can and should encourage them to have their say.

(ix) He should see that his servants, magistrates and other officers perform their duties diligently and well.

(x) He should not be overpowered by any false sense of pride.

The above characteristics provide a broad and a comprehensive view of those graces of human character which lead to kindness, sympathy, equality, and dignity. Ibn Abi-Rabi defines justice as a condition of correctness in life, dominance of reason over animality in man, and integrity in public affairs. It also means defense of the rights of man with courage and conviction. Weak and inefficient officers have very little chance of performing their duties in a just manner.

Justice in Islam also connotes a sense of balance in conducting affairs of the state and society. The Quran says, "He raised up the heavens and He set the Balance." Another verse says, "Allah it is who sent down the book with truth and the Balance." Imbalance of any kind is against the principle of justice. Islam has not provided any definite framework or procedural code, by which work in government can be conducted in a balanced manner. But an examination of the spiritual values enunciated by Islam leaves no doubt that if they are permanently embedded in human character, chances are that imbalances can be avoided.

Thus, in every discussion of Islamic ethics and administration, justice is highlighted as one of the basic characteristics of good administration. It creates a sense of proportion, encourages ethical behaviour and saves men from impious acts of arrogance, self-glory and self-aggrandizement.

Caliph Ali in one of his sermons, proclaimed that promulgation of justice and truth was the cardinal feature of his mission as a ruler. Impiety and injustice lead to the erosion of societies, and the Prophet's main purpose was to establish a moral climate in which people could be administered in a just manner. Ali said :

> "My mission today is the same as it was at the time of the Prophet. I shall strive till I eradicate impiety and injustice and till I establish a rule of Justice and Truth—a humane and heavenly regime."

In another letter addressed to Muhammad son of Hazrat Abubakar (the first caliph) whom he appointed governor of Egypt, Ali insisted on just administration in the following words :

> "Be fair, just and impartial in your dealings, so that even the influential persons may not dare take undue advantage of your leniency and the uninfluential and poor may not be disappointed in your justice and fair dealings."

The Veracity

Love for truth and fairplay has been the theme of practically every ethical system. In no other institution is there greater need of veracity than in administration, because decisions being made in it have deep and far-reaching repercussions. Any effort to misrepresent the facts or make a false statement could be extremely hazardous. If veracity is adopted as an integral part of administrative behaviour, and decision makers consciously insist on truthful assessment of every situation, there is every possibility that the climate within an administrative agency would be free from many suspicions which so often plague internal and external environments of complex organizations. This ethical quality demands that a person in making a decision or providing an information should not be motivated by selfishness. Veracity, in order to be effective, however, has to be spontaneous and should be a continuous habit of mind, rather than an act of expediency resulting from some kind of fear or injury. It has been noticed that men in organizations have the tendency to camouflage realities for self-interest, or withhold information intentionally to harm the interest of someone else. If an empirical investigation is made, ample evidence will be found to how, the inadequate information, a misstatement, and deliberate distortion of facts contribute a great deal in making wrong decisions. All philosophical and ethical systems have emphasized that search for truth should be the continuous professional and intellectual preoccupation of those, who make and execute public policies. The Quran says :

> "The witnesses—among the true believers shall not refuse to present themselves whenever they are summoned to give witness; and conceal not true testimony, for he who conceals it has surely a wicked heart."

> "When you speak a word or pronounce a judgment, be true and just, though the person concerned be your relative, speak not falsely, although the declaration might be against your own interest or against your parents or your near relatives."

In one of his sermons, Hazrat Ali listed faithfulness, truth, and veracity as virtues, which protect mankind against evils. This is in his opinion is the primary object of Islam. Discussing human behaviour in one of his sermons, he said :

> "He is wise who carefully meditates over what he hears (and then accepts only truth) who tries to see things in their real and actual perspectives."

Truth, in Ali's opinion, has precedence even over safety of life and property.

> "A true Muslim is he from whose hands and tongue other Muslims are safe, but not at the cost of truth and justice."

Truth is the foundation of human character and a basic factor which strengthens human faith. The Prophet once said, "No man can attain a firm faith, unless he develops strength of character and that cannot be achieved unless one acquires the habit of speaking truth." Rulers and administrators, who love truth and plain speaking will never become prey to sycophants and courtiers, who are always ready to gather around men of authority.

The Courage

It is by courage alone that individuals in their personal and collective lives can achieve something worthwhile and creative. Cowardice is an ailment of human soul. Courage on the other hand is a spiritual tonic and its value is universally recognized in all areas of organized life. But courage is not to be confused with spontaneous acts of bravery. Bravery is an accident, but courage is a permanent moral virtue. Courageous action is a product of reason and reflection. Rules of propriety and logic play a decisive role in courage, and it does not entail a violation of discipline or decorum. In Islam, control of passions, sublimation of emotions, and curbing of irrational and immoral tendencies are included among courageous deeds. The Quran says :

> "The true brave are those, who lose not their hearts, but stand firmly and behave patiently under ills and hardships and in battles—those are they who are true (to themselves) and those are they who guard themselves against the displeasure of their Lord."

In Islam hierarchical organization is not rigid and excessively formalistic. Distinction among juniors and seniors is maintained, but they are all accountable to God, whose all-embracing sovereignty forms the cornerstone of the Faith. This mitigates formalized subservience of the subordinate to the super ordinate, which is a cardinal feature of all formal hierarchies. The fact that juniors and seniors, irrespective of rank, status, and position are accountable to God for their actions and decisions, changes the climate of human interaction in an organization. Each officer is answerable to God for his own trust.

It is the religious duty of a junior to point out any omission on the part of his senior, which is contrary to religion and morality. Healthy criticism is a sign of courage and shows that the system is stable, tolerant, and progressive. Hazrat Abu Bakr, the first Pious Caliph, in his inaugural address, clearly impressed upon the people that, they were free to exercise strict vigilence on his affairs and if and when he deviated from the path of righteousness, they were under no obligation to obey his commands.

Courage to criticize and large heartedness to accept criticism are certainly counted among the salient features of Islamic administration. There are instances in Islamic history when caliphs and kings were openly castigated for their policies. The critics in doing so always felt that they were performing a religious duty and had not the slightest apprehension about reprisal or punishment. Hazrat Umar I, once while preaching, said, "O, people let him among you, who sees any deviation in me set it right." A man stood up from the congregation and said, "By God if we saw in you deviation we would rectify it with our swords." Umar I answered, "Praise God who created in this Umma him who would rectify with his sword my deviation."

Similarly, Al-Ghazzali in his Ihya has narrated an incident when Muawiya did not pay allowances to the people. Abu Muslim al Khawlani openly told him that royal possessions were not a part of his patrimony. Muawiya, it is said, did not fly into rage and instead said, "Abu Muslim is right. This is not the result of my toil nor my father's. Come forward for your allowances." Authority which is not restricted by certain built-in moral restrictions turns intc a naked aggression and forfeits its right to govern people. Ibn-i-Khaldun in his discussion of the incident says :

> "Since kingship is an expression of the essential grouping together of humans and its basic characteristic is domination and force, both of which stem from irradicable strength rooted in mankind, the judgments of the holder of authority usually turns aside from the right and are unjust to whoever is under him, for he usually demands of them that, which is not within his power. This is because of his appetites. For this reason it is difficult to obey him."

Ibn Khaldun not only preached courage and sagacity, but also practiced it during his stay in Egypt. He was one of the signatories of the Fetwa which the Qadi's and scholars of Egypt drafted against the Mamuluk ruler Barquq on the 11th of November, 1389. In this fetwa, the ruler was declared guilty of unlawful appropriation of people's property, murder and several other charges of misconduct. He did so in spite of the fact that Barquq was one of his greatest benefactors from whom he had received all kinds of favours. For a healthy and constructive use of authority, its good and bad attributes should be exposed. Exposition of good that has been accomplished by a man in authority, will mobilize support for him and strengthen and increase his effectiveness, while uncovering of wrongs committed by him, will put him on the path of rectitude. There is more courage involved in blaming a man of authority than praising him, but the criticism should be free from malice and ought to be based on proper assessment of the whole situation. Similarly, in-appreciating good, one ought to be watchful, that he is doing so not as a sycophant, but as a person fully convinced of the righteousness of the acts performed by the decision maker.

The Politeness

This is a quality which has been universally acclaimed as a sign of culture and refinement. It engenders confidence and ensures peace and unity. In organized life where chances of friction are so frequent, politeness helps individuals to save themselves from many ugly situations. All religions and ethical disciplines have vigorously advocated politeness as an essential characteristic of human behaviour. The Quran applauds this quality as follows :

> "They are most honoured by God, who are the best in conduct those, who are most dutiful to God and are fraternally polite with one another."

Arrogance and attitudes of exultance are forbidden in Islam.

"To walk not in the earth exultantly or arrogantly."

This is a quality particularly useful for those, who exercise authority over others and have the power to be rude or harmful. Authority in itself is a blessing, provided it is used with benevolence for the perpetuation of right and avoidance of wrong. Al-Ghazzali is of the opinion that authority is essential for all organizations in a state, but one who holds it should be watchful that his decisions and actions do not betray malice or callousness.

In Akhlaq-i-Jalaly, the author, has quoted a tradition in which the Prophet is said to have prayed the following :

> "O Lord God, the officer who is benevolent to my followers in the exercise of authority connected to him, be then benevolent to him, and the officer who is severe with my followers in the exercise of authority committed to him, with him thou be severe."

Hazrat Ali in the instrument of instructions issued to Malike-Ashter on the latter's appointment as governor of Egypt said, "Malike, you must create in your mind kindness, compassion and love of your subjects. Do not behave with them as if you are voracious and ravenous beast."

Ibn-Khaldun has listed harshness as one of the fundamental causes of the decline of political systems. He points out that masses in general are not interested in the personality, fame and figure of their rulers. Their primary interest lies in how generous, good and benevolent they are in catering the needs of the subjects. He says :

> "Good rulership is equivalent to mildness. If the ruler uses force and is ready to met out punishment and eager to expose the faults of people and to count their sins (his subjects) become fearful and depressed and

> seek to protect themselves against him through lies, ruses and deceit. This becomes a character trait of theirs. Their minds and character become corrupted. They often abandon the ruler on the battlefield and (fail to support him) in defensive enterprises. The decay of sincere intentions causes the decay of military protection. Thus the dynasty decays and fences that protect it lie in ruin."

Politeness helps men in authority to win confidence, disarm resistence, and win support for government. It rescues rulers from excesses so commonly associated with power. Politeness, however, is to be exercised with caution and in a discrete manner. Indiscriminate use of it is likely to be understood as weakness of character. Islam has emphasized *modus vivendi* in this matter as the best course of action. Ibn Khaldun has elucidated this principle as follows :

> "In the case of all human qualities, the extremes are reprehensible, and middle road is praiseworthy. This for instance is the case with generosity in relation to waste and stinginess, and bravery in relation to foolhardiness and cowardice."

The Forgiveness

A forgiving man is always held in high esteem in a group. It is a manifestation of one's large-heartedness, and saves individuals from the corrupting influence of power. It cements social ties and ensures group cohesion. In all human situations this moral quality can help to create an atmosphere of fraternity. It is a quality which makes leadership effective, spacious and dignified. A leader who is magnanimous and forgiving is always respected and people render compliance to his commands willingly. The Quranic views on the subject are as follows :

> "Praised are they who restrain their anger and pardon the faults of others; and God loves those who do good to others."

> "God loves those who shun transgressions and indecencies, and whenever they get angry they forgive."

In understanding the ethical connotations of forgiveness in Islam, one important point should always be kept in mmd. Islam avoids extremes like "tooth for tooth" or "turning the left check when the right is smitten" because both are contrary to justice. Muslims are asked to practice a middle course avoiding everything which is impractical. The object is to create a climate of thought and action in society in which maximum good of the largest number of people can be ensured. Indiscriminate use of forgiveness can be as ruinous as stubborness, or excessive sternness. Forgiveness as a trait of politics and administration has to be exercised in the light of logic and rationality. The Quran says :

> "The recompense of an evil deed is punishment proportionate to it, but whoever forgives and amends he shall have his reward from Allah."
>
> "Take to forgiveness and enjoin good and turn away from the ignorant."

The Holy prophet once said, "There may well be persons, who through forbearance and forgiveness get the same degree (of merit) as those, who keep the fast and perform the prayer." Vengence and pride are against Islamic ethics. The tendency to lose one's temper quickly, and the inability to forgive people for their minor lapses, creates an atmosphere of awe and despair and brings disrepute to administration and government. Therefore, Muslim statesmen and writers have frequently referred to forgiveness as an indispensable quality of a good administrator. Hazrat Ali said :

> "Do not feel ashamed to forgive and forget. Do not hurry over punishments and do not be pleased and proud of your power to punish. Do not get angry and lose your temper quickly over the mistakes and failures of those over whom you rule. On the contrary, be patient and sympathetic with them. Anger and desire of vengence are not going to be of much help to you in your administration."

The Patience

Many evils in society stem out of hasty and miscalculated decisions. Errors of judgment and faults in policy-making can be reduced considerably if the decision makers have the habit of patiently investigating and reflecting over the issues in hand. Without entering into its psychological ramifications, one can say with some kind of certainty that patience as a characteristic of human behaviour has been preached by nearly all religious and ethical codes. Islam has also applauded patience, as one of the noble qualities of human character. In the words of the Quran :

> "We shall prove you, by afflicting you in some measure with fear, and hunger, and decrease of wealth, and loss of lives and fruit. Those who prove patient under such misfortunes are to be given good tidings of God's reward—to those who, when a misfortune befalls them."

Ibn Taimiyya has pointed out that patience includes "fortitude, restraint on anger, willingness to pardon people, check on evil desire and abstention from indulgence (in luxury), and from frowning." Because of its significant and vital role, in the formulation of human character, Quran has bracketed patience with prayer. It says :

> "And seek assistance through patience and prayer."

> "So hear patiently what they say, and celebrate the praises of thy Lord before the rising of the sun and before the setting."

A tradition of the Prophet has been narrated by Abdullah bin Abbas which says :

> "When God wishes the welfare of a community he blesses it with officers, who are patient and large-hearted."

In one of his sermons, Umar I condemned ignorance and impatience among officers as despicable public sins." So did Ali in one of his letters said :

> "This virtue of patience is one of high values of morality and nobility of character and is the best habit which one can develop."

The Peacefulness

Aggression has been condemned because it disrupts normal and peaceful conduct of human affairs. Peace has been advocated as a great blessing and a cherished asset for fruitful social evolution. It is a natural inclination, and if human beings do not cultivate this quality, society would be under constant threat of dislocation and anarchy. According to Islam, love for peace is a great embellishment of human character and individuals and communities get dignity and respect through it. The Quran is very eloquent and emphatic on this issue. It says :

> "Live peacefully with one another. If they (the other party) incline to peace, do you also incline to it ? There is much good in coming to agreeable reconciliation, i.e., to live peacefully. And the servants of the Compassionate (God) are those, who walk peacefully on earth."

It has also been pointed out that, men tend to practice violence on many trivial matters. This tendency is extremely detrimental to peace, stability, and general welfare of the community. Unless the material injury is heavy and stakes exceptionally high, the Muslims are ordered to adjust their claims by peaceful and conciliatory means. This quality of ignoring trivialities for the larger good of the society has been praised by the Quran in the following words :

> "And when they hear frivolous discourse, which they fear might lead to some quarrel, they do not listen to it, but pass on with dignity, and do not pick up quarrels on trifling matters."
>
> "Repel the evil deed which is vain or frivolous with such a better answer, as to make the person between whom and ourselves there was enmity or discord to become as though he was a bosom friend."

There is a general complaint against bureaucracy that its members tend to isolate themselves from people. They are not readily available to the members of the public. There are procedural and psychological barriers, and very often inaccessibility is paraded as a status symbol. With this attitude civil servants can never have the awareness of the needs of the masses, and this ignorance can make public policy hollow and ineffectual. A closer and constant contact between the public servant and the public can breed an atmosphere of trust and confidence, which is so essential for the success of governmental policies. A cloistered bureaucrat with no awareness of the needs of the people is certainly a misfit Public servants who are self-opinionated, secluded and arrogant can never implement public policies effectively. An administrator, who is easily accessible gets a greater fund of information and better perspectives for his decisions and avoids temptations. A life of seclusion makes an administrator extremely vulnerable to corruption. An officer who meets people readily, sits in a goldfish bowl. His activities are so transparent that he cannot indulge in any dishonest deal. An officer who is constantly interacting with members of the public, has to be extremely watchful about his reputation and performance.

Free and Easy Access

According to Islamic traditions of administration, officers at all levels and in all circumstances have to provide free and easy access to the public. During the Pious Caliphate, special emphasis was laid on this aspect of administrative behaviour. Umar I, in a letter to Muawiyya bin Abu Sufyan, gave special instructions that, he should not isolate himself from the people. He was ordered to maintain easy and facile communication with the masses. Knowing fully the evils that stem out of inaccessibility, Umar I warned his public servants to watch their behaviour continuously so that it did not smack of isolation or arrogance. In this connection his letter to Saad bin Abi Waqas deserves special consideration in which this high-ranking official of the state was administered a severe warning by the Caliph for his inaccessibility to the public.

"I have come to know that you have built a place for yourself which looks like a fortress wherein you live in complete isolation from the people. The doors of this place are closed to the public, and I assure you this place is an edifice of your foolishness, demolish its gates because it hampers peoples access to you and they cannot bring their needs directly to you."

The relationship between civil servants and the public is extremely crucial for social and political stability. If the people know that decision-makers in government are prepared to listen to them, the bonds between the governors and governed would be cemented with trust and confidence. Any political system where the relationship between the subjects and the rulers are polluted with suspicion cannot last very long. In the literature on administration repeated discussions have been unrolled regarding the causes of inaccessibility of the bureaucrats. According to Umar I, inefficiency is one of the major causes of inaccessibility. With arrears piling up every day, an officer does not have enough time to receive people as they flock to his office with complaints or petitions. Umar I, in a letter to Abu Musa, wrote as follows:

> "Let there be no doubt about it that efficiency depends on not postponing todays work until tomorrow. If you do that it will create confusion in work; you will mix priorities and nothing will be accomplished; shun as much as you can from worldly love and lust and imbibe deep-seated interest in the affairs of the masses. Give them audience for justice, even if it be only for one hour daily."

Similarly, Hazrat Ali in his famous letter to Malike-bin-Ashtar emphasized in unequivocal terms that officers must provide every possible facility to the public to vindicate their grievances freely. He wrote:

> "Out of your hours of work find a time for complainants and for those, who want to approach you with their grievances. During this time you should do no other work, but hear them and pay attention to their complaints and grievances. For this purpose you must arrange public audiences for them. During these audiences, for the sake of God, treat them with kindness, courtesy and respect—do not place a prestige curtain between you and those over whom you rule."

According to Nizam-ul-Mulk, accessibility should be a universal characteristic of administration in a country. In his opinions, every officer from the Head of the State to the functionaries working at the lowest level must cordially welcome people, who come to them in connection with some official work. If the highest officers are willing to communicate with people freely their subordinates in his opinion refrain from practicing oppression. Rank, status and position of a functionary should not tend to isolate him from the community, whose interest he is supposed to serve. In certain quarters, genuine apprehensions have been expressed that, if the people are endowed with the privilege of visiting officers at will, it might become an excruciating burden on the time of the officers. But a careful examination of the issue, however, will prove that this apprehension is ill-founded.

Accessibility does not mean unending flow of people in offices all the time. Its primary purpose is to inculcate among officials awareness about public needs and willingness to serve the masses. To this end, proper procedures can be adopted, which without impeding the efficient working of administration would provide the public easy access to the officials. Islam has not laid down any operational framework for this vital aspect of public administration. The emphasis is mostly on the attitudes of the administrators. Officers can organize any machinery, which in their opinion would reduce their isolation from the people. In other words the climate, within the political system should be such that strong and weak, confident and timid, all could have access to public authorities. The Holy Prophet once said, "Tell me always of the needs of those, who cannot reach me with their needs, he who transmits to the man in authority an account of the needy of those, who cannot satisfy their needs by themselves, Allah will render firm his feet on the bridge to Paradise on a day when most feet are never firm."

Akhlak-i-Jalali has also maintained that social systems get additional stability if the rulers take personal interest in the affairs of their subjects. Equity, in the opinion of the author of this treatise, depends on the frequency of interaction between the members of the community and public servants. He says:

> "The maintenance of equity is to be methodically conducted only where the prince himself inquires into his subject's circumstances, and conducts each of them to his due share of provision and dignity. And this object can only be realized where subjects and complainants have access to their prince in time of need."

It was a common practice among kings of ancient Persia and rulers of Muslim dynasties to fix a specific day and time when common men, irrespective of rank, status, and privilege could have direct access to them. Akhlak-i-Jalali refers to a tradition which mentions that Pharoah, in spite of his unbelief and tyranny, had two good qualities. Firstly, he was easily accessible to the people and secondly, he was generous and large-hearted to his subjects. The tradition further points out that there came a time when he discarded these qualities and "he made his "dwelling entirely in seclusion, or rather it may be said like the sulking bat in the den of aversion and repugnance, where none but Eblis (devil) and his attendant demons could obtain an interview." This was the time when the wrath of God descended upon him and this ultimately led to the disintegration of his empire.

Ibn Khaldun is also of the opinion that social organizations move very fast towards decay and dismemberment if the men in authority work in seclusion. He points out that inaccessibility of the rulers is symptomatic of their indolence and incompetence. A ruler of this kind, he says :

> "Seeks to keep away from the common people as much as possible. He employs someone at his door to admit (only) those of his friends and of the people of the dynasty whom he cannot avoid, and to prevent people (in general) from having access to him."

A weak and indolent ruler establishes court etiquette in a manner that only a limited number of people can have an access to him. Very often the members of the Inner circles, in order to perpetuate their own domination, contrive means to withhold information from the rulers about the actual state of affairs in the kingdom. All these are signs of political decay and inefficiency of the administrators.

A frustrated individual, who does not get a chance to unburden his grievances before the proper authorities, loses all interest in the welfare of the government. As this frustration multiplies, the system is bound to decline and deteriorate in efficiency.

The Sympathy

Philosophers and sages have labelled sympathy as one of the sterling excellences of human character. Fellow feeling is considered to be a natural element of man's nature. Sympathy stems out of several factors. It can be due to residence in a common territory, similarity of religious views, loyalty to the same profession, ideological and intellectual affinity, similarity of objectives and membership of a caste or a cult. There is also something called human sympathy in which the above elements are not involved. It is a sentiment which rises above all personal affiliations and is a manifestation of simple love for humanity. Sympathy can be instinctive as well as moral. As an instinctive passion, it is common to men and animals, but as a moral quality, it is a particularity of the human race alone. This quality, however, is not to be expended on sinners and wrong doers. The Quran explains this point as follows:

> "Sympathy and cooperation are enjoined upon you towards deeds of goodness and piety, but you must not cooperate towards sinful or transgressive deeds."
>
> "And plead not on behalf of any people who deceive themselves; God does not love anyone who is treacherous and sinfull."

Moral Quality

This shows that in Islam sympathy as a moral quality is subject to fundamental condition, that the one to whom sympathy is being extended is not a sinner or evil-minded person. Its indiscriminate use is disallowed because it is likely to encourage sin and crime in society.

In government and administration, it is not the individual act of sympathy which is so important. Emphasis here is on the general climate of thought and practice in which people can satisfy their needs without generating acrimony or hostility. If the government functionaries are unsympathetic and callous in their attitudes, a social system will remain unstable. Frustrated masses will be reluctant to provide the required fund of loyalty which in essence is the main support of healthy politics. Hazrat Ali, in one of his sermons, said, "The greatest of these reciprocal rights is that of a ruler on the ruled and that of the governed on the governing authority, but remember that no subject will be happy and contented unless the system of government is sympathetic, humane and congenial."

Sympathy, in order to be effective, has to be universal, and free from racial and sectarian prejudices. All sections of the population, even the religious minorities, have a right to receive sympathy from administration. Islam has accorded a special and privileged status to minorities in a Muslim kingdom. Their life, property, honour and privileges should be of special concern to the rulers. They should be recipient of the same kindness and sympathy which are reserved for the Muslims in an Islamic state, Hazrat Ali administered a severe warning to a governor who maltreated a religious minority. He wrote:

> "Remember Malik that, among your subjects there are two kinds of people : those having the same religion as yours and they are brothers unto you and those who have other religions than yours and yet are human-beings like you. Men of either category suffer from the same weaknesses and disabilities that human flesh is their to; they commit sins, indulge in vices either intentionally or foolishly or unitentionally without realising the enormity of their deeds. Let your mercy and compassion come to their rescue and help in the same way and to the same extent that you expect God to show mercy and foregiveness to you."

10

Economic Development

Historical Review

For the Classical economists, Smith (1723-1790) Malthus (1766- 1834) Ricardo (1772-1823), and Mill (1806-1863), the output depended on the size of labour force, the stock of capital, the amount of land available (known and economically useful resources) and the level of technique. Most classicists probably thought of the production function as linear and homogenous, that is, they expected the output to double if the quantities used of all the factors of production were doubled at once. There is an indication of circularity in their argument. The level of technique depends on profits, and profits depend partly on the level of technique. This circularity is no accident or oversight; it is precisely what the classicists, and most later economists, have wished to stress; in economic development nothing succeeds like success and nothing fails like failure. Thus a rapid rate of technological advance will tend to attract a level of investment that will permit the rapid technological advance to continue, but the reverse is also true.

We can break into the circular flow anywhere and show how the system will evolve under various conditions. An increase in profits brings an increase in investment, and so an addition to the stock of capital, which permits capitalists to take advantage of the steady flow of improved techniques and also raises the wage fund; that brings a rapid population growth, which causes decreasing returns to labour on the land, raising labour costs and reducing profits. In turn, reduced profits mean reduced investment, retarded technological progress, a diminished wage fund, and slowing down of population growth. Eventually, in a mature economy, diminishing returns to land, and the consequent rise in labour costs, will outrun effective technological progress. The profits fall, investment drops, technological progress is retarded, the wage fund ceases to grow, and so population also ceases to grow. In the classical model, the end result of capitalist development is stagnation.

The dialectical materialism of Karl Marx (1818-1883) is well known. For Marx, capitalism is merely one of a series of stages in the evolution of society towards the socialist state, which is the inevitable final form of economic, social and political organization. Each stage, of social evolution, with its characteristic technology and style, breeds its particular kind of class struggle which leads to its breakdown and the emergence of the next, higher form of social organization. Thus feudalism arose out of primitive communism, but feudalism led to a struggle between serfs and feudal lords, out of which arose a class of emancipated serfs, who became merchants and launched the first phase of capitalism. Capitalism brings a very high stage of technological advance. But capitalism leads eventually to a better class struggle between workers and capitalist, from which the workers will emerge victorious and establish the "dictatorship of the proletariat". This transitional phase will lead gradually to the full fledged Socialist (Communist) society. Poverty will disappear. The state will "wither away", as a superfluous institution in a society without conflict. Each will contribute to national income according to their abilities and receive from it according to their needs.

Marx considered technological change the prime mover of the whole system. The technology of each era in a country's development determines not only the economic situation, but also the style of the whole society. Obviously Marx did not foresee a process of economic growth in which technological progress brings such increase in productivity and total output that both wages and profits rise together. So far as its pure economics is concerned, Marx's system is less directly applicable to problems of underdeveloped countries than that of Malthus. Marx did not realy think of underdevelopment as an enduring state; underdeveloped countries were simply pre-capitalist ones, which, unfortunately would have to go through the Capitalist phase before they could attain the Elysian Fields of Communism. The Marxist sociological and political theory, however, provides some clues to the economic history of underdeveloped countries. It suggests to us that we look at power relations among social classes and see whether these relations are of a sort that impose barriers to spontaneous growth.

Essence of Development

To Schumpeter the essence of development is a discontinuance disturbance of the circular flow of economic life. The discontinuance disturbance comes in the form of an innovation, whilst the innovation is exploited by business leaders; the enterpreneurs. Schumpeter believes that unless business leadership of new men is forthcoming to build up new firms for the exploitation of innovations, Capitalist economics may suffer more or less chronic depression. For us it is particularly intersting to note Schumpeter's contribution to the role of entrepreneur: "the entrepreneur is, among other things, a social deviant, he is egocentric, untraditional and ambitious. The impulse to fight, to prove oneself superior to others, to succeed for the sake, not of the fruits of success, but of success itself. From this aspect, economic action becomes akin to sport - there are financial races, or rather boxing-matches. Finally, there is the joy of creating, of getting things done, or simply of exercising one's energy and ingenuity."

Whereas the classical school believed that capitalist development would end in stagnation, Marx and Schumpeter thought it would end incomplete breakdown.

It is of particular interest to us when Professor Higgins after a survey of theories of Development discussed above says, "we might do well, to abandon the search for a truly "general" theory at this stage, and content ourselves with a quest for a "special" theory of underdevelopment. Such a theory would be tailor-made for the institutional, technological, sociological and psychological conditions common to under-developed countries."

Max Weber's explanation of the "rise of capitalism" is at once most facinating and most controversial. According to him the reason for Capitalistic development in the sixteenth century was that the Reformation provided the proper philosophical and ethical setting for the "capitalist spirit" to flourish.

"The chief reward for making money was the feeling of having done the job well". This concept is to be found in Luther's doctrines under the name of the calling, the idea that each individual is called to do a certain job and to do it as well as possible. The highest form of moral conduct is the fulfilment of duty in worldly affairs. A similar but more general explantion of the rise of Capitalism was introduced by Tawney. Perhaps the most forceful critic of the Weber-Tawney thesis is H.M. Robertson. The capitalist, he says, is and always has been a purely secular creature who sees no reason for religion to meddle in his business affairs. Men do not need to be called to the pursuit of riches. If is clear that much of Robertson's criticism is justified, but he goes rather too far in his nihilism with respect to the Reformation. It is fairly generally agreed today that the Protestant ethic was one clement in the acceleration of of capitalistic development. The relationship between predominant religion and per capita income is too close for religion to be dismissed out of hand as a factor in past economic history. If we refer to any relevant volume of U.N. statistics, we can see that the six countries with the highest per capita incomes are Christain and Protestant. Of the twenty-two countries with per capita incomes above $ 600 per year, all but seven are predominantly Protestant, the others are predominantly Roman Catholic. The countries with per capita incomes between $ 250 and $ 600 are mainly Roman Catholic; those between $ 100 and $ 250 are mainly Roman Catholic and Muslim; those below $ 100 are Hindu, Budhist and Pagan. We cannot reach any conclusions about causes and effects on the basis of these facts, but these facts are worth pondering along with other facts. It is also to be noted that in other parts of the world or in other times, quite different relgions have produced the spirit of enterprise.

Those who associate the "rise of Capitalism" with the development of medieval commerce tend to stress the Crusades as a series of events leading to rapid progress. These basically religious movements had as their chief results the colonization of unsettled Continental districts, the opening of new Mediterranean markets and ports, the development of the European luxury trade with the Near East, the introduction of new commodities and new techniques into Europe, improved navigation and ships, better organized capital and foreign exchange markets, the beginning of the absorption of the old feudal aristocracy by the new commercial capitalists and the economic development of Italian cities. Indeed, if one wants to risk picking a single cause for the "rise of capitalism", the Crusades would seem to be the choice, for out of the commercial capitalism of the middle ages and the capital accumulation that it made possible grew the industrial capitalism of later periods.

W.W. Rostow " has explained economic growth in terms of various historical stages viz; (1) traditional society, (2) pre-condition for take off, (3) take off, (4) the drive towards maturity and (5) the age of high mass consumption. It has, however, been forcefully advocated by many critics that the history is not so obliging as to fall neatly into stages. There is again a circularity in Professor Rostow's reasoning. For example Rostow says:

> "For a society to a absorb new production functions, in ways which generate the spread effects on which the take-off depends, requires massive prior change away from the pattern of the traditional society. Before take-off can occur there must be changes in the economy's infrastructure, working force, agriculture, and foreign exchange earning or borrowing capacity. There must also be "changes in rules of behaviour", particularly in the form of emergence of a minimal initial group of entrepreneurs."

All that Rostow seems to be saying here is that for a take-off to occur, the conditions for a take-off must be present.

Rapid Growth

Sociological, as well as economic and political factors coincided to favour rapid economic growth of the Western World in the eighteenth and nineteenth centuries. There is a whole literature purporting to show how the Reformation raised the propensity to save. The byword of Puritanism was "make as much as you can, but save as much as you can". This attitude helped produce a flow of savings sufficient to finance the introduction of new commodities and new techniques brought by the Industrial Revolution. This attitude is lacking in most of the developed countries today. Not only are these countries poor so that large volumes of savings entail real sacrifices, but even among the higher income groups, both the propensity to consume and the propensity to import are high.

Dr. Doulas Lee analysing relationship between climate and economic development has reached the conclusion that geographic factors have some bearing on per Capita incomes, but we cannot explain development or underdevelopment in purely geographical terms.

Dr. J.H. Boeke has tried to understand the problems of under-development in terms of socio-economic dualism and in terms of limited wants and backward sloping supply curve of efforts and risk taking. Boeke considers Western economic theory as totally inapplicable to under developed areas. He admonishes "not to try to transplant the tender, delicate hothouse plants of Western theory to tropical soil, where an early death awaits them."

Professor MacClelland has related his concept of achievement to economic development. He feels that recent researches in the measurement of human motives have improved the capacity of psychologists to provide economists with the "hard facts", which he thinks they should have, if they are to interweave psychological analysis with their economic analysis. In most general terms, McClelland hypothesis that a society with a generally high level of achievement will produce more energetic entrepreneurs who, in turn, produce more rapid economic development.

Based on recent psychological researches, Professor Hagen has presented his theory of the transition to economic growth in form of a model wherein various economic, political, psychological, historical and cultural variables have been linked. According to him the Capital formation is frequently regarded as the process immediately responsible for continuing economic growth — growth in per capita output and income in a society. But it is clear that capital formation is important only as it is the carrier or agent of technological progress. The essential task, he says, is to isolate the forces which bring about the transition from virtualy stationaryy technology to continuing progress.

According to Professor Hagen the Schumpeterian entrepreneurship arises from the lower echelons of a relatively elite group. The dominant group has no incentive to go into risky financial ventures. The question is, then "why should the members of a group in the lower echelons of the elite turn vigorously at a certain time in history to economic development?" He reviews the common characteristics of all the groups which have done so in various countries to find the answer. This principle that only a group driven by an urge to regain or maintian a rightful social status will carry out the revolutionary actions which complete the transition to continuing technological advance. Hagen calls "the law of subordinated group". The members of the innovating group, Hagen continues, must have the "combination of world view and motivational structure", which results in a vigorous attack on their problem rather than resignation to their fate. He then states his law of relative social blockage: "a requisite for economic growth in a traditional society is not merely that upward social mobility by new means is possible, but also that upward social mobility by traditional channels is not possible".

Motivation Essential

Professor Hagen seems to be saying that if people are to have economic growth they must want it — in the sense that a suficient number of the subdominant elite are motivated towards economic activity of a sort bringing technological progress and economic growth, while the motivation of the rest of the society is such as to permit technological progress to spread throughout the society, if this reaction is to occur, Hagen syas, "the society as a whole must have common cultural bonds to be innovated. They must not be so alien, so different from other groups that their activity creates emotional antipathy rather than desire to achieve equal success by doing likewise". In this context it is interesting to note the central importance given by Ibn Khaldum to 'group solidarity or 'group conciousness' in the rise and fall of nations.

Finally, Hagen suggests that an external threat to a nation as a whole may be a powerful force towards development, especially if combined with internal factors in pushing the country toward technological change. This kind of combination of internal and external pressures, in Hagen's view, explains the relatively rapid transformation of the Japanese society from a stagnant one into one with sustained technological progress.

Commenting on the theories of MacClelland and Hagen, Professor Higgins syas "there seems to be no very clear way of creating the required attitudes, unless we revert to MacClelland's process of gradual change through education, a process which would certainly take a generation or two. Will underdeveloped countries wait that long? Some readers may recall that we have already come across Hagen's Laws. Schumpeter described his innovating entrepreneurs in much the same terms nearly half a century ago. He did not, of course, attempt to provide a complete psycho-sociological theory to support his view of the nature of the entrepreneurial class. Arthur Lewis also explains the rise of an entrepreneurial class in similar terms." The resemblance of these laws to Toynbee's" challenge and response thesis is also apparent.

Professoı Gunnar Myrdal has tried to explain under-development in terms of circular causation, "back wash" and "spread" effects. Professor Lewis has also admitted in passing the importance of leadership when he says: "the most plausible of all the explanations is the accident of leadership. If a community is fortunate to have a good leader, born at a crucial time in its history, who catches the imagination of his people guides them through a formative experience, he will create traditions and legends and standards which weave theselves into the thinking of his people, and govern their behaviour through many centuries. This is to some extent a biological accident".

Partial theories of economic growth viz; balanced growth, unbalanced growth, big push, etc., try to explain various problems involved in the dynamics of growth. It is none the less clear that none of these theories provides an adequate explanation of the real forces which stimulate the process of economic development, although some germs of the theory which we are developing here have been traced in Schumpeter, Weber, Tawney, Lewis, Marx, Hagen and Toynbee.

Towards a New Theory

In developing the thesis the pragmatic view of history is rejected, because pragmatic view takes seriously the dictum that in the long run we are all dead. It is essentially a short run philosophy. Pragmatic dreams are little dreams. And little dreams would not help us today. For all practical purposes, we live upon this earth but once, and at best we see but a small segment of it during a very brief existence. And what we see, we see through limited senses, clouded by the mists of particular ideas of the time we live in. Thus man-made doctrines of immutable truth are likely to confuse our thinking more than clarify it. Therefore, in the grand strategy of human life, the place of divine guidance cannot be substituted by any man-made philosophy.

After a prolonged and sustained study of economics and philosophy of history, the fact dawned upon me that inspite of the apparent reasons for economic malaise in Muslim and the underdeveloped countries i.e. the vicious circle of under-consumption, low productivity and poverty, the ultimate truth must lie somewhere else. The present state of underdevelopment is not primarily due to lack of adequate capital formation. Besides being short of even to start the process of economic growth; impetus, such as human endeavour and sacrifice that gave birth to dynamism of Islam the Renaissance, the Reformation and the Industrial and French Revolutions. It was this historical impetus that finally laid the foundation of the present sustained development in Europe.

But here impetus means faith, using the word in its broadest sense. The faith may be the gift of god or may comprise certain man-made ideal such as Marxist philosophy or Parliamentary democracy and so forth. You will see that all the poorer countries of the world are suffering from a lack of faith. It is amply clear that economic development requires more than physical inputs and their rational combination.

In the history of the Orient, the faith or impetus to progress-spiritual and economic — had largely come from the Prophets, whose career in this world was sealed many centuries ago. The Muslim Countries, therefore, cannot look forward to this source of direct inspiration. The faith of Islam is, however, there for all times to come. Does it need rekindling, and who will rekindle it? It is interesting to note the numerous references in the poetry of Dr. Muhammad Iqbal to a man of destiny, who regenerated the forces which led to the glory of Islam in the past. It will also be interesting to note here that as far as our own brother-in-faith are concerned, they always have a lingering hope that someone will come and put the things right rather putting things right themselves. The Western writers have referred to this as fatalism, indolence, lethargy, etc. However, this can claim certain historical causes, as countries of Islam had somewhat of a monopoly as far as Prophets were concerned.

Speaking in more mundane terms, it seems to me that in the final analysis economic development is a function of leadership.

The Western economic development inspite of the Western democracy can be related primarily to leadership of certain classes representing both thought and action and an all pervading faith generated by this leadership in the Western Institutions. The final truth, therefore, is to be found not in the tool-kit of the economists, but in the factors which lead to creation of leadership, and if its creation is at all to be left to human beings, it will necessarily be a very long process.

Before carrying the analysis any further it is essential to reach a conclusion as to what is what is the most essential quality of leadership.

The qualities of leadership have been enumerated by many in various ways, but in all the schemes certain facets such as faith, integrity, intelligence, selflessness, courage and so forth are common. In the present discussion we take such qualities as given. What then is the most essential and over- riding quality of leadership? This quality is the "sense of history", which means a perceptive insight into an objective significance of history.

O God! Bless me with a heart awakened and with an eye able to see mellowness in the wine.

(Iqbal)

Sense of History

The sense of history can be attained by two means; one is a high quality education and second is a prolonged discipline of struggle, particularly in face of physical danger. An enumeration of the top leaders of history will show that they all fall in one of the above two categories, that is, either they had attained the sense of history through a deep and penetrating scholarship or they had gone through a prolonged discipline of struggle in fighting for the liberation of their people and countries. As far as the latter category is concerned, unfortunately our country's struggle for independence was too short to offer any worth-while ground for evolution and tempering of the leadership. We are, in any case, now left with the second alternative only, that is of a high quality education.

Poor quality education creates its own problems and impedes the progress of economic development, which requires that policy makers, administrators and managers in particular, and the educated elite in general, should possess the qualities of clear and independent thinking. But in general this is what they seem to lack most glaringly, with the result one continuously finds our printed literature including Government reports on our economic and social problems full of mistakes of logic, inconsistent and self-contradictory arguments and fallacies of composition. Most of our graduates do not seem to attain the ability of the logical use of language; nor are they able to distinguish clearly between cause and effect and relevant and irrelevant. Our education system does not seem to cater for these qualities, which are the very hall-mark of an educated person. There is no doubt that the main reason for the poor quality of our education is the use of an alien language as a medium of instruction, which is also hardly conducive to the objectives of national coherence. As language is a tool of analysis and expression, a lack of control over it results in unclear and muddled thinking, and due to it, the elite which is responsible for introducing socio-economic changes is itself not clear about the objectives. This is, indeed, a great drawback. Nourished by this system, our leadership is also bound to suffer from a tainted vision and a faulty sense of history, leading to grave consequences.

The nations which lose their self-confidence and self-respect and do not have a clear concept of national purpose eventually fall to pieces. It is a paramount function of a leadership to create a sense of national purpose and national identity. If is very clear that the only thing which binds all Muslims is Islam. Its true presentation and extension is, therefore, extremely important."

The above model thus has supported the hypothesis that in the last analysis, the economic development is a function of leadership, which perhaps is a more adequate explanation of the dynamic process of development than has been offered so far.

Part - III

Present Scenario

11

Muslim World Today

The Muslim world is no isolated social group that could achieve its evolution in a closed vase. Its double participation as actor and witness, in the human drama demands an adjustment of its material and spiritual existence to the destinies of humanity. For integrating itself efficaciously in the world evolution, it must know the world, know itself, make itself known and proceed to an evaluation of its own values as well as all the values that constitute human patrimony. It is, doubtless, a difficult task in a world whose evolution does not obey any criteria. Noting these fact Gibb remarks in his usually exaggerated manner that:

> "... Instead of a broad current of soundly based and rationally acceptable arguments, modernism, lacking the discipline of controlled thinking often loses itself in a maze of subjective impulses and is ever liable to the danger of plunging headlong over some unseen precipice".'

However, as we have noted in the preceding chapter, this empiricism seems to be replaced, since the Palestine affair, by a critical spirit and a care for method; and the judgements and actions of the governments seem more and more oriented towards a better understanding of itself and the other, and by a deeper appreciation of the West and its spirit, even if it has not yet resulted in concrete social action, extending to the entire Muslim world, and in a consciousness of its resources. The Muslim world has not still arrived at technical action which alone could accord it a place in the modern world where a sense of efficacy stands first in the scale of values. This necessity has become all the more imperative for the world stands today at the, end of a term that has lasted for centuries and the commencement of another, marked from the very outset by the Shakespearien, dilemma: To be or not to be.

Equally Divided Chances

In fact, the present conditions are so contradictory that the chances of humanity seem to be equally divided between the one or the other alternative. If scientific and economic factors have put the world in a state of prefederalism, the ideas on the contrary, have maintained, therein, all the ferment of discord and conflict. One finds again here, at its most violent, the imbalance that has always existed between a retarded consciousness and a progressive science. Only this time the imbalance has become incompatible with the very existence of the species. The economic conditions created by the 19th century have gradually imposed, in various fields, positive measures that have given the world a planetary character. The birth of international organisations, social, economic and political, bears witness to the growing necessity felt by people all over the world, to organise their lives in common. Thus every day one sees the outline of a universal federation asserting itself. This tendency has become even more pronounced since the Second World War and today assumes many new aspects, not the least picturesque among them is that illustrated by the "citizen of the world".

It is most of all the technical factor that has accelerated this movement. Technique has abolished space, leaving only the distance of their culture among the peoples. But the latter seems only to have increased, when one thinks of the poor wretch in Algeria where none bothers to educate him, and the man who disintegrates the atom in U.S or Russia. Science has abolished the geographical distances between men but an abyss persists between their consciousness. Thus the facts and the ideas contradict each other. The world has become a tiny, extremely inflammable ball wherein the fire that touches one end could instantly spread to the other. It is no longer possible to divide the problems and the solutions, to treat Europeanism in separation from colonialism. Only twenty years before, the Indo-Chinese conflict would have been confined to its geographical borders. Today, it is as much the concern of a docker from Oran—interested as a colonised, as that of a Japanese, interested as a consumer of rice. The world has been shaken from top to bottom. A new page commences in history under the heading: Humanity must be one or cease to exist.

Peaceful Solution ?

Would the world leaders find a happy and peaceful solution to this dilemma? Unfortunately, if one could judge from their actions, they give the desultory impression of somnambulant painters busy in repainting an old worm-eaten building while pick-axes attack its foundations to pull it down. The painting brush is a ridiculous and out of the place instrument on a ruined site where one needs shovels and trovels for clearing the debris of the old world and for building the new. But if men would refuse to build the new world, it would come into being itself, in its own manner. Certain ideas still maintain colonialism, but the factors of its annulment would, in the end, prove decisive. But for the moment this contradiction is tragic. One might well wonder, what could the proclamations of the "respect for the human person" and the "declaration of human rights" signify to men, domesticated, nativised and "civilised" in the colonialist manner? At the basis of all this we find the common denominator, a materialist culture that could promote an empire or imperialism but not a civilisation.

Inertia of the Matter

Endowed with all the inertia of the matter, this culture is incapable of following the evolution of its own products. It has immured itself in this even by its own Cartesian method. One is pre-occupied not with finality but with causality. The problem of the destination of the object with regard to man has yet to be posed to the Western conscience—one produces, but is incapable of distribution. The rationalist Europe that has created the machine, finds itself incapable of posing the human problems. All non-measurable relationships escape his consciousness. One knows how to fashion the matter but does not know how to render it useful to man. The process of production in Europe does not define the object by its relation to man, but defines the utility of man with regard to the fabricated object.

No Morality

Europe has become technician, but has ceased to be moral, no longer able to discover human, perspectives beyond the numbers, the quantity, beyond the limits of a world solely defined in material terms. A civilisation finds its equilibrium between the spiritual and the quantitative, between finality and causality. As soon as this equilibrium breaks down in one direction or the other, there comes the vertical fall. The Muslim civilisation lost its equilibrium, the moment it ceased to observe the just relation between science and conscience, between the material factors and the spiritual order, thus, foundering in pure metaphysical anarchy and maraboutic chaos that have formed its decadence. We are witnessing today, another disequilibrium—the Western civilisation that has lost the sense of the spiritual, finds itself, in its turn, at the brink of the abyss.

No Separating Values

Thus for the Muslim world, it is no longer a question of separating values, but of coupling science and conscience, ethics and technique, physics and metaphysics, in order to realise a world according to the law of its causes and the imperative of its ends. But for reviving its vigour to the world, their must be a new man capable of assuming the responsibilities of his existence. morally and materially, both as a witness and an actor. The post-al-Muwahhid man is certainly too old, too decrepit; but the Muslim world, nonetheless, contains a large share of this necessary youthfulness. The Muslim has retained, in fact, despite his colonisibility an essential sense of the moral value which the old modern spirit lacks. At the same time, Islam is on the way to renew itself, thanks to the Cartesian value.

This synthesis which is slowly taking place, would no doubt gain momentum once problems begin to be tackled with the scientific spirit that has become the factor of the acceleration of history. This method singularly shortens the stages and eliminates those unnecessary. The medieval, traditional Japan that opened its doors to Commodore Perry in 1868, cleared in one stage the distance that separated it from the 20th century. But it has done so technically, methodically, by tightening its schedule and scientifically utilising man, soil and time. The Muslim world must, in its turn, jump over the interval of its retardation by tailoring its means and activities. The Palestine affair has brought home to it the necessity of such a course while indicating certain new paths. It now seems willing to commence a new experience, taking into account the drawbacks and errors of the past, without which the lesson of history, more particularly of the last years, would lose all significance. Certain stages, like nationalism, which once appeared necessary are no more than archaism bypassed by history.

Inevitable Disintegration

The present world is a product of the inevitable disintegration of the colonist and colonisable world that we knew ten years ago. But, at the same time, this disintegration has laid bare the profound sense of history; on the one hand, it has revealed the unity of problems and needs in the world, and on the other, highlighted the necessity of re-adjusting relations among peoples. Colonialism and nationalism are alike condemned. Colonialism is no longer compatible with an international existence which could not be based on force; the universal conscience would solemnly condemn it as the cause of troubles, regression and war. Hitherto the colonial compact could attack the life, consciousness and even the very existence of the colonised and one turned a blind eye in the "civilised" countries. Now international diplomacy finds itself faced with a dilemma: the colonial compact or the human compact. One could not form part of a human order when one is either colonised or coloniser.

The world is well on the way to realise itself on a planetary scale, to totalise itself, its resources and its needs. It is in a fair way to realise institutionally the direction of history. "Liberalism" cedes place to a rational order that tends towards general harmony, not in accordance with vague Utopian plans, but with strict law of vital necessities. The Muslim world would have to take into account this decisive step of history in its own evolution. Formulas such as pan-Arabism and pan-Islamism are, henceforth, just as obsolete as pan-Europeanism that one wants to resurrect at Strasbourg.

Of course, optimism and pessimism are alike forbidden as regards the chances of peace. But it must be stated that countries do not seem to understand the significance of the decisive stage which the World is about to clear as expressed by the title of the work "The World is One". Still its author seems concerned only with the spatial aspect of this unity that cannot but strike a person crossing the 360 degrees of the globe in a few hours. But the unity of the world has always been the essential phenomenon of history while the divisions constitute mere accidents, the epi-phenomena. If it escapes the Cartesian mind, it is because its formative culture ascribes the commencement of history to the foundation of Rome, and of thought to the academies of Athens. It is curious how, even the greatest European minds seem incapable of rising above the hellenic thought. As soon as they cross the frontier of "Greco-Latin humanities", they seem to be wandering on another planet. One must, all the same, note a new tendency evident in the work of a Guenon or a Huxley, systematically studying and bringing to light the common foundations of mystical thought in the world. These efforts are doubtless still fragmentary and too recent. Moreover they only touch reality at the top; therefore, it is as yet hard to determine their effects on the daily relations and direct contacts between men and peoples. However, converging with the facts already mentioned, they provoke humanity to resolve its dilemma.

In any case, the Muslim world is already, by its very atavism, half-way towards the new world. However backward, the Post-al-Muwahhid man realises better than the civilised man the psychological' conditions of the new man, the "citizen of, the world", or according to the prophetic expression of Dostoievski, of the "Omni-man". To be sure, he must still attain the material level of the present civilisation by applying all his faculties of adaptation to the temporal order of the atomic era, so deeply marked by the technical spirit. But his role remains, above all, spiritual, as moderator of the excesses of materialist thought and national egoisms. Already, while tracing the path of its spiritual renaissance, Iqbal had called for the Muslim world a turn of mind capable of considering things and institutions "not from the standpoint of social advantages or disadvantages to this or that country, but from the point of view of the larger purpose which is being worked out in the life of mankind as a whole .... ". This metaphysics of Iqbal could undoubtedly shock minds warped by a rationalism to which all that escapes the known dimensions seems irrational; but the question is worth posing since it governs the attitude of the man in the new world and the future of civilisation.

It would be proper, here, to adopt the cosmic point of view for seizing the integral sense of history. The eminent Swiss historian, Custave Jecquier, after studying a four thousand years' slice of Egyptian history, arrived at certain significant conclusions:

> "We ascertain" he says, "that among this people, the civilisation, once its path had been traced, follows it without ever straying from it. Even political upheavals failed to force it out of the path climbing in gentle ascent. The great historical crises, however, permit us to mark a certain number of stages in the history of civilisation and by grouping them in periods, to discern better the progress realised in the course of centuries...."

Here is a view that envisaging quite a large perspective of history, seems to embrace two distinct orders of facts: On the one hand, a civilisation that follows "a path mounting in gentle ascent", and on the other "the political upheavals" with all the inherent human contingencies, the triumphs, the fanfares, the births, the funerals and the sorrows.

On the one hand, a harmonious line traversing without a break the millenaries, and on the other, the human drama with its upheavals. But this clearly marked distinction between the two orders does not break their unity. The link between the two is of a dialectical nature: man is the fundamental condition of all civilisation and civilisation constantly fixes the human condition.

Seized in their total human perspective, even the most ordinary facts acquire a significant complexity. For example, in a town a wedding is a commonplace event; evidently, it has a meaning for the married couple and their families, but it also matters to the simple beggar, since the Muslim tradition offers him on this occasion a meal that would sustain for a day his precarious existence. Thus the same event could concern different lives and link up different orders of facts. These liasions are sometimes very subtle; a man could die in Algeria because another man has done or not done such and such a thing that day in Sidney. This remark becomes all the more true when an event gets more complex and goes beyond the individual, local or even national plane. Certain events surpass the framework of simple, rational interpretation founded on immediate human factors, material, moral or political and appear rather to partake of an irrational order whose content could not be seized by Cartesian reasoning.

Beyond Human Design

Among the many such examples furnished by history is that of Tamerlane, whose epic clearly extends the historical perspective beyond that of simple human design. For a "rational" construction of the history of this epic, one would, of course, re-assemble its elements and coordinate them in accordance with the central figure of its hero. One would perceive, however, that the rational elements pertaining to the man and his personal factors do not give us a satisfactory explanation of his career. In fact, this man was no mercenary or a simple bearer of sword. His religious and political sense, his military and administrative genius make him a complex but perfectly defined personage. Yet we find him wielding his sword against the Golden Horde that was in a fair way to conquer Europe, under the energetic direction of Toghtamich. We see equally the redoubtable blade of Tamerlane descending, neither on China, the legacy of his ancestor, Chengis Khan, nor on India, the future conquest of his descendant, Babur, but on the Ottomon empire where Bazajet had assembled an army of five hundred thousand men for conquering Vienna. Why this singular behaviour? The dynastic right, ambition, the unique chance of an easy victory, religious sentiment, that is to say, all the human factors of policy and military strategy were on the same scale of the balance. Why then do we find the other scale inclining? The Golden Horde as well as the army of Bazajet, is destroyed. One has right to demand what imponderables could have acted here to tilt thus the balance of history? Such a question may be regarded as surprising under the pretext that it belongs to the metaphysical order. But for giving to the events an integral interpretation compatible with all their contents, one must envisage them, not only in relation to the causality but of their finality in history. Under this relation, it might be necessary at times to reverse the historical methodto see the phenomena in perspective instead of seeing them in retrospective, to consider them in their culmination rather than in their point of departure. For understanding the epic of Tamerlane, for example, one must ask what would have happened if Toghtamish had occupied Moscow and then Warsaw and if Bazajet had planted his standard on the monuments of Vienna and thereafter of Berlin? In such a case Europe would have inevitably passed under the triumphant sceptre of Islam. But then, does not one see quite another perspective surging out of history? One sees the renaissance of Europe-still in gestation-melting into the "Timurid renaissance". But while equally brilliant, the two did not have the same significance. The one was the dawn that shone on the genius of Galileo and Descartes, the other was but the beautiful twilight that had already enveloped the Muslim civilisation in its decline. The one was the commencement of a new order, the other, the end of an order drawing to its close. Nothing then, could have saved the entire world from the night that was softly stealing over the Muslim countries. Had Tamerlane but followed his own impulse, nothing could have stopped the end of civilisation.

Howsoever that may be, the tenor of historical facts is not so simple as might appear from a merely individual or national point of view. There is according to Iqbal a "plan d'ensemble" that reveals the direction of the events. Why did Tamerlane prevent Bazajet and Toghtamich from planting Islam in the heart of Europe? So that Christian Europe may pursue the civilising effort which the Muslim world, at the end of its last breath since the 14th century, was no longer capable of doing. The epic of the Tatar Emperor illuminates a finality of history since it has had a conclusion conforming to the continuity and perenniality of civilisation; so that its cycles may succeed each other, and the perpetual relay of genius may continue to operate on the path of progress. A cycle born in certain psychotemporal conditions develops therefrom, and when the human civilisation has outstripped them, it is the end of a cycle. Another commences in new conditions that would, in their turn, be passed by. It is this law that traces across the millenium of history, this "path mounting in gentle ascent" that humanity slowly scales. The finality of history mingles with that of man.

Internal Factors

The life does not analyse; it integrates. When the elements available are compatible and assimilable, it makes a synthesis of them; if they are heteroclite and disparate, it makes them a syncretism, an accumulation, a chaos.

Mixed Product

Today the Muslim world is a mixed product of the inherited residues of the post-al-Muwahhid epoch, and the new cultural deposits of the Reformist and Modernist currents. As seen above, this product is not the result of a reflected orientation or scientific planification, but it is a motley composition of crude archaisms and non-filtered innovations. This syncretism of elements from different periods and different cultures, without any natural or dialectical link, has engendered a world with its head in twentieth century and feet in fourteenth century, and that carries in its intestines all the intermediary epochs.

A heteroclite world afflicted with such incompatibilities and contradictions that even a great spirit like Iqbal was assailed by uncertainty over the problem of women as expressed in this melancholy couplet:

> "I too at the oppression of women am most sorrowful.
> But the problem is intricate, no solution do I find possible."

Iqbal could neither bear her present plight, nor approve the deplorable condition of her European counterpart. His anguish is a reflection of the general trouble that reigns in Muslim spirit after half a century of reform and attempted adaptation. The current aspect of Muslim renaissance is marked, above all, by the fact that it has adopted "objects" and "needs" in place of "notions" and "means". Thus, one would find chairs and desks introduced in the madarsah, without any change in the centuries old curriculum. The advocates of Arab culture show a paradoxical attitude, desiring certain ends, but not wishing to adopt the means necessary for their achievement. For instance, they have not even decided in the field of modern instruction to return to Arab numerical system, adopted by the West since Gerbert. The common denominator of six centuries of decadence brings round the modernist and the reformist tendencies to the syncretist confusion of borrowed novelties and inherited residue. This chaos of unassimilable elements results in discordant and violent contrasts, such as that presented by the sight of a copiously turbaned gentleman sipping an anisette at a bar counter.

Vague Idea

Such gross, simple examples could, however, furnish only a very vague idea of the chaos. In every new-born society that sets to organise itself, there are traditional elements beside those of modern inspiration. The latter, borrowed in general from a society already organised, demand for their proper assimilation an effort of analysis and adaptation that in reality constitutes an effort of creation and synthesis. A precise determination and constant vigilance of the critical spirit is needed to impose upon the necessary borrowings, the indispensable conditions of compatibility, utility and convenience. The early Muslim society found itself faced more than once by such problems, and in each instance resolved them in a conscious and happy manner, as in the matter of adopting a mode of the call to prayer. This new "necessity" in the Muslim society already existed in Christian society where the call was made by the sound of bells, and one could simply borrow this means. However, the Prophet and his Companions after reflection opted for an original mode of call: the human voice, thus avoiding the import of bells. Here is an example of a new society that creates its own "means" to responed to this new need. To take another example: the choice of the *minbar* is in all probability, an adaptation of the Christian pulpit. But this adaptation did not take place just simply as a 'newneed', but as a psychological necessity and artistic possibility for Muslim society.

Deliberate Choice

Other usages and "traditions" were similarly admitted in the early Muslim society, but only after a deliberate choice between one means and the other, between diverse procedures and conceptions. In these conditions, the borrowing became naturally integrated to Muslim life, since it responded at the same time to its objective and its means. In the scientific field we find Farabi and his school admitting the philosophy of Aristotle into Muslim thought after having Islamised it, just as later on Thomas Aquinas de—Islamised, Aristotle for adapting it to the Christian society that, in its turn, was being born and organised. Now, since the last century, Muslim society finds itself once again confronted by the same problem.

The Muslim dilemma concerns, on the one hand, the crucial problem of borrowings from modern civilisation and falls in the bio-historical order, and on the other, constitutes a psychological and dialectical problem, concerning the attitude of the Muslim towards his current life.

As to the first problem, one finds that just as in biology, blood transfusion is possible only between similar organic constitutions, the sociological elements that characterise different cultures are not all and always interchangeable. One could ascertain it in 1933 in America, when the temporary introduction of the "dry regime" produced a social trouble as grave as the alcoholism which it sought to remedy. One cannot, however, say that American conscience or psychology were by nature opposed to the "dry regime" or that the jahili organism was better predisposed in this regard: the prohibition, nevertheless, succeeded in establishing itself in Muslim countries, thanks to the Quranic imperative that introduced it in the psychology and usages of the jahiliyyah.

Consequently, new sociological elements could be assimilated only in certain determined conditions provided by an imperative need or a superior imperative. But the Muslim society has failed to take count of these conditions since half a century, making its borrowings without any criteria, or criticism, pushed sometimes by force, but mostly by snobbism and bankruptcy of the spirit. The confusion reigning in the intellectual, moral and political domains results from a melange of decayed ideas, inherited from the past, and borrowed ideas, all the more dangerous because of their displacement from their historical and rational context. For instance the adage "each for himself and God for all", found its necessary antidote in European social organisation, but it could only prove fatal in Muslim society where it replaced the essential social principle of Islam, "each for all and all for each". Sometimes the fatal principle is borrowed from a scientific context acquiring thence a pernicious prestige. Thus the Darwinian principle of the "survival of the fittest" has become an adage of our modern moralists who never doubted that, what was true in zoology could be false in sociology, where "the best" often signifies the "worst". Even in Europe this principle torn from its scientific context had engendered the racist philosophies of Gobineau and Rosenburg. Initially the cause of the concurrence and emulation that favoured the material development of the Western world, it soon transformed the "best" into a rotten man who did not recoil from any means that would ensure his triumph over the "idiots" hampered by their scruples, resulting in veritable gangsterism in this Western society that had erected a zoological principle into a moral principle. It is such ideas, pernicious even for the civilisation that gave them birth, that frequently pass into Muslim renaissance, thus accumulating in a society already encumbered with the residue of its own decadence, the residue of another de-composition. A filteration of dead and deadly ideas constitutes, therefore, the basic task of a veritable renaissance, that must be undertaken consciously and systematically.

Incapacity to Act

The incapacity to think and act characterises also the second aspect of the problem, and may be witnessed in the psychological domain by the absence of a dialectical link between thought and its concrete finalisation. One finds, on analysis the process of an activity in the private or public order wanting in one respect or the other. For example, the Islamist thought aims at the reform of man, but one never sees the reformer in the places where the object of his reform is to be found—in the cafes, market places and other public venues where the social evils he wishes to correct are directly in evidence. Likewise the programme of an Islami madrasah does not differ essentially from that of a traditional school and the word "Islam" becomes a simple etiquette that may cover useful activities but is truncated from the doctrinal idea.

Besides this divorce between thought and action, the inertia of the Muslim spirit is also imputable to a confusion between the essence of phenomena and their appearance which has, from the beginning, characterised the modern intellectual movement, The science that it has borrowed from the Western universities is not a means of "being better", but of "appearing better". Its inefficacy in the life of the Muslim world can be judged by its failure to produce any outstanding personality in the realm of human knowledge. Gibb wrongly ascribed this weakness of the Muslim intellectual movement to the natural characteristic of a spirit solely directed towards the "known"; in fact, its organic cause lay in the absence of the "intellectual tension", a weakness peculiar to the post-al-Muwahhid spirit. The Reformists too, like the Modernists, failed to modify essentially the intellectual attitude in this respect. Intelligence is constantly the function of the spirit: when the latter no longer possesses its purity, the former no longer has all its depth. The Islamist did impress the soul with a certain dynamism, but the latter has remained sterile for want of a systematic orientation. It is the drama of a movement that wishes to liberate itself from apathy, of the spirit struggling against its incoherence of the man who has been awakened, but does not know what he must do.

This organic impotence is reinforced by moral, social and political paralysis, the former being the gravest since it, in a certain measure, determines the others. From the indisputable verity "Islam is a perfect religion" the post-al-Muwahhid man drew the deadly syllogism: "We are Muslims, therefore we are perfect", that tends to sap all perfectibility in the individual by neutralising in him all concern for attaining perfection. It is a long time since Umar Ibn-al-Khattab regularly took stock of his conscience and often wept over his faults. One finds today reigning among the ruling class the most perfect moral quietitude, and no leader would be seen making his mea culpa in public.

So, the Islamic ideal of "life and movement" has foundered in the pride and complacency of a bigot who believes to have realised perfection by performing his five daily prayers, without trying to amend or improve himself. The beings immobilised in their mediocrity and their imperfectible imperfection become, thus, the moral elite of a society where verity gives birth only to nihilism. The difference is essential between verity as a simple theoretical concept enlightening abstract reasoning, and active verity that inspires concrete facts. Verity could even prove disastrous as a sociological principle when it no longer inspires action, but paralyses it; when it no more conicides with the motification of change, but with the clibis of individual and social stagnation. It could then become the origin of a paralytic world which Renan and Father Lammens denounced, saying that Islam is "a religion of stagnation and regression".

Intellectual Paralysis

Moral paralysis results in intellectual paralysis: when one ceases to perfect himself morally, one also ceases to modify the conditions of his life. Gradually thought finds itself petrified in a world that no more reasons, since its reasoning has no longer a social object. The "taqlid" or moral conformism implies a renunciation of the intellectual effort, of this "jihad" that was the essential directive of the Muslim spirit in the great period. After 'Abduh, "tajdid" in the Reformist movement became basically a literary renewal tied to the rules of a stifling traditionalism and classical themes. On the Reformist side, it has remained tied to classical themes: theology, law, philology, scholastic; and in none of these fields, it has gone beyond the landmarks left by the masters of the Reform. On the Modernist side it seems to have moved further with Taha Husayn. Though the work of this writer could not be termed a doctrine whence new tendencies could emerge, yet its very singularity has led to an agitation of ideas, paving the way for discussion and a movement of thought. However, this movement has remained fragmentary and without articulation, for the Muslim world still lacks academies that would direct its intellectual life and establish mutual contact and dialogue as once existed. between the Ghazalian and Averroist schools. Thus it comes about that the work of Taha Husayn has barely touched the literary milieus of North Africa, while that of Iqbal does not even find an echo therein. Even in independent Muslim countries, thought has not still acquired its personality, its right to be stated, "and its social value as the essential basis and means of action. In Algeria particularly, the thought is not an action, but a motif of decoration, that is to say, something that does not come under the law of formal or practical logic, but rather under that of the post-al-Muwahhid aesthetique.

The absence of a direct relation between thought and action implies blind, incoherent action and results in a subjective appreciation of facts-in their over-estimation or under estimation. In the modern Muslim world, it has given birth, on the one hand, to a psychosis of the "easy thing" that leads to blind action, and on the other, to a psychosis of the "impossible thing" that paralyses action. In Algeria the latter is based on three well-known axioms:

— We cannot do anything, because we are ignorant.

— We cannot realise that, because we are poor.

— We cannot undertake this work, because there is the colonialism.

While men of good faith thus explain their incapacity, the charlatans use them for justifying their lucrative enterprise of mystification, under the complacent regard of colonialism. However, the least effort of investigation would reveal that these supposed "verities" are but a cover for certain myths.

We are ignorant — it is a fact, and it stems from colonialism. But what is the role of the existing educated cadres? Do they use their education as elementary and immediate means to fight general illiteracy? One has seen how under German occupation, the Israeli intellectuals, despite strict surveillance, were concerned to use their learning for the benefit of their people. There are very few Muslims, pharmacists, doctors or professers who think - in Algeria and beyond their profession of popular education. Of course, on the electoral plane, the Muslim elite has not failed to demand an increase in the number of schools. But what is the good of multiplying the schools, so long as one does not 'ameliorate' the teaching? By multiplying the nullity, one can never obtain anything but the nullity. If the educated individual is himself inefficacious, if his education is without social efficacy, the myth of 'ignorance' is a dangerous myth because it masks under the problem of the illiterate man, the more profound problem of the post-al-Muwahhid man, whether ignorant or educated.

Myth of Poverty

Equally dangerous is the myth of poverty. It would suffice to consider the social efficiency of the financial means of the rich Muslim bourgeoisie that ranks even below that of the poor class. Very few rich Muslims would suffer to lower their standard of living to help the intellectual or technical formation of a poor child, or to sustain a work of public utility. This bankruptcy is not particular to the individual, but is also found at the level of so-called cultural organisations that would not give up certain wholly superfluous expenses for the sake of encouraging and aiding culture. It is a course of useless spending. It also seems that in this field the poor have no cause to envy 'the rich, One can, in fact, ascertain the usage that the "poor" make of their money anywhere. I have had recently a chance to ascertain it once again in a small town in Constantine where a madrasah, the only work of public utility, balanced itself precariously on a modest budget of six hundred thousand francs. Now an overall, on the spot, survey allowed me to calculate that the "poor"and they are really so, had spent in one single evening more than two hundred thousand francs, in between two cinemas, a circus, a travelling booth and a number of cafes. Basing on figures of this sort, one could appreciate the rate of efficiency of the Muslim capital, that is to say, the relation between the budget of utilities e.g. that of a madrasah and the budget of futilities such as those of we have just enumerated. In this case, the wastage was 95%. It is an indication of the entropic evolution that reigns in all the fields of modern Muslim life. The wastage ratio mounts even higher during the ceremonies—marriages, circumscisions, funerals, that cause frightful budgetary haemorrhages in the life of Muslim families. The same is the case in public life. In 1948 the U.N. delegation of Arab League in Paris disposed of a 500,000 dollar budget, yet it failed to publish a single document on the Palestine issue, while the Israelis inundated the world with their propaganda. This enormous disproportion between the means and the results is typical of all the Muslim public activity. We are no doubt "poor" but we show no concern in remedying it by a more judicious utilisation of the available means. The case of the Arab League is no exception. In all domains, public or private, wherever money exists, it is ill utilised. Even if the budget of the Arab delegation had been increased, it would'nt have resulted in an augmentation of their means and efficiency, but only of their needs, and expenses. For the problem before the Muslim world is not financial, but psychological and technical, that of the "orientation of the capital".

There is finally the third myth which, under the name of colonisation, paralyses all good wills, often justifying veritable moral and political swindlings. It is important to note concerning the myths under discussion, that the inhibiting cause does not come from outside, but from within, born of the psychology of the men, the ideas, the tastes and usages that constitute the post-al-Muwahhid spirit, in a word, from their "colonisibility"

Role of Colonialism

The role of colonialism is certainly crushing, since it strangulates each thought and intellectual effort, each tentative of moral or economic recovery, that is to say all whatsoever that could give an impetus to "native life." It technically inferiorises the humanity delivered to its law, this law that we have designated the "colonising coefficient". But this coefficent does not affect the fundamental worth of the individual that escapes his power. Now, we find the individual inefficacious and inert even in domains where the colonial pressure cannot be incriminated. Thus colonialism acts, at the same time, as a reality when it effectively inhibits action, and as a myth when it becomes an alibi or a mask for colonisibility. There is a historical process which must not be overlooked if we are concerned with the essence of things rather than their appearances. This process does not commence with "colonisation" but with "colonisibility" that provokes it. Moreover, colonisation is to a certain degree the most fortunate effect of the colonisibility because it reverses the social evolution that has engendered the colonisible being: the latter becomes conscious of his colonisibility once he is colonised and thus finds himself obliged to "de-indigenise" himself and become incolonisible. It is in this sense that one can understand colonisation as a "historical necessity". Here a distinction should be made between a country simply conquered and occupied and a colonised country. In the former, a pre-existing synthesis of man, soil and time, implies an incolonisable individual; in the other, the existing social conditions betoken the colonisibility of the individual, and foreign occupation inevitably becomes a colonisation. Rome had not colonised but conquered Greece. England, while it had colonised 400 million Hindus, could not colonise Ireland. On the contrary, Yemen though never colonised, could not profit from its independence because of its colonisibility. Morocco though independent till 1912 did not profit from the experience of Algeria, colonised on its very frontiers since a century. It is from the moment of its own colonisation that it has embarked on a real effort of recovery under the inspiration of Sidi Muhammad ben Youssef.

Thus colonisation is not the primary cause to which one may impute the bankruptcy of men and the listlessness of spirit in Muslim countries. For carrying a valid judgement in this field, one must follow the colonial process from its origin,rather than to take count only of the present moment; that is to study it as a sociologist and not as a politician. One would then ascertain that colonisation introduces itself in the life of a colonised people as a contradictory factor that helps it to surmount its colonisibility. By the intermediary of colonisation, colonisibility thus becomes its own negation in the consciousness of the colonised; the latter then forces himself to become noncolonisable. For more than half a century, the history of the Muslim world has merely represented the development of this contradiction introduced by colonialism in the state of things that characterised and constituted colonisibility. There is thus a positive aspect of colonisation in that it liberates potentialities that have for a long time remained dormant. Even if it constitutes, on the other hand, a negative factor since it tends to destroy the very same potentialities by applying to the individual the "colonising co-efficient", one fact is significant: history has never recorded the perenniality of the colonial fact. The essential forces of the man finally surmount all the contradictions. Naturally, coloniser does not come to "promote" but, like a spider, to paralyse its victim; but at the end of the count, it so radically changes the conditions of his life that by its very force, it transforms his soul. Hence, while examining the situation in a colonised country, it is fundamental to consider, turn by turn, these two concurrent yet quite distinct notions 'colonisation and colonisibility' and to determine in what measure the cause of inhibitions relate to the one or the other. This is the only way for the Muslim world to arrive at appropriate means for making an end of the deficiencies that have hitherto blocked all its enterprises.

The entire success of a method—whether it concerns a Political doctrine or Islam depends, in the first place, on a simultaneous consideration of these two aspects of the problem. Seeing the one without the other is to falsify the problem.

Disguised and Masked

Unfortunately, this fashion of truncating the problem is, in general disguised under the mask of patriotism, a patriotism loquacious and vain. Is it not, however, the best means of serving colonialism since it helps perpetuate the deficiencies, the paralyses and the abscesses which have already constituted for three or four centuries the obvious signs of a society in a state of pre-colonisation? We are then, forced to the logical and pragmatic conclusion, that, for liberating oneself from an effect: 'colonisation' one must first get rid of its cause: 'colonisibility.'

Colonialism is responsible for the dearth of the desirable means for developing their talents and material resources, but the unwillingness of the Muslim to utilise the available means, and to exert the required over-effort to raise his standard of life denotes colonisibility. An analysis of the causes of inhibition that hamper the evolution of the Muslim world, would reveal that they are overwhelmingly the result of the internal factors, that is, of colonisibility. This may best be ascertained in the political field which resumes the moral, intellectual and social content of a milieu and of a people, because of its direct relation with life, the one being the planification of the other. For politics is, in its essence, the enterprise of regulating the successive transformations of the condition of men. This, relationship, while defining the condition of the individual as an end of all politics, also designates him as an agent in the pursuit of this end, thus doubly implicating him in the political enterprise as both subject and object. Now the condition of post-al-Muwahhid man is that of a colonised and a colonisible. The relation of subject with object is, here, between the colonised and the colonisible and not between the colonised and the coloniser. This remark exposes the shallowness of the "politics" in practice in the Muslim world—particularly in North Africa, where it addresses itself exclusively to the coloniser. On the other hand, the colonised is naturally in need of means for acting on the condition of the colonisible. There, again, the politics in question constitutes a heresy since it demands their means of action from the coloniser himself: paradox of a captive who would demand from his jailor the key of his cell.

It is essential to know the given stage of the evolution of a people to determine the politics that would correspond to it. It is a question of the *"stage of civiliation"* and not of "political status" the second aspect being only a certain projection of the first: there are monarchies where one is down at heels and republics where one dies of hunger. One could study the degree or stage of civilisation by observing the manner in which man adapts himself to his milieu. At the stage of vegetative life, man adapts himself by a sort of *under-effort* that involves the least amount of exertion and movement. While, at the stage of active life, he adapts himself by an *over-effort,* that is, by a conscious and technical organisation of his life against cold, hunger and other contingencies. This passage from the vegetative to active life, that marks the commencement or re-birth of a civilisation presents no incomprehensible phenomenon, but comes about through means furnished by the man's own milieu and realised by the most natural powers of man as applied to himself, his soil and his time.

So the colonised man must, despite colonisibility and colonisation, find in his own milieu the fundamental rudimentary means. The soil, time, and his own genius are at his disposal; these original means could be transformed into more perfect means in the measure he transforms himself and becomes conscious of his humanity and the responsibilities that it implies. For being an applied sociology rather than a simple demagoguey, political activity should then imply two postulates:

— to make the politics of its means;

— to procure the means of its politics.

Two successive stages would result therefrom:

(1) A politics compatible with the primordeal means immediately available, the man, soil and the time. This condition would not exclude, however, the secondary means furnished by chance, or as one calls them today, the conjunctures. But it must be borne in mind, that the latter do not constitute the fundamental bases of a politics, but just simply its chances, the supplementary possibilities presented by hazard. If one leaves too much room for uncertainties, one would land oneself in a sort of political romanticism.

(2) The progressive transformation of original means into perfect means, capable of modifying in turn the various circumstances of the milieu. This stage would naturally end in the suppression of all forms of colonialism, whether occult as in Yemen, or declared as in North Africa.

The above two principles do not imply a form of politics but a content, the label could be indifferently, parliamentary or autocratic, but its positive content alone determines if it is applied sociology or a simple mythology. Unfortunately, while following the general evolution of Muslim politics uptil the Palestine affair, one does not have the impression that it rests on well-determined principles and clearly established postulates. Nor could one find real and realistic objectives controlled by a doctrine that would indicate ways of achieving them technically. Even the traditional principle that Jamal-al-Din had already formulated by designating "Islamic fraternity" as the basis of all politics in Muslim countries, is continuously combated by diverse nationalisms which are, in fact, only "partyisms", that is to say, the expression of the elites in no way concerned about the relations that they should establish between Muslims, caring only for their own interests. It is difficult to apply the term *politique* to the anarchical initiatives of these different elites, and it would be preferable to apply to them the term *"boulitique"* that the Algerians employ for denoting the confusions, illusions and the myths that masquerade under this label. It exposes the entire difference between chance and sentiment, and a precise direction distilled from human experience in the course of history. The "boulitique" is only the confusion of the possible and impossible, and the abandonment of the accessible and direct means for those inaccessible and imaginary, inevitably leading to the contradictory psychoses of the "impossible thing" and the "easy thing".

Political Mythology

This political mythology still masks from Muslim consciousness the true facts of the problem, indulging in mere words when action is needed, denouncing colonialism instead of colonisibility without any effort to transform effectively the condition of men. Even the most serious leaders wait for conjunctures, that is, chance, and in the meanwhile are content to voice their demands by appealing to, no matter what myth: the U.N.O. or the "universal conscience". For the partisans of such an attitude, moreover, the theory of conjunctures is no more than a simple word, a vain hope in face of events that always come to pass unexpectedly. Evidently, one would not know how to discover the sense of the conjecture if one did not possess a sense of reality, stripped of all romanticism and sentimentalism. Unfortunately judgements are most often no more than sentimental professions of faith. One does not judge, but either condemns, hates or loves. Even Sheikh Ben Badis in 1934 merely deplored the "shedding of Muslim blood" in the Arabian peninsula as if he did not discern the grandeur of the conflict wherein the forces of decadence led by Imam Yahya, backed by the colonial powers wrestled with those of the Islamic material and spiritual renaissance incarnated by the Wahhabi thought. This judgement neglected the instructive side of the drama—the rapidity of the manoeuvre of the young Saudi army that foiled the colonial plan in twenty-four hours by taking Hodeiba, and the attitude of Mussolini who would have willingly installed himself in Yemen for "protecting Islam". More recently the Arab press in general dismissed Chikakly's coup-d'etat (1949) with regret over the continued instability of the young Syrian republic, when it betokened in fact the first political move in the country taken independently, and in defiance of the British intelligence.

Glaring Effects

The most glaring effects of "boulitique" are to be seen in the Palestine debacle. The British knew well what they were doing when they surreptitiously quitted Jaffa, without previous transfer of power to a regular authority organised to protect the entire civil population. Bernard Shaw-but it was generally believed that he spoke only to make a witty remark, said some days before the event, that "the Arabs and Jews should be left alone to settle their differences by arms". It was certainly the opinion of a well-informed man, or of one capable of reflecting before forming an opinion. With the exception of Ibn Saud, all the Arab League members were so stunned that they did not even dream of denouncing the British evacuation which, in the given circumstances, could only benefit the Israelis. Nor did they think of forestalling events by creating a legal situation through the proclamation of a Palestine state. Deceived by the psychosis of the "easy thing", the Arab League counted on U.N. alone, all the while grossly underrating the diplomatic, financial, technical and even the numerical superiority of the Israelis, who could mobilise 300,000 men as against the combined Arab total of 200,000. The Israeli victory was, indeed, easy to foresee for all, but the victims of the "boulitique", the latter being neither a science, nor an experience, but a misleading ignorance that goes on repeating its errors.

Thus we find that even when it became evident that the League of Nations was not charged to apply the celebrated "fourteen points" of the American statesman, but to distribute fresh mandates and protectorates, no practical conclusion was drawn and the game recommenced with eulogies of the Atlantic Charter and the U.N. as the panacea for all international problems. Pakistan and Indonesia's access to 'easy' independence, that is, independence acquired without great constructive effort, and so to speak, without means, further helped to re-envelop the Muslim consciousness in the enervating, vapours of mythology. One failed to see the precarious nature of liberty that did not stem from a liberating principle, but was linked to demands of international strategy liable to change at any moment. One could see it in Indonesia where Queen Wilhelmina changed attitude twice or thrice at the whim of circumstances. Japan must be crushed: the Queen grants independence. Japan is vanquished: the Queen sends an expeditionary force "to cull" the nationalist leaders from their beds and to put an end to the republican euphoria. And when

Mao-Tse-Tung finally reaches Canton, the same Queen modifies anew her policy towards Java.

Examined from close quarters, the situation in Pakistan appears as confused. It seems that Churchill wanted to attain in India three distinct objectives, that is, to deprive the Soviet Union of an effective propaganda weapon, to provide a security zone in Asia against Communism and to create an India-Pakistan antinomy that would, on the one hand, isolate Islam from the Hindu mass, and on the other, prevent the formation of a powerful Indian Union. The irritant of Kashmir was further designed to guard against a reconciliation between two brothers enemies. Would they understand, in particular, the Machiavellian sense of the declaration made by a Zionist leader: "Relations would have to be established between the state of Israel and the Hindu state for removing from Islam its virulence." In plain language it signifies that the two states that partake the sub-continent must be at war with each other.

It would seem then, that the peoples of North Africa could only liberate themselves from colonialism as a result of similar international circumstance. But they would not achieve a veritable liberation unless they themselves technically prepared the conditions of their liberation. It would be wrong to assume that the liberation of one country renders "inevitable" the unconditional liberation of another. There are two possible attitudes: wait for the conditions to realise themselves or prepare them in a positive manner.

The capital problem remains: for ceasing to be colonised one must cease to be colonisible, cease to indulge in mythology. While writing these lines, the author still finds the politics of North Africa centred on appeals to U.N. and diatribes against colonialism; there seems to be no new orientation, no indication of concrete means of definition of daily effort needed to change the factors of colonisibility, and thereby those of colonialism.

The Palestine affair, nevertheless, seems to have somewhat troubled the general euphoria and may well mark the historical turning point leading the Muslim world towards a positive orientation.

External Factors

"Verily, when the tyrants enter a city, they pervert it, and humiliate its elite. So do they act."

Quran (27:34)

While the internal aspect of the chaos in the modern Muslim world is attributable to colonisibility, its external aspect relates to colonisation. Here, colonialism not merely manifests itself as an inhibiting myth, but also under the tangible form of eliminating acts which tend to destroy the values of individual and the possibilities of his evolution, as may best be seen in countries under "totalitarian" colonialism as was prevalent lately in Indonesia and Tripoli and exists today in North Africa. The above two aspects interfere and confound with each other, but it is necessary to treat them separately in order to determine their relative importance. One must also define "totalitarian colonialism". Unlike, what may be termed "liberal" colonialism that in appearance at least, leaves a free hand to the colonised, the former intervenes directly in all the domains of the life of the colonised, penetrating even into the details of his religious life. This interference extends to all. One would assign to the children of the colonised a 'native' school that would 'indigenise' his spirit; and if the colonised is a cafe-owner, one would assign to him a social sense that would 'indigenise' his commerce.

This totalitarianism has its academies (Schools of Colonial Sciences) its general plan, and periodical congresses, masking their objectives under various names—Volta Congress, Amis de Nostradamus etc.,—that keep up to date its colonial policies and technical planning of moral and material colonisation.

It is not only through its direct contact between the coloniser and the colonised, that colonialism acts as an essential element in the Muslim chaos, but also, in an occult manner, through rapport of Muslims among themselves. Its "presence" the word is a whole programme manifests itself in the most insignificant details of daily life. One may witness it any day in the streets of Algiers, where a policeman could be seen chasing away a poor boy selling oranges while turning a blind eye to the degrading spectacle of beggar boys spinning out a doleful tale" for a few pennies, or a turbaned "soothsayer" grovelling before a foreign tourist. The Quranic verse, "Verily, when the tyrants enter a city, they pervert it and humiliate its elite", illustrates well the colonial philosophy. Colonialism is methodic: all its work is a stage-production, a trick for giving to the country an "indigene" air. All danger that could encounter its work is systematically set aside. It eliminates the veritable elite-not the one its particular favour has designated for representing the people, but the natural elite that testify to the highest virtues of a people. That it may not reform itself, that it may not emerge anew, there is installed a system of perversion, debasement and destruction directed against all dignity, all nobility and all modesty. This technique of disorientation adapts itself continuously to new situations, sabotaging all initiative. The "Muslim renaissance, particularly since Afghani shattered the post-al-Muwahhid equilibrium, could not but excite its most passionate interest, and its unbounded power and ambition has inspired it with the mad and tragic idea of halting the march of civilisation in the colonised country. To counter tajdid it has set up an artificial archaism as a theatre scene wherein its puppets -marabouts, pashas, fake alems or University degreeholders must play the scene of the "Islamic tradition", "tradition" that has become the pass-word of the entire colonial policy.

Boisterous Obscurantism

One sees on the other side, the reformist effort countered by a boisterous obscurantism that continuously resucitates dead and buried anachronisms and myths. Since colonialism tries tirelessly to re-edify the ruined pantheon of maraboutism, one would find parading in certain capitals the mummified figurines drawn from the post-al-Muwahhid middle ages to represent the "traditional Islam" in the retrospective scene of native politics. At each instant colonialism shouts at the history of the colonised people the words of Joshua, "stat sol!", "Stop Sun!". This singular pretension which never entered the brain of any Genghis Khan or Attila, is today the political formula of the most odious form of human despotism in this twentieth century of Christian European civilisation.

Guided by the sacrilegious idea of halting the march of the peoples towards light, colonialism has not hesitated to confuse the sacred with the profane. Early in the twentieth century a number of falsified scripts of the Quran were circulated in Egypt in order to sap the very base of Islamic renaissance. When the deception was discovered, those responsible did not scruple to make a joke of the whole thing. The author himself heard an eminent professor in Paris declaring: "Why should the Muslims worry to protect the Quran, since Allah himself has undertaken to safeguard it?" It is indeed difficult to describe all the discordant details introduced ceaselessly in the Muslim life as the grains of sands in the wheels of a motor: the resurrection of maraboutism even when rejected by the people, the choice of morally and physically deformed persons to "represent" Muslims in various assemblies, putting the stamp of "indigene" on the housing projects for Muslims designed to efface the memory of the beautiful Arab style immortalised in the monuments of Spain, the compulsory labelling of native-owned cafes as "cafe maure" where, as in Tunisia, one may be obliged to cater for hif smokers so as to make them forget their past, present and future. The colonial work is in fact an immense sabotage of history.

If the world has not been definitely demoralised, and has not lost all moral sense, it is because the human soul is indestructible and eternal, and theologians of all confessions owe thanks to colonialism for demonstrating imperatively the immortality of the soul. No other age has known better to regenerate in the man the attributes of the brute by concoctions of its well-run and well-provided laboratories: laws, banks, administrations, journals and "native" schools. Thanks to them, the dreg of Muslim society has come on top and its elite is at the bottom. Even the intellectual life of a colonised country is a mere ferment for distilling certain ideas that the coloniser carefully culls, for turning them into the guiding ideas of the "boulitique".

Ever since his primary certificate examination, a child becomes the unconscious object of a conspiracy by the "honourable" examiners who take good care to ensure that a "little native" might not get a more honourable mention than his European comrades. The same applies to the soldier in the ranks. As Marshal Franchet d'Esperey said in the course of a review: "for the native officer, the grade is not a right but a favour". For the little child at school as for the Muslim intellectual the diploma or situation are not rights but favours. One can well conceive, the pitiable samples of Muslim elite that are considered worthy of such favours. On the contrary, if a remarkable intellect appears, one tries to break him by all means and if he proves too hard, one would break his family to paralyse him.

Economic and Social Plane

On the economic and social plane, the policy follows the same procedure: to destroy the existing armature and to prevent its reconstitution by all means. Thus one finds Britain in Egypt, effacing the thought of Muhammad Ali and the work of Khedive Ismail who tried to build a national industry in Egypt—not to speak of the 50% shares of Suez wrested from a terrorised government. Similarly, in Algeria social and charitable institutions functioning at the time of French occupation were made to disappear in one way or another. Today, the precious art of miniature painting in the Muslim world has been left with rare representatives, like Omar Racim in Algeria: when these artists will disappear, their art will perish with them, since the administration far from supporting it, has done its best to obliterate it.

So, one finds appearing together in all domains of life, the twin faces of the chaos - colonisibility and colonisation. If the cultural life itself does not escape from the control of colonisation, it is because the latter knows that religion remains the sole and ultimate means of rebuilding the moral health of a people that in the crisis of its history has lost all moral sources. If there is something that vibrates still in Muslim soul, that renders him capable of transforming and surpassing himself, it is Islam. Hence this power of resurrection becomes everywhere the target of attack and an object for all sorts of restrictions and surveillance. It is today infinitely easier in Algeria to open a gambling house or a cafe than a Quranic school. On the other hand, the administration itself appoints the personnel of the cult, who are chosen not on account of their piety or knowledge, but their utility to the administration, thus confronting Muslim conscience with the profoundly disturbing phenomenon of an Imam who is an informer, a corrupt and corrupting Mufti and a prevaricating Qadi. One wishes to make of Islam itself a picturesque aspect of the "native life", thus piling up obstacles and impediments in the path of Muslim renaissance.

But here at least, a direct confrontation becomes possible between colonisibility and colonisation as factors of paralysis, permitting us to realise, very vividly, that the colonised could always rid himself of his colonisibility in the measure he aplies his intelligence to surmount difficulties, avoid pitfalls and to break the shackles. Here at least, for even at the post-al-Muwahhid stage, a Muslim will not suffer attack on his religion, we see him, notably in Algeria building new mosques and schools, where he can pray freely, and his children could freely pursue their studies. These initiatives have proved to us that it is not a question of discoursing on the liberty of the cult of the extension of education, but of performing social works and accomplishing imperative duties. It is, of course, excellent to obtain the rights that one has demanded but it is not a question of reversing the order of values by putting the 'rights' before the 'duties' this could only increase the confusion, the disarray and the chaos by multiplying the faux pas of the "boulitique".

Colonialism still rings midnight, but in the Muslim world, the hour of sleep and phantoms has irrevocably passed away.

12

Initial Exposure to West

> "Verily, we created you of a male and female, and made you into nations and tribes, so that ye may know each other".
>
> Quran (49:13)

Since time immemorial, the Europeans has sought their nourishment from the soil. This vital necessity helped them to develop the bases of an agrarian, or as a French sociologist puts it, of a "civilisation de P herbage". The original synthesis of men and soil having been realised at an early stage, the latter found themselves disciplined in terms of very close neighbourly relations that created the notion of property, strictly delimiting it as the fixed space of a human life, of a hearth and a family. Internally this space of life, this "vital space" is essentially conditioned by regular seasonal activities that engender a very precise notion, that of the daily work. The social notion of time, in its turn, incorporated itself in the original synthesis. The climate would lead man to adopt fire as an essential element of his life, and to furnish his interior in terms of his daily work, climate and fire. The table and chairs became the conditions of a very intimate family life wherein the individuals gathered at fixed hours for the common meal.

Gradual Promotion

Externally, this family space necessarily articulated on neighbouring spaces similarly conditioned. The church spirit born of these local agglomerations would little by little give birth to communal life, thus realising the integration of the individuals to an order responding to the conditions and aspirations of a static life.

Neither Roman imperialism, nor Germanic nomadism succeeded, in the course of centuries, in modifying this original canvas of European life. Christianism and Cartesianism came to complete the physiognomy of this society, profoundly, perhaps excessively, penetrated with the sense of utility. The former brought to it the sense of the universal, and through it the dynamism that its static temperament lacked; the latter tailored its fundamental activities for efficiently integrating them in the industrial vitality that was going to surge from its evolution. In this society of centripetal virtues that practised mutual aid, but did not know hospitability. Christianism also deposited the ferment of moral expansionism that would serve as a justification for the Crusades and the colonial enterprise.

The Crusades offered the European civilization an opportunity to turn towards the exterior, and to reap a profitable harvest in the Muslim civilization. The same tendencies pushed it to the discovery of America, and one could here discern the beginning of a profound rupture between a dominating Europe and the rest of humanity, that explains the politics of the world for the last four centuries as well as its present disequilibrium. Howsoever it may be, it was this society marked with the genius of the soil, but where the possibilities of inter-human relationships were almost completely stifled that, towards the 18th century, discovered the Muslim world.

In this world, the individual did not originally seek his nourishment from the soil-which could not furnish it, but obtained it from the beast. He was a shepherd, a nomad or a warrior. The space of his life, his vital space, was as indefinite as the zone, the nearest to his habitat, where the last rain had fallen. This habitation itself was mobile by necessity and could dispense with furniture.

Why settle on a soil that did not give food? The man thus on the move, did not have regular activities, and though he well knew the effort, at times exhausting, that his profession of shepherd and warrior demanded, he had no idea at all of an organized, daily work, which only the soil teaches to those who work on it during the seasons. Content with the warmth of the sun, he did not adopt fire as an accessory of his life. Moreover, this errant life did not impose relations of orderly neighbourhood since the individual did not own landed property. As his nurture did not depend on such relations, his gregarious instinct was little developed, and he did not seek to integrate himself to a social order. The tribe of which he formed a part, was not an order determined by social reasons, but rather by biological causes. The relations of the individual outside the tribe, that is, his properly social relations were non-existent.

Divided World

A world divided in the extreme and atomised into individuals, a world of centrifugal virtues that did not know mutual aid, just as it ignored the efficacy of the matter, but practised hospitality, honoured generosity, loved vanity and poetry. Its dynamism explains the extreme rapidity of Islamic expansion, the cause of which the historians have vainly sought in the external conditions. On this canvas Islam came to embroider its admirable civilization, giving to a world dominated by individualism a cohesion and a sense of the collective that determined its historical orientation. The Quran transformed the Beduin into a sedentary, who left in Spain and the south of France, the evidence of a perfect agricultural science. This fixation of the man to the soil immediately produced its effect. Science and art appeared and developed in a disciplined society where the individual no longer obeyed his vagrant humour, but submitted to an order and to the laws.

In the 18th century, this civilization had long finished the cycle of its civilization, and the individual found himself once again in the conditions of life offered by an atomised society of abolished activities, save for certain enclaves such as Fez, Qayruwan and Damascus, prestigious vestiges that alone bore witness to a finished past since in general the post-al-Muwahhid man preferred a return to the nomadic life of his ancestors to a sedentary life. Just as a European engineer or artist once seeing the cycle of his civilization nearing its end, would again become a cultivator or a gardener, the Muslim world had reverted to a tribal, nomadic state when the West made its discovery, more than a century ago.

It would be convenient not to forget that Europe which looked upon itself as the sole depositary of the human destinies had already, since the age of Boccaccio-even while its cradling civilisation still drew its first nourishment from the Arabs, disowned purely and simply the Arab civilisation. On this point, it would be doubtless more fitting to quote a European himself. Here are, for example the melancholy reflections of D. Gustave Lebon that conclude his study on the *Arab Civilisation:*

> The reader would ask himself why under these conditions, the influence of the Arabs is so ignored today by the scholars whose spirit would seem to place them above all religious prejudices.... In reality, this independence of opinion is much more apparent than real and we are by no means free to think as we wish on certain subjects. The hereditary prejudices that we profess against Islam and its disciples have been accumulated over so many centuries, that they have become part of our organism.

This text indirectly, but clearly illuminates the position of the European civilisation vis-a vis the Muslim, at the debut of the colonial era, position to which corresponded the attitude of this Muslim world towards the "things" and "notions" of Europe which it, in general; covered with a sovereign scorn-pretending as it did, to be the sole depositary of Divine grace. From these given facts, one could easily imagine the internal contradictions which the modern West was going to introduce in the archaic world of the post-al-Muwahhid man.

Reformist Movement

> "Verily, God will not change the condition of men, till they change what is in themselves."
>
> Quran (13:11)

While implanting himself in the Muslim world ... beginning of the last century, the European pres... Christian morality, only certain dispositions of his soul... soul if one viewed it from the interior, from the p... convergence of his centripetal virtues, but which wo... closed and impermeable to the Muslims.

In fact, from the exterior, that is to say, in its actu... with the Muslim world, the Christian soul was, above a... a coloniser who, before embarking for the Barbary coast, ... or the Islands of Java, had heard, in the course of evenin... re-unions by the fire-side, of the fabulous Eldorados. In h... he had parted in search of Peru, and never was the thirst fo... so violent as after the discovery of the "Colony".

If one views it as a sociologist and not as a moralist, the salutary role of the Europeans in the history of the world since the last two centuries, becomes apparent. However detached he was from the rest of the humanity that he disdained, viewing it only as a sort of stepping stone - the European did, nonetheless, pulled the Muslim world out of the chaos of the occult forces, wherein every society that substitutes for the spirit, its simple function, founders, shadow deformed by the imagination of the visionaries who have lost, along with their sense of the real, the very genius of the soil. By causing the social order, wherein the post-al-Muwahhid man peaceably vegetated, crack on all sides, the activism of the European would give him a . new revelation of his social worth. The man from Europe unknowingly played the role of the dynamite that explodes in a camp of silence and contemplation. The post-al-Muwahhid man, like the Buddhist of China and the Brahmana of India, felt himsef jolted and finally awoken.

He found himself thus in a new order that was not of his making, and before two imperative necessities. Despite his bankruptcy, he must assure himself of the minimum of dignity that Islam demands of all his adepts, even in the primitive societies of central Africa; and he must assure himself of a vital minimum in an implacable social order that no longer nourished either the plunderer living on the razzias, or the hermit living on public charity, or the son of the family living on familial patrimony all

Al-Afghani found himself, by an accident of history, the incorruptible witness and the implacable judge of a society that slowly attained its decomposition, while colonialism installed itself on its soil. It was the sepoy revolt and its bloody ending that seems to have catalysed in the conscience of this man, the will to reform his milieu. He saw in this drama the moral and material bankruptcy of the Muslim society, as implied, in the failure of the revolt and confirmed, in a way, by the Aligarh movement that appeared in the wake of these bloody events and, in the eyes of Al-Afghani, took on the character of a betrayal of Islam. He forthwith launched an offensive against antiquated institutions and fatal ideas.

Powers Undermined

On the first plane he sought to undermine the existing powers in order to realize a political re-composition of the Muslim world, founded on "Islamic fraternity" that was breached at Siffin and finally destroyed by colonial regimes. On the second plane, he led the struggle against "naturism", the term under which he denounced the materialism that he allegedly detected in the teaching of Sir Syed Ahmad Khan at Aligarh and attributed it to the occult influences of the West. Al-Afghani's attitude appears reactionary, the more so since the University movement later proved to be an eminent factor of Muslim renaissance in India. However, it supplied the necessary corrective to the future orientation of teaching at Aligarh, just as a century later, the opposition of Azharite scholars, notably of Rashid Rida, to the thesis of Taha Husayn, far from proving merely negative, exercised a salutary influence not only on the future orientation of Egyptian culture, but also on the writings of Taha Husayn himself.

Anyhow, Al-Afghani's impetuous temperament made of him a militant rather than a thinker who would carefully examine problems and work out solutions. His extraordinary culture was only a dialectical, even demagogic, means of revolutionary action that had a psychological and intellectual, rather than political, impact on a still totally apathetic Muslim world. It must needs make the Muslim drama manifest in the Muslim conscience itself. It does not seem that this recall to the Muslim conscience of the drama that it carried within itself formed part of a systematic plan:

his quite rare written work, mostly polemics directed against the naturists or against Renan, do not allow any affirmation in this regard. But if he was neither the leader, nor the doctrinaire of modern Reformist movement,.he was its initiator, at the same time gathering and transmitting, all along his life of a pilgrim, this anxious inquietude to which one owes the modest efforts of the present renaissance.

Fully conscious of the rottenness of his milieu, Al-Afghani sought to cure it through a suppression of its institutional framework rather than through a reformation of the post-al-Muwahhid man. He might have achieved his objective if such a revolution was accomplished, for every revolution is creative of new values, and, as a result, susceptible of transforming the man. But the lever of this revolution was ill-forged; it could be efficacious only if the sentiment of "Islamic fraternity" was transformed into an act: "the Islamic fraternisation", such as it once had existed in the days of Ansars and Muhajireen—the first constitutional act that laid the foundation of early Muslim society.

So, while Al-Afghani had been the promoter of the Reformist movement and remains the legendary hero of the modern epic, he was not himself a "reformer" in the exact sense of the term. That role was reserved for Shaykh Abduh, an Egyptian Azharite. Immemorially attached to the soil, Egypt has always been a society, that is to say, a milieu where the individual is constantly merged into a collectivity, and endowed thereby with the instinct of social realities; Al-Azhar has always furnished dogmatic spirits. Having taken cognizance of the Muslim drama Abduh was obliged to transform it into a social problem, whereas his master with his tribal and empirical spirit had seen it from a political angle.

The Disposition

These original dispositions of the Egyptian Shaykh explain the entire genesis and orientation of the Reformist school. Yet, it appears, that the instinct of the soil-which is the quintessence of social sense—and the Azharite spirit separately suggested their solution, perhaps even due to what Gibb calls "the atomism". Abduh knew that for realising a reform of Muslim Society, one must first of all reform the individual. He found for this concept an important reference in the Quran: "God does not make any change in the condition of a people, till the latter has not previously changed what there is in its soul" (Quran, 13:10). In this verse, that became the watchword of the school, notably in North African Islamism there is a vigorous statement of the entire social problem 'which is essentially linked to the soul of the individual. But how to transform this soul? Here the dogmatic spirit of Abduh intervened. He thought, as Sir Muhammad Iqbal thought that a reformulation of Muslim theology was indispensible.

But the word "theology" became the fatality of the Reformist movement resulting in a partial deviation, and devaluation of certain of its leading principles, such as the "Salafiyah" or a return to the original purity of Islam. For theology touches the problem of the soul only in the realm of credo. or dogma. Now the Muslim, even the post-al-Muwahhid Muslim, had never abandoned his credo. He had remained a believer or more exactly a devotee; his faith had become inefficacious because it had lost its social radiation, becoming centripetal, individualist: the faith of the individual disintegrated from his social milieu.

Consequently it was not a question of teaching him a faith that he already possessed, but of restoring to this faith its efficacy. In a word, it was less a question of "proving" God to him than of "manifesting" Him to his consciousness, filling his soul with it as with a source of energy. Transforming the soul is to make it surpass its ordinary bounds. This task did not lie in the domain of theology, but in that of a mysticism, or more exactly of a science that still has no name, but what may be termed, the nenewal of alliance or union. In an effort of renaissance, mysticism that has led to Marabutic mystification—could not furnish the necessary basis for Reformist action. The mystic did, in fact, aim only at the spiritual condition of certain souls of the elite, while it was a question of general reform, of providing an internal impulsion to the masses thirsting for a (call of) sursum corda (Lift up your hearts) for vanquishing their own inertia.

These considerations would not have failed to appear to the Reformist school if it could have achieved a synthesis of its ideas by establishing a link between the dogmatic views of Abduh and the political and social views of Al-Afghani. It would have indicated quite another path than that of a simple reformulation of theological principles. Moses, Jesus and Muhammad were not the theologian constructors of abstract propositions, but essentially the accumulators of this moral energy which they communicated to simple souls.

Theology restored respectability to discussion and exchange of ideas, but at the same time it de-naturalised the Muslim problem by transforming the "Salafite" principle even in the spirit of the reformers. This unconscious transgression substituted for the psychological problem of renaissance, a scholastic problem. For with theology the "social function" of religion is not posed, as the believing man does not learn anything from a school that teaches him solely the existence of God, and does not, in any case, teach the return to the Salaf.

Reformist Deviation

To explain fully the Reformist deviation, one must, perhaps, add to the reasons already enumerated what Gibb calls the "superimposition". It existed in European culture in the epoch of Thomas Acquinas under the form of a purge of Muslim influences. Today the same phenomenon is evident in the traditional Muslim culture in the form of a resistence to Western ideas: the theological work of Abduh is finally apologetic because of the 'superimposition'.

A sum-up of this criticism would risk to show us only the lacunae of the Reformist movement, so that the latter would lose in our eyes, if not its historical value, at least its social value. However, the present Muslim world, with all its realisations and virtualities, is, for a great part, the other being that of the Modernist current that we would examine later on the work of Shaykh Abduh and his school. Even if the great Egyptian Azharite failed to place the problem exactly in the Muslim conscience, he succeeded in posing it on the intellectual plane, provoking an intellectual ferment not only in Egypt, but almost in the entire Muslim world. For theology was, in fact, the first effort of Muslim intelligence to disengage itself from its secular lethargy. One must not underestimate the significance of the appearance of Risalat-al-Tawhid in a field where nothing had happened since Ibn Khaldun.

For the first time since many centuries, a Muslim brain had fathered a thoughtful work. For the first time discussions broke the silence that had reigned in the old universities of the Muslim world. One of them, Al-Azhar, where the debates opened by Al-Afghani and Abduh had come to resound, was to show itself particularly sensitive to the new mood—not in its programmes and methods which, despite certain superficial tentatives, still await their re-statement, but in its spirit. Al-Azhar, that is to say, the intellectual centre of the Muslim world had at last admitted the law of movement and progress and realised that there was no such thing as an immutable perfection, but only a state of perfectible things, even under its imposing domes.

Thus, the modern Muslim thought set itself to work in the immense field that the Reformist action had opened before it.

However this field, left fallow for centuries, was overrun entirely by parasitic vegetation, and a thorough clean-up was necessary in the spiritual as much, if not more, as in the intellectual domain. To the lacunae inherent in the post-al-Muwahhid man, there came to be added the lacunae attaching to the institution. An institution has its life, its history and traditions; in a word, its own inertia that at times defies the will of man. To the atomism, dogmatism and the apologetic tendency-that the Reformist spirit could not spontaneously shake off-were added the blemishes of an institutional order: the *mujadalah,* literalism, hysterics and poetism peculiar to the post-al-Muwahhid culture. How could one move under the weight of centuries and the burden of traditions that had pell-mell accumulated themselves. For building anew, one needed either a revolutionary spirit like Jamal-al-Din, partisan of the "clean slate" or a systematic spirit that would have methodically proceeded towards the necessary ruptures to liberate the institution from its traditional shackles. One must have first of all, made a balance-sheet of these indispensible ruptures by a discrimination of the traditions. The word "tradition" *(taqlid)* is a magical Arabic word that could cover up all sorts of superstitions and mystifications under the prestigious varnish of Islamism. 'By a methodical confrontation of tradition with Islam, Muslim culture would have been rid of a great number of sacrosanct *taqlids.* Shaykh Abd-al-Hamid ibn Badis would thus succeed in extirpating the false tradition of *"Marabutism"* from Algeria. But this task of detection could hardly be the work of an isolated individual, and in his time Shaykh Abduh was alone. As a thinker, he had furnished the example of intellectual work to a world unaccustomed to thinking; as the rector of a university, he had given to his institution the movement that made it amenable to new ideas. In addition to the ruptures that he operated in the Islamic culture, he had revealed Western culture to the Muslim world by introducing it in the re-organization of his university and in his written work which thus bore its first reflection. From all these initiatives must need gush forth the intellectual upsurge of renaissance. But while the "Meiji" upsurge oriented Japan towards the sciences, Muslim renaissance remained confined for a long time to the domain where the natural inclinations of the post-al-Muwahhid man, who cared little for efficiency, and the notions attached to cultural institutions that had since long lost their social objective, helped to maintain it.

The reformers-I am talking of the continuers-themselves contributed to maintain this state of affairs. The *mujadalah* would subsist for a long time in literary debates. One did not look for verities, but for arguments: one did not listen to his interlocutor, but flooded him with a verbal deluge. The *mujadalah* was all the more dangerous since it depended, in general, on a senseless love for words, leading to another lacunae of post-al-Muwahhid spirit "litteralism". The Arab genius that had created the most beautiful of languages, resembled a sculptor who becomes amorous of the statue that his chisel has created. Unfortunately the passion for words is more dangerous than that for bronze, marbel or stone.

It commences by making one lose the sense of proportion indispensible for all positive constructive effort. The least headline of an Arabic journal is edifying in this regard. Recently, a Tunisian journal announcing the arrival of a leader from abroad, greeted him with five or six laudative epithets- *karim, jalil, zaim,* etc. It betokened, doubtless, an apologetic bouquet, but Arabic words carry an irresistible attraction for the postal-Muwahhid spirit. The Arabic language thus divinised could no longer evolve. The adoration of its adepts has rendered intangible a syntax irrevocably reduced to a dozen of forms, and it has become sacrilegious to constitute new forms through adapted prefixes-something that would be in accord with the very spirit of this language.

Defying Time

In the independent Muslim educational institutions, the syllabi and methods of instruction also seem to defy time; the principles have remained the same since the Christian Middle Ages. For all that these principles constitute the mental canvas of action, the activities remain in the periphery and at the rhythm of a world that has gone by. One believes sometimes to have changed an entire world of ideas by certain superficial retouches, such as the introduction of chairs and tables in independent Algerian schools. It was, of course, the first step to take, but it would be naive to stop at that.

In the circumstances, it is not astonishing that modern Arab thought has still not acquired the sense of efficacy. The despotism of words and forms impresses a superficial character on every translation of renaissance. One could witness it at the Congress of Islamic Culture at Tunis where a Shaykh, while making a discourse consecrated to the Traditions on "clemency", spent more than an hour in counting out the chain of narrators. Needless to specify that its content remained finally unperceived while the listeners yawned-with admiration. Here one comes across an important aspect of post-al-Muwahhid psychology: all is still more grave while the orator and the audience are in accord over the inefficacy. So much so that the living verities that had once fashioned the visage of Muslim civilization are henceforth but dead verities, buried under beautiful phrases and a vast erudition.

It seems that the idea remains the same as it has been since the decadence; the famous "well of science" wherein science is swallowed up and loses the sense of its social role. Just any discourse on Commentary could furnish the occasion for ascertaining the inconsequences of our present culture which, subjugated by the verb, does not express a concern for *acting,* but the simple pleasure of *talking.*

The Orientation

There is another reason for this orientation that the apologetic tendency has impressed on the intellectual effort. In its pre-occupation with the apology of the past, the culture takes on a character of archeology where the intellectual effort is directed not forward but backwards. This retrograde tendency imprints on the entire teaching a retrospective character, incompatible with the exigencies of the present and the future. There results therefrom, in the ideas a sort of the phenomenon of "hysteresis", of a constant obsession with the past.

Two other lacunae would complete this picture of the deficiencies of the post-al-Muwahhid culture: a puerile "quantitatism" evident even in the element bearing a "polish" of Western culture, and a "poetism" that is the particular apanage of Zaytunian youth of purely maternal culture. Quantitatism consists in estimating efficacy and value in terms of a book by the quantity of paper written. As for poetism, it is the aesthetics or rather the coquettishness of litteralism and the apologetic tendency. It is the means, more or less elegant according to the case, of masking the imperfections and insufficiencies, of gilding the errors and placing before the incompetences the screen of rhetoric.

It is clear that all these lacunae, we have analysed, were not of a nature to favour the efforts of the Reformist school that did not or could not know how to eliminate them, systematically, thus leaving intact the problem of post-al-Muwahhid, residues in the Muslim renaissance. Moreover, since the disappearance of its last two great figures, Rashid Rida in the East, and Ben Badis in North Africa, the movement as a whole, finds itself at a new turning. In Egypt, the fundamental idea of creating a new moral basis for Muslim life finds itself transformed and deepened in a new movement, that of Muslim Brotherhood, which would be treated further on. In North Africa, it has been more and more superseded by a very important institution, that of independent education, that has timely fulfilled the enormous gap of official instruction. On this path the Islamist idea more or less subsists. Certain young teachers are animated with a salafite zeal, but some others are already no more than simple functionaries. This instruction has the merit of attacking the mortal defect of the post-al-Muwahhid world-illiteracy. But in the absence of a doctrine on culture, Islamism propagates a complacent alphabetism that dreams of transforming the conditions of life by communicating, above all, the taste for "Muslim things" and Arab "belles-lettres".

Translation into Reality

It appears from this balance-sheet, that the Reformist movement did not know how to transform the Muslim soul or to translate into reality the "social function" of the religion. All the same, it did succeed in breaking the static equilibrium of the post-al-Muwahhid epoch by introducing in the Muslim conscience partially and on the intellectual plane only the notion of its secular drama. But there remained the task of posing the problem of culture in its generality if the renaissance were to emerge from its embryonic state.

As already noted, the development that goes under the name of "Muslim civilization" was only an accommodation of doctrinal Islam to the state of facts that followed Siffin. The juridical schools were put hard to realise such an accommodation in face of a dynastic hence extra, Muslim power that was exclusive and tyrannical. So much so, that it is not the Muslim civilization that is the issue of Islamic doctrine, but on the contrary, the doctrines that have accommodated themselves to an imposed temporal order.

Any attempt for the reconstruction of Muslim culture must begin with the re-establishment of pure doctrine over the le fait de prince (political power) that has stemmed from Siffin. This reconstruction implies a return to Islam, that is to say, in particular the extrication of the Quranic text from its triple matrix of theology, jurisprudence and philosophy.

But the Modernists seek to drag the Muslim world in quite another direction by breaking-sometimes violently as Kamalism did in Turkey with a "tradition" that is often no more than a cover for the post-al-Muwahhid myth.

Modernist Movement

> "Would'nt I have been, moreover, flagrantly inconsistent, if wishing to ameliorate the country, I would have balked before the idea of ameliorating man?"
>
> H. De Balzac

Far from bringing its entire soul to the Muslim world, Europe brought there only that much of its civilization as concerned the immediate commodities of the colonist. On the "native"' plane, however, it had brought what one calls the "native school". It is from this very small contribution that the Modernist movement of the Muslim world had started.

The school, on the plane of Modernism formed a counterpart to the *madrasah* on the plane of reform. While the madrasah presented a relatively rejuvenated Islamic thought, the school introduced new cultural elements in the Muslim world. The former would operate a rupture with the post-al-Muwahhid past, the latter would establish a contact with Western thought. Envisaging this new fact, Iqbal remarked that "the most remarkable phenomenon of modern history... is the enormous rapidity with which the world of Islam is spiritually moving towards the West". But was this really the case ?

It could have been so only if Europe had brought its soul and its civilization to the world of Islam, or the latter would itself have gone to discover it on the spot. It does not seem that many Muslims, have gone in search of the West. Instead, Europe came to the East not as the bearer of a, civilization but as a coloniser, and the young bourgeois Muslim went to Europe only for getting a university diploma or for satisfying a wholly superficial curiosity. A Zaytunian student, who after finishing his Islamic studies asked for a scholarship to complete his education in Europe, was told by the concerned cultural organisation that "for studying the French language one need not go to France." That is how the Muslim milieu envisages the role of a student who is going to the West. It is just a question of studying a language or learning a profession, not of discovering a culture. Only the aspect of immediate utility counts.

But this way of looking at things must not be exclusively imputed to the indifference of the Muslim vis-a-vis the West. The "native" school did not disperse elements of European culture, but only certain rudiments susceptible of rendering the "native" fit for European economy. There was no question of detecting and stimulating intelligences, but of forming auxiliaries, of a capacity at once sufficient and limited.

Despite all this, the conscious being-student or simply a governed, even when treated as an "object" did nevertheless remain a "subject". And it is as a "subject" that the Muslim judges the European order that he sees around him or squeezes from his insufficient readings. His ideas on European "civilization" must need flow from this rudimentary judgement and from the superficial contact, administrative or commercial, that he has had with it.

On the other hand, the little Musalman who goes to the native school, is the brother of the one who goes to the madrasah. Consequently, the same mental habits, the same sociological heredity that marked the Reformist movement have come to mark also the Modernist movement, intermingled with the new elements, bookish or empirical borrowings from European life as viewed from the exterior.

Muslim Spirit

For centuries the Muslim spirit has been incapable of delving beneath the surface of the phenomena; the Muslim no longer understood, but only learnt the Quran. Now, having judged grosso modo the utility of European products, he was not going to criticise them! He did not bother himself to find out how they were created, but how they could be acquired. Thus the first stage of modernisation of the Muslim world that would adopt the forms without their content, took shape. This disposition would inaugurate an entropic evolution that did not accumulate its means but solely its needs. And the infatuation for the things "modern" went to absurd length in all social classes, among both men and women. One could see towards 1925, during the years of prosperity, motor cars parked under the tents where the fowls were kept. The ceramic wash-basin made its appearance in bourgeois homes where it adorned the "modern" bed-rooms. A significant clumsiness, 'obviously inspired by the hotel style, that is to say, by a way of looking at the European from the exterior. The woman also partook in this euphoria. Instead of acquiring the art and the taste for a 'bit of frippery', she was content to buy it, according to her condition, from needlework parlours or ready-made garments stores run by shrewd and gracious European saleswomen. Apparent evolution, that often masks a simple transformation of post-al-Muwahhid content from an archaic to a modern form. This tendency seems to develop in Muslim society as the elite, the offspring of Western school, grows more numerous at the top.

New Stage

This elite has gradually passed beyond the stage of native school, a certain number of young intellectuals have now spent a term in the Western universities. Naturally, it is in this new stage that the Modernist movement approaches its perfection, if this expression could possibly be used-and its moral and social content becomes quite significant.

Because of the psychology of his maternal post-al-Muwahhid milieu where one passes from the sacred to the profane without stopping at the sublime, from Islamic ilm to modern education without pausing at the notion of culture, the Muslim student starts with blinkers that prevent him from contemplating the civilization otherwise than from an abstract or futile side in accordance with his disposition for the serious. He generally registers himself in the university of a capital. The Quartiers Latin are the same everywhere: one finds there the bookish and controversial or the superficial aspect of culture, its distractions and its pleasures. From one side as from the other, he can see only the culmination and not the evolution of a society. He does not see the woman who is picking a wild flower, but the one who colours her nails and hair and sits smoking on the cafe terraces. He does not see the artist or the artisan bending over his work to translate an idea into matter. Oriented, from the start, with the sense of utility, he does not remark the energies, obscure, but creative and creative, above all, of moral and social values that render a civilized man superior to the primitive man culture commences when the intellectual effort goes beyond the objective of individual need. Nor would he have the chance to seize the generous aspect of the civilization, that which nourishes the affectivity of the civilised man and gives the creative impulsion to his genius so true it is that "the great thoughts come from the heart". Descendant of a world that has sold its relics and manuscripts to the American tourist, he would not discern, besides, the healthy cult of the "old thing" that links the past with the future. He will not see the child learning the sense and respect of life as he caresses a cat or cultivates a flower, nor the labourer stopping at the edge of a furrow for judging his work, in communion with the soil which is the embryo of the synthesis of every civilisation. He would not draw, any more, the lesson of certain follies as that of Bernard Palissy burning his last piece of furniture and his floor for obtaining the enamel.

His unconscious materialism and obsession with the "utile" would not let him see, either, the horrible aspect of this civilization that holds in bondage men, whom the machine commands, exhausts and wears out and transforms into "robots of human flesh". He will not see the woman forced to leave her hearth to gain laboriously a loaf of bread in a debasing atmosphere that masculinises women and emasculates men. He will not see this odious side that makes even the degraded post-al-Muwahhid society appear in certain respects frequently superior to a civilization that has lost the sense of the human.

Generally speaking the Muslim student has not experienced Europe, but has been content to read it, that is to say, to learn rather than to understand. He thus remains ignorant of the history of its civilization; he cannot know how it was formed and how it is in the process of disintegrating itself, by its internal contradictions and its incompatibility with the laws of human order, and because its culture is no longer that of a civilization, but has been transformed by colonialism and racism into the "culture of the empire". Even if sometimes guided by curiosity he sets out in search of reality, he finds himself in contact only with the twentieth century Europe, shorn of its secular tradition, nickled, chromited and polished; the modern Europe and the practical materialism of its bourgeoisie and the dialectical materialism of its labouring class. And the intellectual who has not even acquired sufficiently the sense of real efficacy at the European school, by which a Christian still distinguishes himself from a Muslim, would more readily borrow from the materialism of Europe its bourgeois tendency—that is to say, the materialist tastes, rather than its proletarian tendency, that is to say, a dialectical discipline. Having never considered the ontological liaison of European "products" with the natural framework of Europe, he would not care to bother if these tastes had any relation with Muslim life, thus encumbering the latter with a thousand borrowings that possess no raison d'etre whatsoever.

Rudimentary Aspect

This disposition for accumulating indiscriminate borrowings denounces the rudimentary aspect of the Modernist movement. Civilization is not an accumulation, but a construction, an architecture. Concentrating only on its products, one overlooked the structure of Western society, and did not seize its positive symbol at the level of its virtues, incarnated equally by the artisan, the scholar or a simple labourer, but of its temporary signs such as the aeroplane and the bank. One does not see them any more clearly in the structure of the Muslim world, being content in the one case as in the other, to regard what appears the most easily.

It is not astonishing in these circumstances, that the words themselves have been drained of all the contents that form their social value. Certainly the "parole is divine", but only so far as it is an act and not a simple collection of words as happens during election campaings. For exercising its seduction, this litteralism has at its command an entirely new terminology, favourably received in a society, under strain of an effort of recovery. The parole here betrays its mission: instead of directing this "effort" in the direction of over-effort, necessary for confronting the tasks of the present, it degrades it to an under-effort into gestures barely sufficient for securing a seat or an honourable position. The man who pretends to direct public life does not conceive things for doing them, but only for saying them, and talking about them eloquently. This word is purely a verbal act without social potential or moral "tension".

However, it is this moral tension that essentially characterises all efficacious intellectual, moral and physical attitudes. It is the man in his plenitude who "strains" himself, goes beyond his nature because he constantly modifies it. In such a case, his word is a will, an act that expresses a just relationship between words and realities. But when this relation between word and the act makes default, the former is no more than mere talk. If the liaison between the word as an expression of thought—and the act—as its concretisation does not exist in our spirit, we would - no more seize the reverse relationship of act to thought, and will miss this perpetual dialectic that goes from new conquests to new words and by these words to still new conquests.

If with the Reformists (particularly since the disappearance of its last great representatives) the word is not founded on a social imperative, with the Modernists it does not aim at efficiency or implicate the practical tension of words towards acts. The common cause of the error of the two movements is that neither went to the very source of its inspiration. The Reformists have not in reality gone back to the origins of Islamic thought, any more than the Modernists to the origins of Western thought. However, on the psychological plane, a discrimination between the two is altogether indispensible. The "Salafist" individually carries the notion of renaissance. Even if he does not methodically realize therefrom the practical conditions, he at least does not lose sight of the essential objective. He has enough awareness of his milieu to demand only the "duties", leaving "rights" for the Modernist. In peforming his work, however naive, he reaches an understanding of his milieu through his own "reformist" effort. With the Modernist, on the contrary, the very notion of renaissance makes default or is relegated to a secondary position. The Modernist engages himself in the life of his country only on the political plane. For him the primary question is not the regeneration of the Muslim world, but of pulling it out of its present embarrassment. It is a borrowed notion that does not, in fact, envisage the Muslim problem of the man, but the European problem of the institution. This results sometimes in distressing scenes. I have seen in the streets of Algiers, a young man bending over a dustbin in search of his pittance, while a wall-poster a little above his head, invited him to demand a "Sovereign Constituent Assembly". It well seems that the inspirers of this sinister inconsistency had never regarded from near the man of the people, for seeking to know exactly what would have really and immediately referred to his sad fate.

Precise Doctrine

The modernist movement does not in fact reflect any precise doctrine: it is as indefinite in its means as in its ends. Its only precise path that leads the Musulman to be a client or imitator without originality, of an alien civilization that more readily opens the doors of its shops than of its schools, where the students could perhaps learn to utilize their personal genius for their own benefit. It would suffice, in this regard, to consider the very composition of the student missions that Egypt annually sends to European universities. One of the most recent group consists of some sixty students, none of whom was destined for technical studies, and of whom the majority was, besides, Copt. This example, like so many others, shows that the Modernist movement is not oriented towards acts and means, but towards fashions, tastes, and wants. When its representatives attribute to colonialism their own inefficiency, it seems that it is for them chiefly the question of an alibi and that they wish to run away from their true responsibility. This subterfuge is also employed by the Reformist movement which instead of seeking the internal causes of its insufficiencies, contents itself to impute them to foreign political powers. Neither the one nor the other cares to remedy its own shortcomings, but only to mask them from the eyes of the people.

However, a certain spirit of initiative-sole criterion of the efficacy of the individual has begun to manifest itself in certain intellectual circles, notably in Algeria. In Constantine, for example, a number of doctors have arranged to observe a weekly social day to attend to the poor—an instance of the intellectual seeking to enter the life of his people otherwise than through the customary thereshold of elections. The intellectual and the political effort could thus resume normal significance of being the means and not the end.

This does not mean, however, that the political effort of the Modernist movement has always been in vain. It has succeeded in the crystallisation of a collective consciousness that as we have seen-has been missing in the Muslim countries since Siffin, and has constituted in these countries a sign-post which designates, if not the essential objective, at least certain, more or less, practical ends capable of drawing the masses from their indifference and apathy. On the intellectual plane, if the movement has not brought-for lack of a real contact with modern civilization and an effective rupture with the post-al-Muwahhid past the elements of a culture, it has, nevertheless, given birth through its borrowings from the West, to a current of ideas which though debatable have nonetheless the merit of bringing into question all the traditional criteria.

13

West in Peril

"And they devised and God devised. But of *those who devise is God the Best".*

Quran (3:54)

In noting the "enormous rapidity with which the world of Islam was moving towards the West", Iqbal merely referred to a particular aspect of a phenomenon that Ibn Khaldun had seized in its generality. "The conquered people", the great medieval historian wrote, "adopt the forms, the ideas and the manners of the conquering people." It is this same phenomenon, known as the "law of adaptation" in modern phraseology that confronts today the Muslim world. The anguish and hesitation that, as earlier mentioned, had troubled Iqbal in his quest for a solution to the problem of women, point to the general perplexity of the modern Muslim consciousness before two solutions that appear equally deplorable. It seems that in most cases one is searching for a third solution that would be compatible, at the same time, with the spirit of Islam and the demands of modern age. The hesitation and anguish involved in the search have resulted in a sort of pause in the evolution of ideas, a "historical no man's land", since the Muslim society could neither return to the post-al-Muwahhid stage, nor make a blind thrust forward in its movement "towards the West". For the latter no longer exercises the irresistable fascination and influence it wielded in the epoch of Mustafa Kemal and Iqbal; the West in its turn, represents to-day the spectacle of but another chaos, wherein the Muslim spirit in its search for an "order", does not find a model to imitate or the source of external inspiration that could guide its progressive march. It is thus forced to fall back on its own values, and so one remarks in the writings and discourse of young Muslim intelligentsia a renewed interest in Islam which is, in no sense, a withdrawal. Indeed the Muslim world seems to open itself in a more conscious manner towards the modern world, with the knowledge that though the West could not provide it with all the solutions, as it had fondly believed in the Kemalist epoch, yet one would find therein the results of a highly edifying experience, that constitutes at once the most perfect achievement and the gravest failure of human genius-prodigious lesson of history for understanding the destiny of peoples and civilisations. This double intelligence of events becomes all the more necessary as the Muslim world in its present pause,since the Palestine affair, seems to strive at a real comprehension of its problem through a more objective evaluation of the factors of its renaissance as well as those of its chaos.

One has remarked already a tendency to try to grasp the sense of the European historical process, rather than to copy it purely and simply. By seizing the relativity of the European phenomena, one would find it easier to understand their imperfections as well as their real grandeur, and the contacts and exchanges would become more fruitful with this Western world which must, for a long time still, provide the canvas of one's thought and action.

Universal Radiation

In fact, it is the universal radiation of the Western culture that makes its present chaos a world problem, that has to be understood and analysed in its liaison with the human problem in general, and by consequence, in its liasion with the Muslim problem. Such an analysis could not fail to give the Muslim a chance a placing himself as man, and not as indigene with regard to the European order, and to the purely material inter-dependence that at present constitutes the essential relation between a more or less colonial Europe and a more or less colonised Muslim world. Thus, there would succeed a state of mutual esteem and more fruitful association. Such a modification would not be solely beneficial to the Muslim world, for colonialism weighs as heavily on European life: colonialism that materially kills the colonised, also destroys morally the coloniser.

While one could note a tendency among the colonial nations to modify their political relations with the colonised countries, a sort of fatality seems to neutralise this awareness of the colonial peril. The colonial habit seems to be too deeply ingrained in European society to allow the new turn of mind to modify the psychology and the usages that lie at the basis of its moral chaos. It would suffice here to point out the relation of the latter with the chaos in the Muslim world.

Double Aspect

The European chaos, like the Muslim, presents a double aspect. The first is merely the simple and ineluctible culmination of a historical moverment, while the second is an accidental aspect that results from the incidence of the colonial fact on the life, habits and the ideas, for more than a century. These two aspects merge together in a phenomenon common to all the civilisations: the retardation of consciousness over science and the march of thought. Consciousness is, in fact, the psychological resume of the history, the distillation of the past in a human "ME", a crystallisation of habits, prejudices and tastes. All acquisitions of thought, therefore, if they have no direct link with the past, the tradition and habits of a people remain beyond the grasp of its consciousness. Herein lies the origin of the drama of modern civilisation where the consciousness has failed to assimilate most of the realisations of science.

The same retardation had caused the rupture of Siffin in the Muslim world. The Quran as a philosophical system was a science singularly beyond the horizon of the jahili consciousness. This resulted in a reputure between those who had assimilated the new thinking and those who remained attached to their old conceptions and conditions of life that the Quran sought to abolish. This has been the underlying phenomenon of Muslim history for thirteen centuries. Masked by historical trappings, it has nevertheless been periodically surfacing in one crisis or the other, through internecine struggles. The Kharijism and the Mutazilism were but-the one on the political and the other on the intellectual plane, the tentatives to catch up with the Quranic thought that still escaped from a retarding consciousness. In all these conflicts, it was always a question of divorce between the temporal Muslim world and the Quranic thought. If the decadence denoted an imbalance between the temporal Muslim world and the Quranic thought, the renaissance marks the effort of the Muslim consciousness to regain its retardation over the Quranic and modern scientific thought.

The same process could be observed in the history of Europe. The first rupture therein, took place on the moral plane in the name of Reformation, but various schisms as that of Al bigenis had already indicated that the Christian consciousness could no longer span the gulf that divided it from a rationalism derived from scientific development. The second, on the political plane, appeared with the French Revolution; it shattered the traditional social structure and replaced it with a statute founded on the equality of individuals. However, this theoretical equality merely established a precarious equilibrium, and one could already discern in the bosom of the third Estate, champion of the new order, 'a working class tendency among the Jacobins, opposed to a bourgeoise tendency. The execution of Robespierre, and the liquidation of the First Commune of Paris resulted in a bourgeoise triumph. However, the conflict remained latent between the two wings of the new society, the bourgeoise who inaugurated the new era of capitalism, and the workers who prepared the advent of a new class: the proletariat.

But the world born out of this double development is full of all the contradictions and ready for all ruptures. In fact, the Third Estate eventually found itself definitely split, when in face of the practical materialism of the European bourgeoisie, the proletariat would set up its "dialectical materialism".

For the moment the conflict was confined on the summit, between the economists of the bourgeoise tradition, mainly Adam Smith and Ricardo and the economists of the new school, Engels and Marx-without taking account of the doctrinaire anarchist-syndicalists, like Bakunin. But with the set up of the First International, after the preparatory congresses at Brussels and London, and the Paris Commune in 1871, the disputes between the two opposing forces were carried from the philosophical into the political arena. It was this period in European history marked by a moral, political, and social schism that was contemporaneous with the zenith of the colonial era and the first manifestations of the Muslim renaissance. It was by this double material thrust-bourgeoise and proletarian, that the Muslim world became conscious of European influences in its political and intellectual evolution. It was chaos not civilisation that it discovered in this Europe where the ruptures were going to aggravate in terms of the two growingly preponderant factors: the rapidity of scientific development and colonial expansion. These two factors, scientism and colonialism, joined together to become the "fatality" of Europe, just as theology had become that of the post-al-Muwahhid society. Under their influence the slide of Europe into materialism could not but accelerate with the soaring of a prodigiously innovating science. Each invention, each discovery deepened still more the gulf between an overwhelming science and an overwhelmed traditional consciousness.

Drunk with the new forces that it had unleashed, 'the European "ME" was enticed by its own genius, becoming a slave to the machine that he had created but could not control. Reality became calculable and happiness measurable in quantities of calories and hormones. It was the era of quantity, of "quantitatism" in the consciousnesses. It was also the era of moral relativism, of the commencement of a century that had for its maxim the famous, "all is relative..." One no longer possessed the sense of the "obsolute" since the 20th century positivist like the brain of the machine, no longer understood what went beyond the "relative" perspectives of the matter. The sense of the "absolute" died in the same manner as did the concept of justice, the day it was declared in Europe that a "bad settlement is worth more than a good proceeding", and one dared affirm that "commerce is authorised theft". Thus the quantitatist and relativist Europe killed a good number of moral precepts, stripping them of their title to nobility and transforming them into the pariahs and untouchables of language, banished from usage and from consciousness; and dictionaries became cemeteries of words that no longer made sense since they responded to dead concepts.

Quantitatism Aggravated

In Europe the quantitatism aggravated in terms of the multiplier co-efficient representing technical power on the scale of a tentacular industry that multiplied by tens and hundreds the material appetites of men. It marked the vocation of the child who no longer chose his line for what he could give to society, but for what he could get from it. One sought to obtain a sinecure rather than to satisfy his natural inclination-an excellent preparation for the colonial administrator, who did not even need to maintain the relative "dignity" that prevented him going to the end of his moral relativism at home. On the colonial level, the moral relativist found an excellent pretext in "national sovereignty", and the mask of "dignity" that he managed to preserve at home, melted in the heat of the colonial sun and the passion of unchained appetites: one simply got what one desired.

Within Europe itself one came to acclimatise oneself to the habits, tastes and ideas imported from colonial life. All social articulations became numerical: one produced so much, one paid so much, one bought so much and ate so much; the life revolved solely around "how much". In the technical and mechanical society being edified since the beginning of the twentieth century, the number reigns supreme and satistics are unquestionable. The human nature, that is, the conscience itself, does not enter into count, since it could not be deciphered or quantified. The human condition becomes a simple numerical function. The machines tick off, calculate, and drag the man to work in their steel meshes. Even human wants are dehumanised and commercialised, and admitted only so far as they are solvent. The general wants of humanity, more particularly those of the "widows and the orphans", the old and the sick are not solvent, and the machines do not make either moral calculation or metaphysical estimates.

The automatism is admirable: the machines turn, the colonies furnish the raw material and cheap labour, the consumers who can pay, consume, the machines calculate the scales, establish dividends, the salaries, the time-table the automatism is admirable, on condition, of course, that not a single grain of sand entered in the motor.

But there entered more than one in the modern machine. In 1914 there was a sinister grating of brakes. The sources of raw material were not sufficient; there were motors that went idle or did not work to their normal rythm, that is to say, at the scale of an insatiable avidity and voracity. A row broke out among the machine owners. After four years of destruction and millions of dead, a precarious *modus vivendi* was established, and the machines started revolving again. In the consciences, drunk with the money and the champagne, the 1914-1918 rupture did not leave any mark, and the apparent prosperity momentarily masked the reality.

However, since 1930 a new grating was audible in the machines. This time the crisis was going to lay bare the moral canker that devoured the civilisation, and to prove that technique could not alone solve the human problems by simple graphs and equations. The machines stopped turning. The queus lengthened before the unemployment pay-offices, and misery installed itself in homes and hearths. A tragic irony presided over this misery, that for the first time in history, issued, not from a scarcity of riches, but from their superabundance. It is the stroke of genius of the 20th century to have transformed scientifically the conditions of welfare into factors of misery. Wherein lay the mischief? In an excess of the curve of production over that of consumption. A child's play for the technician who knew very well to rectify the calculation by simple arithmetic: One must destroy the surplus, and one destroyed wheat, cotton and coffee, while there existed peoples who totally lacked them. And the civilisation that had invented Malthusianism, undertook to refer no longer to the consumers but to the commodities of consumption.

No Spiritual Authority

No spiritual authority existed to denounce the scandal. Those who could save Europe from its economic chaos did not have "solvent" wants: the colonised people, who were naked and hungry, and could'nt buy anything because in considering them as mere instruments of work, one has overlooked to take account of them as consumers.

In the, genesis of the phenomenon resulting from the simultaneous impact of scienticism and colonialism, the conflagration of 1939 was only a return of the flame: the moment when Machiavelli turns against himself and Satan destroys his own work. It is the moment when destiny breathes in human veil, which unfolds itself, so that the oracles may be fulfilled. Prophet Muhammad, had said in fact: "He who digs a well under the feet of his neighbour shall himself fall into it." And fearing more for a nation the injustice that it commits, than the injustice that it suffers, he added: "The power even of the unbelievers shall endure if it is just, but the power of the believers perishes surely, if it is unjust".

The Oracles

The history of our period tragically illustrates these oracles. Europe that should have used its torch of civilisation to guide the march of humanity, employed it to set aflame the colonial world. But it has harvested therefrom, the same chaos, the same disorientation, and the same fatalism before the evil powers of mythology on its own soil, that it has sown in the rest of the world. Because, the Cartesian, learned, industrialised and polished Europe has also its myths, inhibitive in a different manner: while the paralysis of the post-al-Muwahhid society is apathetic and silent, that of Europe is convulsive and hurling. Its myths are infinitely more dangerous since they hold the power of machine and matter, and thus risk to destroy scientifically the countries and the peoples.

In Europe, the mythology is learned and has its academies, doctors and poets. A little before the Ist World War, a young artillers officer, Ernest Psichari, felt himself transported by emotion before the simple but profound faith of the Muslims of Mauritania. It was for him a providential opportunity for introspection and meditation. It matters little if the Road of Damascus leads to a temple, a church or a mosque. Transfigured and converted, Psichari took the path of the church, "the party of my ancestors", as he would note later. Nothing more normal, provided he did not turn the back abruptly on him, who had enlightened his path. In the course of a voyage, in fact, he experienced the urge to vaunt before his young Moorish guide, the material power of modern civilisation. The young beduin replied:

— "You have the earth and we have the heavens." Psichari should have smiled at such ingenuity. Instead, he wrote in his diary, this significant exclamation:

— "Ah! that is a word that the Muslims must no longer pronounce!"

Whence came this unwarranted cry from a man recently converted? Psichari, the believer, was the nephew of Renan, and his thinking here strangely accorded with that of his uncle (whom he had renounced because of his atheism) who, after the 1871 war wrote the following lines, that express, in another form, the same racism and contempt for humanity:

> "... A race of masters and soldiers, that is the European race. Compel this noble race to work in the slaves' prison like the negroes and the Chinese, and it will revolt. Each rebel among us is more or less a soldier who has missed his calling, a being made for heroic life.... Now the life that revolts our workers would render happy a Chinese, a fellah, beings not at all martial. Let each do that for which he is made, and all would go well."

Let us overlook the intellectual mediocrity of these lines-the great erudite has more than once thus let his pen wander. One may ascertain, however, that it errs here right into mythology, incidentally betraying the supreme myth that has hierarchically dominated, since the last century, all other myths of Europe.

The uncle and the nephew had received the sacrament from the same fountain: the superiority of the "race of masters", source of the bloody myth, of the monster that has fathered the anti-human colonialism and anti-European Nazism. This myth has demolished the entire Christian moral philosophy and has committed an outrage against God Himself by striving to supplant Him in the European conscience. It resides in the hearts, dwells in the ideas, animates the wills and untiringly inspires the vocations of the young. History of the past century, is a saga of the colonial spirit. The child born in Europe feels himself pre-destined for colonialism, Even if he misses his vocation, he continues, nonetheless to feed his spirit on colonialism, just as he feeds himself on colonial products.

But there is the return of the flame. Colonialism undergoes a transformation in the European consciousness. It engenders a hypernationalism, then moves on, passing through philosophical distillations, refining itself carefully, to become finally the myth of the "chosen race" that would justify the last degree of barbarism. Founded on racial contempt, colonialism engenders a super-racism.

The first world war was in reality only an intermediary term between colonialism and Nazism, a stage in the distillation process. At the time, each invoked for the best of his material interests the propitious entities of modern alchemy: God, the Right, the Man, thus found themselves intermingled with the petrol and the tin. History became an incantation of dead concepts, for recalling them from the hereafter where they had been sent by the civilisation of machine and numbers. This fashion of using religion-as of yore, magic and sorcery— for the safeguard of one's interests is, perhaps, the most monstrous aspect of the Cartesian genius.

But when one invokes God for the performance of fraudulent deeds, for plundering, killing and corrupting, God delegates Satan for perfecting the process and for achieving in the institutions what had commenced in the individual.

Practice of Injustice

The habit of "teaching the native to work", has diverted the coloniser from veritable labour and robbed him of the sense of his civilisation. The practice of injustice has made him forget justice and its fundamentals: respect for law and the sense of the right of the other. The facility of colonial life has made him unaccustomed to all effort, even intellectual, to such a degree that in Algeria the intellectual life, of this community which boasts of nearly a million of colonisers, is less intense and less productive than that of a simple town in France.

Thus the coloniser gradually de-civilises, brutalises and degrades himself. He had wished to de-civilise, brutalise and degrade the colonised, but "whosoever digs a pit under the feet of his neighbour" The oracle is fulfilled. The coloniser is himself today isolated from his own civilisation whose problems he no longer comprehends. His "anti-indigene" racism has exacerbated his individualism on the national plane and his chauvinism on the global plane.

Thus, little by little, a colonial administration ceases to be an impersonal institution and an organisation of state, and is transformed into a company of individuals or a "gang". It becomes like the old East India Company, "autonomous" in its internal regulations, having almost nothing in common with the interests of the colonising nation and no relationship at all with those of the colonised people. One no longer countenances an administration but coteries of civil servants. Each wants his share and trims for himself the portion that he pretends to be his. It is thus that the colon who had abandoned all dignity and moral reserve on the colonial plane is thence brought to abandon all scruple on the national plane.

The oracles are fulfilled .... And in its turn, Europe becomes a field wherein the colonial spirit reigns. To recapitulate the slow but sure march of this process, one could not do better than to allow a colonised to speak.

Let us, listen for instance to Aime Cesaire whose very work testifies to the human riches which colonialism must need destroy."One must, first, tell how colonisation works to decivilise the coloniser, to brutalise him in the exact sense of the word, to degrade him, to rouse his latent instincts of lust, violence, racial hatred, moral relativism and show that each time a head is chopped off in Vietnam or an eye gouged, and one accepts it in France, a young girl raped, and one accepts it in France, a Malgache executed, and one accepts it in France, there is an acquisition of civilisation that weighs down with its own dead weight, a universal regression that begins to operate, a gangrene that settles in, a source of infection that spreads out, and at the end of all these broken treaties, propagated falsehoods, tolerated punitive expeditions, bound and 'interrogated prisoners', and tortured patriots, at the end of this encouraged racial arrogance, and boastful display, there is instilled a poison in the veins of Europe and the slow but sure drift of the Continent towards savagery...."

"And then one bright day, one is awakened by a formidable return shock: the gestapos bustle about, the prisons overflow, the executioners invent, refine and discuss around easels. One is indignant, surprised. One says: '... Bah! it is Nazism, it will pass', and one waits and hopes and does not admit even to oneself the truth that it is a barbarity, but the supreme barbarity that crowns and resumes all the day to day barbarities; that this comes from Nazism, yes, but before becoming its victim, one has been its accomplice; one has supported this Nazism before being subjected to it, one had absolved it, one had closed one's eyes to it, one had legitimised it, because up to now, it had only been applied to non-European peoples; one had cultivated it; one is responsible for it, and that it wells, it pierces and it drips, before swallowing in its bloody waters all the fissures of the Western, Christian civilisation...."

And the ruptures, the corruptions, the transgressions and betrayals multiply and amplify each day in Europe. By the force of utilising justice as means of repression in the colonies, one has degraded it even in the metropolis. By the force of rigging the elections in the colonies, one has contracted even in Europe the taste for falsification in the civic life. By the force of bullying the consciences of the colonised, one does not respect any conscience whatsoever. One is engaged in constant struggle, vying with each other.

Ruthless Struggle

This ruthless struggle is carried on even in the scientific arena. In biology, Lyssenko wished to dethrone Mendel, Wiesman and Morgan. The science, no doubt, gains from such disputes, but, at stake, is not merely a better understanding of the laws of heredity. One fights, more often, for demonstrating that one is stronger. It is not the scientific conscience alone that is torn to pieces, but the conscience of humanity, lending itself to all the ruptures, conflicts and apocalypses. Tragic perspectives open up: a return to the troglodyte age is possible. The atom bomb could inspire, tomorrow, a new urbanism, that of the subterranean era. And in the gigantic mole-holes of monstrous Cartesianopolis, would dwell a human race that has substituted a machine for its brain, numbers for its moral concepts and myths for its God.

Howsoever that may be, the Muslim world can no longer seek guidance in the present chaos from a Western world itself on the verge of apocalypse. For discovering its own sources of inspiration, it must look for new paths. But whatever new paths it might borrow, it could not isolate itself within a world driving towards unity. It is not a question, for it, of breaking with a civilisation that represents a great human experience, but of adjusting relations with it.

Bibliography

English Books

Arnold, T. W. : *Preaching of Islam*, London, 1913.

Assemani, J. S. : *Bibliotheca Orientalis*, Rome, 1719.

Bar Hebraeus : *Chronicon Ecclesiasticum*, Louvain, 1872.

Baumstark, A. : *Ceschichte der Syrischen Literatur*, Bonn, 1922.

El-Beladhuri : *Kitab Futuh-al-buldan, Liber expugnationis regionum*, Leiden, 1868.

Bergestrasser, G. : *Risalat Hunayn ibn Isltaq*, Leipzig, 1925.

Bevan, E. R. : *House of Seleucus*, London, 1902.

Boer, T. J. : *Geschichte der Philosophie im Islam*, Stuttgart, 1901.

Bouyges, A. M. : *Sur le de Scientiis d'Alfarabi*, Beyrouth, 1924.

Brockelmann, C. : *Geschichte d. Arabisch. Literatur*, Berlin, 1902.

Browne, E. G. : *History of Arabian Medicine*, Cambridge, 1921.

Caetani, L. : *Annali dell' Islam*, Milano, 1905.

Cajori, F. A. : *History of Mathematics*, New York, 1924.

Carra De Vaux : *Penseurs d' Islam*, Paris, 1921.

Chabot, J. B. : *L'Pcole de Nisibe*, in JA., 1896.

Csco. : *Corpus Scriptrum Christianorum Orientalium*, Paris, 1912.

Cumont. L. : *Egypte des Astrologues*, Bruxelles, 1937.

Denha : *Histoire de Marouta*, Justinien, Paris, 1901.

Dieterici, F. : *Alfarabi's Philosophische Abhandlungen*, Leiden, 1890.

Doughty, C.M. : *Travels in Arabia Deserta*, London, 1923.

Drfyer, J. L. E. : *History of the Planetary Systems*, Cambridge, 1903.

Droysen, J. G. : *Gesch. de Hellenismus*, Gotha, 1877.

Duchesne, L. : *Early History of the Christian Church*, London, 1914.

Dulsem, P. : *La Systeme du Monde*, Paris, 1915.

Dutt, Nalinaksha : *Early Monastic Buddhism*, Calcutta, 1941.

Goldziher, J. : *Muhammedanische Studien*, Halle, 1889.

Goodspefd : *Athanasius (of Antioch), Conflict of Severus*, 333-590.

Hankel, H. : *Zur Geschichte der Mathematik*, Leipzig, 1874.

Harnack, A. : *Lehrbuch der Dogmengeschichte*, Freiburg, 1894.

Haskins, C.H. : *Arabic Science in Western Europe*, 1925.

Hauser : *Ueber das Kitab al-hijar*, Erlangen, 1922.

Heath, T. L. : *Aristarchus of Samos*, Oxford, 1913.

Hffele, C, J. : *History of the Christian Church Councils*, 1871.

Hirschberg, J. : *Geschichte d. Augenheilkunde*, Leipzig, 1899-1918.

Hoffmann, J. : *De Hermeneuticis Apud Syros Aristotelis*, Leipzig, 1873.

Hogarth, D. G. : *The Nearer East*, London, 1905.

Houtsma, T. : *Encyclopaedia of Islam*, Leiden, 1906.

Huart, C. : *Histoire des Arabes*, Paris, 1911.

Inge, R. : *Philosophy of Plotinus*, London, 1918.

John, D. : In *Migne Patrologia Graeca*, xciv and xcvi.

Jras. : *Journal of the Royal Asiatic Society*, periodical, London.

Labourt, J. : *Le Christianisme Dans l'Empire Perse*, Paris, 1904.

Land, J.P.N. : *Anecdota Syriaca*, Leiden, 1862.

Le Strange E. : *Palestine under the Moslem* (550-1500), London, 1890.

Lyde, L.W. : *The Continent of Asia*, London, 1923.

MacDonald, D.B. : *Development of Muslim Theology*, London, 1903.

McCrindle, J.W. : *Topography of Cosmas*, Hakluyt Society, 1897.

Maneckji Nusservanji D. : *Zoroastrian Civilization*, New York, 1922.

Merivale, C. : *History of the Romans under the Empire,* London, 1896.

Muir, Sir William. : *The Caliphate, its Rise, Decline, and Fall.* London, 1891.

Musil, A. : *The Manners and Customs of the Rwala Bedounis,* New York, 1928.

Neuberger, M. Gesch. : *Der Medizin,* Stuttgart, 1908.

Nicholson, R.A. : *Literary History of the Arabs,* London, 1922.

Poole, Lane, S. : *The Mohammedan Dynasties,* London 1895.

Purgiter : *Ancient Indian Historical Tradition,* 1922.

Ray, Sir Praphulla Chandra : *A History of Hindus,* Calcutta.

Smith, V.A. : *Early History of India,* Oxford, 1914.

Tarn, W. W. : *The Greeks in Bactria and India,* Cambridge, 1938.

Thomas, J. : *Selections Illustrating the History of Greek,* Classical Library, Loeb 1941.

Warmington, E. H. : *The Commerce between the Roman Empire and India,* 1928.

Winer, L. : *Contributions towards a History of Arabico-Gothic Culture,* New York, 1917.

Oriental Books

Abbas Khan Sarwani, *Tuhfa-i Akbar Shahi,* Dacca, 1964.

Abdu'i-Fazi 'Allami, Shaikh, *Akbar-nama,* Calcutta, 1873-87, English tr. by H. Beveridge, Calcutta, 1897-1921.

Abul Hassan Nadvi, *Nabi-e-Rahmat* (PBUH).

Abul Kalam Azad, *Rasul-e-Rehmat* (PBUH).

Amin Ahmad Razi, *Haft iqlim,* Tehran.

Amir Khwurd, *Siyar al-auliya Fimahabbat u'i-Haqq jall wa'ala,* 1302/1885.

Amir, Shah Khan, *Amir u'i-Rawayat,* Saharanpur.

Anonymous, *A 'ina-i haqq-nama,* India Office, D.P.

Bamawi, 'Ala'u'd-Din Muhammad Chishti, *Chishtiyya-i bihishtiyya* or *Firda-wsiyya-if Qudsiyya,* Panjab University, Lahore, MS.

Bashiru'd-Din Ahmad, *Waqi'-at-i daru'i hukumat-i -Dihli*, Delhi, 1337/1918-1919.

Bhupat Ray, *Insha'-i Roshan-Kalam*, Aligarh, MS.

Chand, Shaikh, *Sawda*, Delhi, 1940.

Fayzi Sirhindi, Shaikh llahdab, *Akbar-nama*, Ethe.

Fazlu'llah al-Amin B. Ruzbihan, *Sulukue-muluk*, Tashkent MS, English tr. by M. Aslam, Islamabad, 1976.

Haydar Malik, *Tarikh-i Kashmir*, Ethe.

Muhammad Kazim Munishi,' *Alamgir-Nama*, Calcutta, 1865.

Muhammad Latif, *Auliya'-i Lahore*, Lahore, 1962.

Muhammad Miyan, *Ulama-i Hind ka Shandar Mazi*, Delhi, 1957.

References

Al-Adab-al-Mufrad, compiled by Imam Bokhari (translated into Urdu by M. Khalil-ur-Rahman Nu'mani), Karachi.

At-taliq-us-Sxbih 'ala Mishkat-il-Masabih, Muhammad Idris Kandhalvi, Damascus.

Commentary on Sahih Muslim: Abu Zakriya, Yahya al-Nawwi. It is appended: to the original Text, published by Karkhana Tajarit-Kutab, Delhi, in 1930.

Fath al-Bari (commentary on Sahih al-Bokhari), Hafiz Ibn Hajar 'Asqalani (852 A.H.), Cairo, 1959.

Jami' al-Tirmidhi: Abu Isa Muhammad b. Isa, Delhi.

Kanz al-Ummal fi Sunan-e-Aqwal wa-l-Af'al, by Sheikh 'Ala' al-Din al-Muttaqi ibn Hisham al-Din, Hyderabad, 1312 A.H.

Musnad: al-Imam Abu 'Abdullah Ahmad b. Muhammad Ibn Hanbal, Ed. by Ahmad Shakir, Cairo, 1949-55.

Sunan al-Darimi: Abu Muhamad 'Abd Allah b. 'Abd al-Rahman, Kanpur, 1293 A.H.

Sunan al-Nasai: 'Abd al-Rahman Ahmad b. Shu'ayb al-Nasai.

'Umdat-ul-Qari, by Badr-ud-Din Mahmud ibn Ahmad, al-'Ayni Hanafi: This is the commentary of Sahib Bokhari according to the Hanifite point of view, Cairo.

Al-Bidaya wa. al-Nihaya by Hafiz 'Imad al-Din, Abu-l-Fida Ismail ibn Umar ibn Kathir Qarshi, 744 A.H.

Al-Jami'li-Ahkam-al-Quran, popularly known as Tafsir Qurtubi. Imam Abu 'Abdullah Muhammad b. Ahmad Ansari Qurtubi.

Insanul 'Uyun fi Sirat al-Amin al-Mamun, popularly known as Al-Sirat al-Halbiyyah by 'Ali, b. Burbanuddin Halabi, al-Shafa'i.

Jami' al-bayan 'an Tawil al-Qur'an, popularly known as Tafsir al-Tabari, by Abu Ja'far Muhammad ibn Jarir Tabari, Published by Matba' Mustafa Albabi al-Halbi, Cairo, 1954.

Kitab-al-Maghazi by 'Ali Abd Allah b. 'Omar al-Waqidi, Edited by A. Von Kremer, Published by Asiatic Society Bengal, Calcutta, 1855.

Tanwir-ul-Miqyas min Tafsir Ibn 'Abbas, edited by Abu Tahir b. Muhammad b. Ya'qub al-Ferozeabadi Al-Shafii, Egypt.

Z'ad al-Ma'ad fi. Hadyi Khair-al-'Ibad by Hafiz Abu 'Abdallah Muhammad b. Abu Bakr, popularly known as Hafiz Ibn Qayyim, Edited by Muhammad Hamid al-Fiqi, Cairo, 1953.

Hayat-i Shaikh *'Abdu'l-Haqq Muhaddis Dihlawi,* Delhi, 1953.

Hayat-i Tayyiba, Lahore, 1976.

Sirat al-Mustafa, M. Idris Kandhalvi, 3 volumes, published by Ilmi Markaz, Anarkali.

Sirat al-Nabi M. Shibli Nu'mani, and *M. Sayyid Sulaiman* Nadvi, 6 volumes, Azamgarh.

Index

J

N

T

❑❑❑